Latin in Modern Fiction

Who Says It's a Dead Language?

Henryk Hoffmann

Series in Literary Studies

Copyright © 2022 Henryk Hoffmann.

All rights reserved. No part of this publication may be reproduced, stored in a retrieval system, or transmitted in any form or by any means, electronic, mechanical, photocopying, recording, or otherwise, without the prior permission of Vernon Art and Science Inc.

www.vernonpress.com

In the Americas:
Vernon Press
1000 N West Street, Suite 1200
Wilmington, Delaware, 19801
United States

In the rest of the world:
Vernon Press
C/Sancti Espiritu 17,
Malaga, 29006
Spain

Series in Literary Studies

Library of Congress Control Number: 2021932158

ISBN: 978-1-64889-315-5

Also available: 978-1-62273-949-3 [Hardback]; 978-1-64889-264-6 [PDF, E-Book]

Cover design by Vernon Press. Background image by Akyurt from Pixabay.

Product and company names mentioned in this work are the trademarks of their respective owners. While every care has been taken in preparing this work, neither the authors nor Vernon Art and Science Inc. may be held responsible for any loss or damage caused or alleged to be caused directly or indirectly by the information contained in it.

Every effort has been made to trace all copyright holders, but if any have been inadvertently overlooked the publisher will be pleased to include any necessary credits in any subsequent reprint or edition.

To my wife Betsy

and

my friends Les Sekut and Patricia Wendland–
three people most instrumental in and most supportive of
my Latin teaching career;

and

to my friends Lidka and Krzysztof Samolej,
the hosts of the Skrzynki Mansion,
where my multi-level, thirty-year-long journey has been repeatedly enriched
through their amazing cordiality and encouragement

Table of contents

	List of Figures	ix
	Preface	xi
I.	Latin in Mainstream Literature	1
1.	**Samuel Hopkins ADAMS (1871–1958)**	3
2.	**Aldous HUXLEY (1894–1963)**	7
3.	**Sinclair LEWIS (1885–1951)**	13
4.	**F. Scott FITZGERALD (1896–1940)**	19
5.	**James HILTON (1900–1954)**	23
6.	**Thomas WOLFE (1900–1938)**	29
7.	**John STEINBECK (1902–1968)**	35
8.	**Irwin SHAW (1913–1984)**	41
9.	**Julio CORTÁZAR (1914–1984)**	45
10.	**Saul BELLOW (1915–2005)**	51
11.	**Morris L. WEST (1916–1999)**	55
12.	**Flannery O'CONNOR (1925–1964)**	59
13.	**Gore VIDAL (1925–2012)**	63
14.	**Herman RAUCHER (1928–)**	67
15.	**Umberto ECO (1932–2016)**	71
16.	**John UPDIKE (1932–2009)**	77
17.	**John Gregory DUNNE (1932–2003)**	87
18.	**C. K. STEAD (1932–)**	91

19.	Jerzy KOSINSKI (1933–1991)	95
20.	John IRVING (1942–)	99
21.	Dermot McEVOY (1950–)	107
II.	Latin in Crime and Detective Fiction	109
1.	Raymond CHANDLER (1888–1959)	111
2.	S. S. VAN DINE (1888–1939)	115
3.	Erle Stanley GARDNER (1889–1970)	121
4.	Brett HALLIDAY (1904–1977)	129
5.	Ellery QUEEN (Manfred B. Lee, 1905–1971; Frederic Dannay, 1905–1982)	133
6.	John Dickson CARR (1906–1977)	143
7.	Ross MACDONALD (1915–1983)	149
8.	William X. KIENZLE (1928–2001)	155
9.	Tom KAKONIS (1930–2018)	161
10.	Joe GORES (1931–2011)	169
11.	Joseph WAMBAUGH (1937–)	173
12.	Robert K. TANENBAUM (1942–)	177
13.	Sara PARETSKY (1947–)	181
14.	Paul LEVINE (1948–)	187
15.	Elizabeth GEORGE (1949–)	197
16.	Scott TUROW (1949–)	203
17.	Joseph FINDER (1958–)	207
18.	Greg ILES (1960–)	211
19.	Ian RANKIN (1960–)	215
20.	Dennis LEHANE (1965–)	219

III.	Latin in Frontier and Western Fiction	223
1.	**Emerson HOUGH (1857–1923)**	**225**
2.	**Paul HORGAN (1903–1995)**	**231**
3.	**Will HENRY/Clay FISHER (1912–1991)**	**235**
4.	**Larry McMURTRY (1936–)**	**239**
	Appendix	247
	Conclusions	255
	Acknowledgments	267
	Bibliography	269
	Index	277

List of Figures

Figure 0.1. The Latin sign meaning "Glory to God in the highest and peace on earth to men of good will" above the altar of Peter and Paul Church in Potsdam, Germany. Photo by Betsy Hoffmann. — xii

Figure 1.1. Polish poster, designed by Waldemar Świerzy (1968), for Michelangelo Antonioni's *Blow-Up* (1966, based on the short story by Julio Cortázar). Courtesy of the "Ikonosfera" Gallery and Transart Collection. — 46

Figure 2.1. The image of Humphrey Bogart (as Philip Marlowe) in the poster "The Cinema According to Chandler," designed by Waldemar Świerzy (1988) for the retrospective organized by the Film Society "Kinematograf 75" (Poznan, Poland). Courtesy of the "Ikonosfera" Gallery and Transart Collection. — 113

Figure 3.1. The jacket of the first edition of *The Covered Wagon* (1922) by Emerson Hough (D. Appleton and Company, New York, MCMXXII). — 227

Figure 3.2. Polish poster for Raoul Walsh's *The Tall Men* (1955), designed by Wiktor Górka (1965). Courtesy of the "Ikonosfera" Gallery and Transart Collection. — 236

Figure 4.1. Polish poster for King Vidor's *Duel in the Sun* (1946), designed by Jakub Erol (1970). Courtesy of the "Ikonosfera" Gallery and Transart Collection. — 253

Figure 5.1. The author standing in front of a store named "Qvo Vadis" in Potsdam, Germany (March 2020). Photo by Betsy Hoffmann. — 265

Preface

> *"Magna est . . . vis humanitatis".*
> ("The effect of liberal education is great.")
> - Cicero

> *"Rident stolidi lingua Latina."*
> ("Fools laugh at the Latin language.")
> - Ovid, Tristia, Book V, Poem 10

When asked what made them take Latin, most students quote their parents, who told them that Latin would help them on the SAT exams. Others say it is important to take the language because they want to be doctors or scientists, and some have decided to take it because of their hope to become lawyers. While all of this reasoning is more or less correct, there are many other, more substantial, reasons why Latin should never be abandoned from school curricula in both Europe and the United States. In order to establish cogent arguments in support of such reasoning, let us, first, have a brief look at the history of the language.

Originated from the spoken tongue of a nomadic tribe wandering north of the Caucasus Mountains around 6,000 B.C., Latin is rightly considered to be one of the "grandchildren," or rather "great-great-great-(...)-children," of Proto-Indo-European, a language thus labeled by historical linguists due to the location where it had appeared (somewhere between Europe and Asia/India) and the lack of a better name. Also influenced by the local language of the Etruscans, Latin took the shape as is known to its past and present students around 1,000 B.C., when some of the descendants of the previously mentioned nomadic tribe, after growing considerably in numbers and repeatedly splitting into smaller groups, moved far west from the Caucasus Mountains and eventually decided to settle down on the Apennine Peninsula and form a nation they themselves called 'Latium.' While the pure and very complex form of the language, which had adopted its grammar system (along with the concepts) from Greek, survived in the Catholic Church, its simplified version, also known as "Vulgar" Latin, gradually, through a blend of different ethnic groups, developed into a number of derivative languages, such as Italian, French, Spanish, Portuguese, Romanian and a few others—the Romance languages which, by using the already applied family metaphor, we can also refer to as the "children" of Latin. By the same token, we can refer to the other modern European languages as the "cousins" of the Romance languages or the "nephews" or "nieces" of Latin.

But the influence of Latin was not limited to the nations where Romance languages developed. Due to the enormous Roman conquests of some other European areas, especially by the army of Julius Caesar, and to the expansion of the Roman-Catholic religion, many other European languages were impacted by Latin, its alphabet, lexicon and syntax. While English vocabulary incorporates over 70% of lexical items derived from Latin, the concept of cases and the system of tenses, along with some vocabulary, were adopted by some other Germanic languages and, even more, by some Slavic languages, Polish being one of them. In fact, Latin had a major impact in Poland between the tenth and eighteenth centuries, first being the only written language (of historical documents, chronicles, scientific publications—e.g., Copernicus's *De revolutionibus orbium coelestium*, i.e., *On the Revolutions of the Celestial Spheres*, 1530—and even literary works) and later becoming the second spoken language among the Polish gentry, which is creatively evidenced in Henryk Sienkiewicz's trilogy, consisting of *Ogniem i mieczem* (*With Fire and Sword*, 1884), *Potop* (*The Deluge*, 1886) and *Pan Wołodyjowski* (*Sir Michael*, 1888).

Figure 0.1. The Latin sign meaning "Glory to God in the highest and peace on earth to men of good will" above the altar of Peter and Paul Church in Potsdam, Germany. Photo by Betsy Hoffmann.

The presence of Latin in the Catholic Church had been strong over many centuries, the Latin Tridentine Mass, also known as the Traditional Latin Mass or *Usus Antiquior*, lasting between 1570 and the 1960s as the most widely used Mass liturgy in the world. Nowadays, Latin can still be traced in religious hymns and Christmas carols—phrases like *Gloria in excelsis Deo* ('Glory to

Preface xiii

God in the highest') used repeatedly—as well as on many old buildings in most European countries (the city hall in Poznan, Poland, e.g., is practically one big plaque of Latin inscriptions). Modern languages, both written and spoken, brim with Latin words, phrases and clauses, not only where people expect them the most, i.e., in the sciences, medicine and law, but also in everyday communication, public speaking and, what is to be demonstrated in this book, in fiction.

However, there is no nation anywhere in the world that currently communicates exclusively by means of the Latin language. And that criterion itself turned out to be decisive for some scholars that have labeled Latin a dead language. Nevertheless, we must ask ourselves if the criterion is correct or fair; i.e., if Latin deserves to be included among some obscure languages spoken in the remote past by some forgotten tribes that ceased to exist for one reason or another. Yes, the only place where Latin can still be extensively heard in a discourse is the Vatican, and the people that use it there do not belong to one nation only. But this should not diminish the importance of the language and make people ignore many obvious facts related to its broad and complex impact in many aspects of modern life. Just to show one illustration, the word 'computer,' made up to describe probably the most important modern invention, is derived from the first-conjugation Lain verb *computo computare* ('to reckon together/calculate').

It is impossible to list here all the English words that have Latin roots. Below are some examples that I am especially fond of, divided into groups according to the three basic parts of speech:

Nouns: 'agent' (from *ago agĕre* – 'to do/act'), 'benefactor' and 'beneficiary' (both derived from *bene* – 'well,' and *facio facĕre* – 'to do/make'), 'factotum' (meaning 'do-it-all' or 'Jack/master of all trades' from *facio* in the imperative form and the neuter form of the adjective *totus, tota, totum* – 'whole/all'), 'gladiator' (from *gladius* – 'sword'), 'tradition' (from *trado tradĕre* – 'hand over');

Adjectives: 'belligerent' (from *bellum* – 'war'), 'cordial' (from *cors cordis* – 'heart'), 'eloquent' and 'loquacious' (both from *loquor loqui* – 'to speak') 'malevolent' and 'malicious' (both from *malus* – 'bad/evil'), 'pugnacious' (from *pugno pugnare* – 'to fight');

Verbs: 'accelerate' (from *ad* – 'to/toward' and *celer* – 'quick'), 'deposit' (from *de* – 'down to' and *pono, ponĕre, posui, positum* – 'to place'), 'procrastinate' (from *pro* – 'forward,' and *cras* – 'tomorrow'). (Note: Here and henceforth in the entire book, Latin nouns are usually listed only in the nominative singular form unless it is sensible to include also the genitive singular form to show the similarity between the base and a given derivative or to indicate its declension number; two principal parts of the Latin verbs are listed unless it is necessary to list all four, occasionally three, in order to show the stem used in the derivative. For similar, practical, reasons, in my explanations, I use diacritics—signs that were not used in the original Latin texts—only when they are grammatically significant: a 'macron,' distinguishing long or heavy vowels/syllables, over the 'a' in ablative singular nouns of the first declension and over the 'u' in genitive singular and nominative and accusative plural nouns of the fourth declension, as well as over the penultimate 'e' in the infinitive of the second-conjugation verbs; and a 'breve,' indicating short or light vowels/syllables, over the penultimate 'e' in the infinitive of the third-conjugation verbs.)

The English language has adopted numerous abbreviations, phrases and some clauses (sentences) without any spelling change. There are a number of abbreviations—such as 'a.m.' (*ante meridiem* – 'before noon'), 'p.m.' (*post meridiem* – 'after noon'), 'A.D.' (*Anno Domini* – 'in the year of our Lord'), 'i.e.' (*id est* – 'that is'), 'e.g.' (*exempli gratiā* – 'for example') and 'etc.' (*et cetera* – 'and others')—that are commonly used in English without any questions asked. All or some of them, just like a host of unabbreviated words or phrases—such as 'alibi' (literally 'elsewhere,' implying the impossibility of committing a crime), 'alma mater' ('nourishing mother,' in fact, referring to 'an educational institution one graduated from'), 'modus operandi' ('manner of operating'), 'quorum' (literally 'of whom,' i.e. 'the minimum number of people required to be present'), 'quota' ('portion/part/share' or 'a fixed minimum or maximum') or 'status quo' ('the existing state')—constitute a normal part of either spoken or written English and, in fact, some other European languages. Their users automatically include them in their vocabulary, frequently unaware of their literal meaning (occasionally—when used metaphorically or as a different part of speech—somewhat dissimilar to the one assumed in their native languages) and sometimes even oblivious of their Latin origin. Because those abbreviations, words and phrases are deeply incorporated in those modern languages, they are not even italicized when used in writing. In addition to these, however, there are many Latin phrases (usually italicized in print) borrowed by English with a higher level of awareness but still without any changes in the Latin spelling; thus, they should be considered to be Latin lexical items widely used in the English language rather than Latin-derived English phrases. Here is an incomplete list of such phrases, divided into categories:

    a) general: *ad hoc* (literally 'for this,' i.e. 'for a particular purpose' or 'only when necessary or needed'), *ad infinitum* ('again and again/forever'), *ad nauseam* (something going on for too long, as a result, 'causing a bad taste'), *bona fide* ('genuine/real'), *de facto* ('in fact/in effect/in reality'), *in memoriam* ('in memory of'), *in situ* ('in position/in original place'), *in toto* ('as a whole/in all/overall'), *persona non grata* ('an unwelcome person'), *post facto* ('after the fact'), *quid pro quo* ('one thing for another'), *sui generis* ('one of a kind' or 'unique');

b) medical: *post mortem* ('after death/of a dead body'), *rigor mortis* (literally 'stiffness of death' or, better, 'postmortem rigidity');

c) legal: *corpus delicti* ('the dead body of the victim'), *habeas corpus* (literally 'that you have the body,' a recourse allowing to report an unlawful detention), *in flagrante delicto* ('in the act of wrongdoing'), *in loco parentis* ('in place of a parent'), *pro bono* ('out of good will/free of charge'), *pro forma* ('as a matter of form or politeness');

d) scientific: *deus ex machina* ('a god from a machine,' i.e. 'an unexpected/miraculous power'), *in vitro* ('in a test tube'), *in vivo* ('in a living organism');

e) religious: *Dominus vobiscum* ("Lord be with you"), *mea culpa* ('my fault');

f) statistical: *per capita* (literally 'per heads,' i.e. 'for each person');

g) literary/art/music criticism: *deus ex machina* (again, this time referring to 'a plot device capable of solving a seemingly unsolvable problem'), *in medias res* ('into the midst of things'), *magnum opus* ('a large and important work'), *pars pro toto* ('a part representative of the whole,' a poetic device also known as 'synecdoche').

And here are some of the most common Latin quotations/proverbs—phrases/clauses/sentences (which definitely should be italicized in writing)—that one can quite frequently encounter in both written and spoken language, be it English or any of the Romance, Germanic or Slavic tongues:

a) *Ab ovo usque ad mala.* ("From the egg all the way to the apples." Or simply "From soup to nuts.")

b) *Ad astra per aspera.* ("Through thorns/hardships to the stars.")

c) *Alea iacta est.* ("The die has been cast.")

d) *Amor vincit omnia.* ("Love conquers all/everything.")

e) *Carpe diem.* ("Seize the day!")

f) *Cogito ergo sum.* ("I think; therefore, I am.")

g) *Errare humanum est.* ("To err is human.")

h) *Et tu Brute contra me.* ("And you, Brutus, against me!")

i) *Festina lente.* ("Rush slowly.")

j) *Gladiator in arena consilium capit.* ("Gladiator makes a plan in the arena.")

k) *Homo faber suae quisque fortunae.* ("Every man is the artisan of his own fortune.")

l) *In vino veritas.* ("In wine lies the truth.")

m) *Ipsa scientia potestas est.* ("Knowledge itself is power.")

n) *Manus manum lavat.* ("One hand washes the other.")

o) *Mens sana in corpore sano.* ("A sound mind in a healthy body.")

p) *Morituri te salutamus.* ("We, about to die, salute you.")

q) *Nemo malus felix.* ("No bad man is happy.")

r) *Nihil sub sole novum.* ("Nothing new under the sun.")

s) *Otium sine litteris mors est et hominis vivi sepultura.* ("Leisure without literature is death, or rather the burial of a living man.")

t) *Stultum est timere quod vitare non potes.* ("It is foolish to fear what you cannot avoid.")

u) *Sursum corda.* ("Lift up your hearts.")

v) *Tempus fugit.* ("Time flies.")

w) *Ubi concordia, ibi victoria.* ("Where there is unity, there is victory.")

x) *Ubi opes, ibi amici.* ("Where wealth is, there friends are.")

y) *Veni, vidi, vici.* ("I came, I saw, I conquered.")

z) *Virtus mille scuta.* ("Courage is a thousand shields.")

In addition to appearing on American bills (e.g., *Novus ordo seclorum* – "A new order of the ages") and coins (e.g., *E pluribus unum* – "One out of many"), besides constituting mottos of states, universities, schools and other civilian or military institutions, Latin words, phrases and sentences have "invaded" numerous books published throughout the centuries in other than Latin languages, including English. Books from previous eras (by Geoffrey Chaucer, Christopher Marlowe, Jonathan Swift, Jane Austen and Oscar Wilde, just to name five authors) or novels about ancient Rome written within the last 130 years (e.g., *Quo Vadis* by Henryk Sienkiewicz, *Spartacus* by Howard Fast, *The Antagonists* and *The Triumph* by Ernest K. Gann) constitute evidence of an extensive impact of Latin amongst numerous writers. However, since they are either too remote in time or too obvious because of the setting, they cannot be used as convincing examples testifying to the fact that Latin is alive TODAY, and, consequently, they are excluded from the scope of this publication. James Joyce, who wrote in the first half of the twentieth century, frequently embellishing his prose with Latin lexicon, is also excluded here for a different reason: his case has already been discussed in a serious book—*Latin and Roman Culture in Joyce* (1997) by R. J. Schork—an excellent and comprehensive work, which cannot be improved and should not be plagiarized. Thus, the scope of this publication covers all the other writers actively popularizing Latin in the twentieth and twenty-first centuries, mostly representing three genres: mainstream, crime and detective, and frontier and western. In order to fit all those genres in the scope, the setting restrictions are somewhat less strict than those of the publication time, allowing books set in the nineteenth century to be included as well.

Latin words, phrases, clauses and extensive quotations have been found in approximately 220 modern works of fiction (published between 1900 and now) by more than 150 authors, the discrepancy in the two numbers indicating the fact that many writers have quoted the language of Vergil in multiple works. Those that habitually include Latin in their prose include such prestigious authors of mainstream fiction as Aldous Huxley, Sinclair Lewis, F. Scott Fitzgerald, Thomas Wolfe, John Steinbeck, Julio Cortázar, Saul Bellow, Flannery O'Connor, Umberto Eco, John Updike and John Irving; such remarkable mystery writers as Erle Stanley Gardner, Ellery Queen, John Dickson Carr, Ross Macdonald, William X. Kienzle, Joe Gores, Sara Paretsky, Paul Levine, Elizabeth George and Joseph Finder; and such distinguished western writers as Emerson Hough, Paul Horgan and Larry McMurtry. These and some other writers (with a moderately impressive number of Latin references)—altogether forty-five—constitute the main body of the book, divided into three parts, each corresponding to one of the genres. All the Latin quotations, as well as the word 'Latin' itself, are put in **bold print**; the English translations and other marginal comments in the main text appear in parentheses; my own translations of the Latin text within the quotations, which are consistently moved to the right (creating thus a double margin on the left), are put in brackets, just like the page numbers in the book from which a given quotation was extracted.

The individual entries on the writers do not aspire to be complete portraits of the authors' lives and works, nor do they try to present the writers' contributions to the thesis of the book comprehensively. While in some cases a given author's bibliography has been researched in an extensive or even, in a few cases, complete manner, most of the entries resulted from random or accidental findings, and no further studies of a given author's work followed. It would be absolutely impossible to conduct thorough research of all modern fiction or even of all the works by the writers included in the Bibliography. Consequently, it needs to be understood that the scope of the database is not precisely defined, but rather instrumental in or conducive to the goal of this project: to present as many examples of Latin references as possible, by as many writers as possible and by writers representing more than one genre (the last assumption, however, somewhat restricted by my individual literary taste). It is not, after all, a book on literature; it is a book on the Latin language as presented in samples of modern fiction. Thus, the reason behind the bio-bibliographical introductions in each entry is, on the one hand, to provide data for establishing the authors' validity/prestige, and, on the other, to offer information that will either tie the quotations with the authors' images or help, at least to some extent, explain their content.

It is a reference book; thus, each entry is a whole in itself. It does not need information presented in other entries to explain what is in it. Hence, repetitions of translations and explanations of the same or similar lexical items, along with comments regarding their cultural or grammatical context, are to be expected, my sincere intention to avoid them notwithstanding. But, if there is an interesting aspect of the data worth addressing but ignored in one entry, it is more than likely that it is discussed in another. Consequently, if someone is interested in obtaining here as much information as possible about a certain Latin word, phrase or clause, the person should look up each of the page numbers listed next to that item in the Index, which is a comprehensive lexicon of all the Latin references discussed in the book. On the other hand, the Index does not include the contributors of the quotations; thus, it needs to be clarified that the basic biographical information about each of the famous people behind the references—especially the Roman poets, historians, philosophers and politicians—can be found in the entry where they are quoted for the first time, and, if mentioned again later in the book, for the second, third or fourth time, their names are followed by a note in parentheses referring the reader to the appropriate entry.

Professor E. Christian Kopff, in his excellent work *The Devil Knows Latin: Why America Needs the Classical Tradition* (1999), offers an abundance of comprehensive and convincing arguments in defense of tradition in general, of Western culture and of the classics, and provides a model of an ideal curriculum for secondary and higher education institutions. The book you are looking at can, thus, be treated as a modest supplement or an addendum to Kopff's masterful treaty, an addendum offering numerous examples and further evidence in support of his amazing, if sometimes wrongfully ignored, conclusions.

I would like to finish the preface with three Latin quotations dear to me not only because they are closely related to my life in America. I spent the first eight years as an immigrant in North Carolina, the state whose motto is *Esse quam videri* ("To be rather than to seem"), a clause interesting from the grammatical standpoint because of the present infinitive of the deponent (passive in form, active in meaning) verb 'to seem' at the end, related to the normal verb *video, vidēre, vidi visum* ('to see'). The motto of The Asheville School, where I taught the last six years of the twentieth century, is *Vitae excelsioris limen*, which needs to be translated backwards as (literally) "A threshold/gateway of a better life" or (better) "A threshold/gateway to a better life." The motto is also of interest due to the comparative form *excelsioris* of the adjective *excelsus* (meaning 'high,' 'lofty' or 'elevated') in the middle of it. Finally, the motto of Perkiomen School, where I taught in the years 2000-2020, is *Solvitur vivendo* ("It is solved by/through living."), alluding to the Aristotelian theory of 'learning by doing.' This motto is definitely the most interesting out of the three because, in order to explain why the two words in Latin need five in the English translation, one must explain a few grammar problems—such as the passive third person singular ending (*-tur*) of the Present/Imperfect/Future Tense: the Present Tense determined by the infix *-i-* (applied between the present stem *solv-* of the third-conjugation verb *solvo solvĕre* – 'to loosen/untie/solve' – and the ending), as opposed to *-eba-* in the Imperfect Tense and *-e-* in the Future Tense; the implied subject (the neuter pronoun selected by elimination as being the only choice that makes sense); the concept of 'gerund' (*vivendo*); and the ablative of means/instrument, which explains why the preposition 'by/through' (absent or implied in the Latin version) is physically present in the English translation.

The Preface would not be complete without referring to one of the possibly most famous Latin songs, the anonymous and over 700-year-old *"De Brevitate Vitae"* ("On the Shortness of Life"), also known as *"Gaudeamus Igitur"* ("So Let Us Rejoice"), popular, especially in the past (not very remote, though), in many European countries, Poland in particular, and sung during university ceremonies. Judging by the significant role the song plays in at least a couple of Hollywood movies—Howard Hawks's *Ball of Fire* (1941; starring Gary Cooper and Barbara Stanwyck) and Joseph L. Mankiewicz's *People Will Talk* (1951; featuring Cary Grant and Jeanne Crain)—it must have been known or even popular also among the American academia. Let me quote several of its captivating lines—without translation, in order to make it a little mysterious or, maybe, to challenge the potential readers of the book:

Gaudeamus igitur
Iuvenes dum sumus.
Post iucundam iuventutem
Post molestam senectutem
Nos habebit humus.

Ubi sunt qui ante nos
In mundo fuere?
Vadite ad superos
Transite in inferos
Ubi iam fuere.

Vivat academia!
Vivant professores!
Vivat membrum quodlibet;
Vivant membra quaelibet;
Semper sint in flore.

I.
Latin in Mainstream Literature

1. Samuel Hopkins ADAMS (1871–1958)

Born in Dunkirk, New York, on January 26, 1871, Samuel Hopkins Adams was educated at Hamilton College in Clinton, New York. He was an investigative reporter for the *New York Sun* and wrote articles for *Collier's* before he started writing novels. In the 1920s and 1930s, he published several risqué novels under the pseudonym Warner Fabian. His major fiction works include *Revelry* (1926), *The Gorgeous Hussy* (1934), *The Harvey Girls* (1942), *Canal Town* (1934), *Plunder* (1948), *Grandfather Stories* (1955) and *Tenderloin* (published posthumously in 1960). Adams died on November 16, 1858, in Beaufort, South Carolina.

The indisputably most important film derived from Adams's writing is Frank Capra's Oscar-winning *It Happened One Night* (1934; starring Clark Gable and Claudette Colbert), based on the short story "Night Bus," which was also the basis of a few other movies, including Dick Powell's *You Can't Run Away from It* (1956; featuring Jack Lemmon, June Allyson and Charles Bickford). The other notable screen adaptations of his works include Clarence Brown's *The Gorgeous Hussy* (1936; featuring Joan Crawford, Robert Taylor, Franchot Tone, Lionel Barrymore, Melvyn Douglas and James Stewart) and George Sidney's *The Harvey Girls* (1946; starring Judy Garland, John Hodiak, Ray Bolger and Angela Lansbury).

Set in the New York City of the 1890s, *Tenderloin* (1960), a novel abundant with Latin references, is a fictionalized version of the battle between Charles Henry Parkhurst (a clergyman and social reformer) and the political organization known as Tammany Hall or the Society of St. Tammany. In the novel, Parkhurst is renamed the Reverend Brockholst Farr, and one of his allies is Tommy Howatt, a reporter of the *Police Gazette*.

One of the first Latin phrases appears in a narrative paragraph describing one aspect of the relationship between Tommy and his boss, the editor of the *Police Gazette*, R. K. Fox (the same phrase is used twice more on p. 339, once again in a narrative paragraph):

> Another effort brought him to the attention of R. K. Fox himself. It was a rewrite job, pat to the *P.G.* formula; a church elder in a New Jersey town, caught ***in flagrante delicto*** ['in the act of wrongdoing'] with a fellow elder's wife. [p. 100]

The literal translation of the Latin phrase is 'in blazing offense,' but it is widely used as a legal term indicating that a criminal has been caught in the act of committing an offense. Thus, it is correct to assume that the colloquial equivalent of the term is 'caught red-handed.'

Several Latin references become an inherent part of a lengthy scene addressing the checkers games between Tommy and Farr ('Dominie'). The other character involved in the scene is Dan Adriance, a reporter for the *Star*. In the first excerpt, Tommy describes Farr to Dan:

> "Guide, philosopher and friend, eh?"
>
> "I don't say that he always takes my tips. Sometimes he just looks at me with that sideways smile of his and calls me an **advocatus diabolis** ['devil's advocate'] or something and jumps two men into my king-row." [p. 197]

While formerly the term *advocatus diabolis* referred to an official position within the Catholic Church, the Promoter of the Faith, who was looking for any character flaws in a candidate for canonization or the verification of a miracle, nowadays the phrase 'devil's advocate' has a more general meaning and is often used to describe any person expressing a contentious opinion to provoke a debate or, to go even further, a sceptic or, like in case of the quoted passage, an opponent or enemy.

The conversations in the next two excerpts take place as samples of the real game keep going. In the first one, Dr. Farr comments on Tommy's complaints regarding his own moves. In the second one, Tommy, clearly an inferior player, is once again defeated, loses his composure and swears in a way unacceptable to the minister.

> "I know what I'd oughta to," Tommy would lament, eying the board. "And then, somehow or other I go and do something else, and it's always the wrong thing."
>
> "An ancient complaint, Thomas. What said the penitent: '**Melior video proboque; deteriora sequor.**' ["I see and approve of the better, but I follow the worse."—Ovid, *Metamorphoses*, Book VII, lines 20-1]" [p. 198].
>
> "It slipped out," he said.
>
> "Good day to you, Thomas," his host replied. "You may return when you can command your tongue."

1. Samuel Hopkins ADAMS (1871–1958)

"Yes, sir." Tommy was meek. Then, with a sigh of relief, "Gee! I thought you were going to give me the bum's rush for good and all!"

Dr. Farr permitted himself a meager smile. "I do not propose to lose my expert adviser for a ***lapsus linguae*** ['slip of the tongue'], however gross." [p. 199]

It needs to be added here that Ovid (full name: Publius Ovidius Naso; 43 B.C.–c. 60 A.D.) was a Roman poet who was active during the reign of Augustus (thus, a contemporary of Vergil), and *Metamorphoses* (in Latin: *Metamorphoseon libri*, "Books of Tranaformations"), written in 8 A.D., is his *magnum opus*. While the quoted excerpts clearly prove Dr. Farr's superior chess skills and intelligence, the Latin references in both, plus some of those quoted below, testify to his more impressive education.

The next excerpt catches the end of an argument between Tommy and Laurie Crosbie, a society girl Tommy is in love with, and then it switches once again to checkers:

"Look, Laurie—"

"I don't ever want to see you again. Ever!" Out she marched.

Her place was taken by Dr. Farr, who set up the checkerboard. In even humor because of his misstep with the girl, Tommy was ready to take it out on his friend.

"Wouldn't take my tip, would you, Dominie! Now look where you've landed."

Dr. Farr shook a doleful head. "***Sero sapiunt Phryges***" ["It is late before the Phrygians become wise."—Zechariah 1.1-1.6], he murmured. [p. 250]

Zechariah, whose book (quoted above) included visions and messages which called for the people of Judah to repent, was a priest and a prophet who lived in the sixth and fifth centuries B.C.

There are some more Latin references in the book that should be presented here, even without their contexts. Here is the list (the first item appears in the motto; the second and fourth are quoted by Dan, the third one by Farr and the last one by the narrator):

Civis Romanus sum. ("I am a Roman citizen." p. 6);

Caelum non animam mutant qui trans mare currunt. ("Those who run across the sea change the sky, not their soul." p. 257—Horace);

argumentum ad hominem ('an argument attacking the person,' p. 286);

particeps criminis ('partner in crime,' p. 319);

persona non grata ('unwelcome person,' p. 344).

In some other sources, the second quotation appears in its alternative form, with the subject *caelum* ('sky/heaven') spelled as *coelum*, and the direct object being *animum* (from *animus* – 'soul'), rather than *animam* (from 'anima' – 'breath'). Thus, based on the second part of the alteration, while Adams's version of the saying refers to the physical part of the body, the other form addresses the spiritual aspect of a human being.

Though relatively an obscure name, especially to the younger generations of readers, Samuel Hopkins Adams is an author of some substance, and quite a few of his works, both fiction and nonfiction, constitute significant items in the American literature of the first half of the 20th century. Furthermore, his Latin references, skillfully intertwined with elements of the story, tastefully embellish his prose, in addition to testifying to the author's scholarship. The motto of his alma mater, Hamilton College, interestingly in Greek, means "Know Thyself." Its seal, however, is in Latin; it reads *Collegii Hamiltonensis Sigillum.*

2. Aldous HUXLEY (1894–1963)

Born on July 26, 1894, in Godalming, Surrey, England, Aldous Leonard Huxley was educated at Eton College, an independent boarding school for boys near Windsor in Berkshire, and studied English literature at Balliol College, Oxford. Deeply interested in philosophy, he started writing as a teenager, but his first published novel was Crome Yellow (1921). His other major novels from that period include *Those Barren Leaves* (1925), *Point Counter Point* (1928) and *Brave New World* (1932). In 1937, Huxley moved to the United States to write screenplays for Hollywood movies. He did not, however, give up writing novels, and the notable ones among those that came out later are *Time Must Have a Stop* (1944), *The Genius and the Goddess* (1955) and, above all, *Island* (1962), his quintessential work reconciling his narrative talent with his unmatched, among novelists, philosophical inclinations. In addition to novels, he published short-story collections; poetry collections; pamphlets; travel books; nonfiction books—e.g., *The Grey Eminence: A Study in Religion and Politics* (1941), *The Perennial Philosophy* (1945) and *The Devils of Loudun* (1952); and essay collections, such as *Music at Night and Other Essays* (1931), *The Doors of Perception* (1954), *Brave New World Revisited* (1958) and *Literature and Science* (1963). Huxley's awards include the James Tait Black Memorial Prize (1939, for *After Many a Summer Dies the Swan*), the American Academy of Arts and Letters Award of Merit (1959, for *Brave New World*) and the Companion of Literature Award from the Royal Society of Literature (1962). He died on November 22, 1963, in Los Angeles, California.

Huxley's most important credits as a screenwriter (working in collaboration) are Robert Z. Leonard's adaptation of Jane Austen's *Pride and Prejudice* (1940; starring Greer Garson, Laurence Olivier and Mary Boland) and Robert Stevenson's screen version of Emily Brontë's *Jane Eyre* (1943; featuring Orson Welles, Joan Fontaine and Margaret O'Brien). The most successful adaptations of his original prose include Zoltan Korda's *A Woman's Vengeance* (1943; starring Charles Boyer, Ann Blyth and Jessica Tandy)—from his short story "The Gioconda Smile" (adapted for the screen by himself); Fergus McDonell's *Prelude to Fame* (1950; featuring Guy Rolfe, Kathleen Byron and Kathleen Ryan)—from his short story "Young Archimedes"; and Ken Russell's *The Devils* (1971; starring Vanessa Redgrave, Oliver Reed and Dudley Sutton)—from John Whiting's play based on Huxley's novel *The Devils of Loudun*.

A strong and insightful commentary on the world in the mid-twentieth century, equally applicable, however, to today's reality, is Huxley's last novel, *Island* ([1962] 1989), which brims with Latin references. Set on Southeast-

Asian island Pala, it depicts a Utopian nation as perceived by an accidental visitor from the West, reporter Will Asquith Farnaby, whose gradual moral transformation is the main theme of the book. A purely adult and realistic novel, it has hardly any action or twists of the plot; it consists of dialogues, both external and internal, which collectively prepare the reader for the inevitable ending. Because of the abundance of Latin quotations, let me start with the presentation of the most interesting ones.

While most of the characters encountered by Farnaby are idealists understanding what is best for the island, two people are in the clear opposition: Murugan Mailendra, the boy whose official title of the Raja of Pala is about to be sealed on his upcoming birthday, and his mother, the Rani, who is responsible for his alternative upbringing, including a fascination with purity, power and technological progress. What is even worse, both the mother and her son conspire with Colonel Dipa, the regime leader in the neighboring country, Rendang, to use his forces to accomplish their short-sighted and selfish goals. A well-known Latin phrase is incorporated in the following conversation between Farnaby and the Rani:

> "I'm not denying their kindness," said the Rani. "But after all kindness isn't the only virtue."
>
> "Of course not," Will agreed, and he listed all the qualities that the Rani seemed most conspicuously to lack. "There's also sincerity. Not to mention truthfulness, humility, selflessness ..."
>
> "You're forgetting Purity." Said the Rani severely. "Purity is fundamental, Purity is the **sine qua non** [literally 'without which, not,' or, better, 'something impossible without something else,' or, still better, 'absolutely indispensable']."
>
> "But here in Pala, I gather, they don't think so."
>
> "They most certainly do not," said the Rani. [p. 52]

A long Latin quotation appears much later in the book during a completely different kind of exchange. Farnaby's interlocutor this time is widow Susila MacPhail, the daughter-in-law of Dr. Robert MacPhail and mother of Mary Sarojini and Tom Krishna (the two children that Farnaby encounters first and benefits from their aid). She is also one of the most prominent citizens of Pala and a loyal fighter for the good cause. In the quoted excerpt, somewhat philosophical, Susila takes Will to show him around and then bring him to the hospital where Dr. MacPhail's wife, Lakshmi, is dying of cancer:

2. Aldous HUXLEY (1894–1963)

Low in the west the sun was shining with a brightness that seemed almost supernatural.

Soles occidere et redire possunt
nobis cum semel occidit brevis lux,
nox est perpetua una dormienda.
Da mi basia mille.

["Suns can set and return;
For us once that brief light dies
The night is eternal and we must sleep forever.
Give me a thousand kisses." Catullus, Ode to Lesbia]

Sunsets and death; death and therefore kisses; kisses and consequently birth and then death for yet another generation of sunset watchers. [p. 246]

Gaius Valerius Catullus (84–54 B.C.), one of the greatest Roman poets, wrote a series (about twenty-five) of lyrical poems addressed to Lesbia (a pseudonym of Clodia, an older and married woman, later a widow), the object of his desperate and tragic love. The quoted lines come from his poem 5, entitled "Vivamus, mea Lesbia, atque vivemus" ("Les Us Live, My Lesbia, and Let Us Love"). The role of the extensive quotation, in addition to the obvious: a commentary on the sadness caused by the loss of someone's true love (Dr. MacPhail's, in this case), is to reinforce the novel's general message, expressing the idealistic philosophy loyally and bravely practiced by the majority of the island's inhabitants.

The lengthy Latin quotation also offers some interesting grammatical input through a variety of verb forms and one verbal form. For it contains two infinitives – *occidere* (from the third-conjugation verb *occido occidĕre* – 'to fall/die') and *redire* (from the fourth-conjugation verb *redeo redire* – 'to return') – both serving as the complement of the main verb *possunt* (from the irregular verb *possum posse potui* – 'to be able to/can') in the Present Active Indicative Tense, third person plural; one Present Active Indicative, third person singular form, *occidit* (from the already mentioned verb *occido occidĕre*), this one meaning '(it) dies'; and one Present Active Imperative, second person singular form, *da* (from the first-conjugation verb *do dare* – 'to give'), meaning 'give.' The verbal form is *dormienda*, a gerundive from the fourth-conjugation verb *dormio dormire* ('to sleep'), meaning 'about to be asleep,' which, in connection with the Present Active Indicative, third person singular form *est* (from the irregular verb *sum esse* – 'to be'), means 'must sleep.'

In the next quoted scene, Farnaby talks with Mary about the basic differences between the education system in Pala and that in the Western world:

> "In the school *I* went to," he said, "we never got to know things, we only got to know words."
>
> The child looked up at him, shook her head and, lifting a small brown hand, significantly tapped her forehead. "Crazy," she said. "Or were your teachers just stupid?"
>
> Will laughed. "They were high-minded educators dedicated to **mens sana in corpore sano** ["a sound mind in a healthy body"] and the maintenance of the sublime Western Tradition." [p. 248]

The famous quotation, emphasizing the importance of physical fitness and thus encouraging people to exercise, comes from a late-first century poem (Tenth Satire) by Roman poet Juvenal (full name: Decimus Iunius Iuvenalis; c. 55 A.D. – c. 127 A.D.) where it is a part of the sentence *Orandum est ut sit mens sana in corpore sano*, meaning "One should pray for a healthy mind in a healthy body." Two grammatical forms are worth addressing here: *Orandum* is a gerundive of the first-conjugation verb *oro orare* ('to pray/beg') and *sit* is the Present Subjunctive, third person singular form of the verb *esse* ('to be'), the subjunctive mood resulting from being a part of the purpose clause.

After Lakshmi's death, narrated in a scene that is both moving and unusual, Will talks with Susila again, this time about Pala's future and the island's enemies:

> "Did you know that Murugan and the Rani were conspiring against you?"
>
> "They make no secret of it."
>
> "Then why don't you get rid of them?"
>
> "Because they would be brought back immediately by Colonel Dipa. The Rani is a princess of Rendang. If we expelled her, it would be a **casus belli** [literally 'the cause of war,' better, 'an act that provokes or justifies a war']." [p. 270]

In addition to the references presented above, there are some Latin expressions in the book that are worth quoting outside of their contexts. Here is the list of such lexical items, along with their translations and page numbers:

vis medicatrix naturae ('the healing power of nature,' p. 24);

De mortuis (a beginning of the proverb *De mortuis nihil nisi bonum*, which means "Of the dead, say nothing but good." p. 51);

Pecca fortiter ("Sin boldly." p. 64);

coitus reservatus ('the postponement/avoidance of ejaculation,' pp. 75, 76);

Noli me tangere ("Don't touch me." p. 78);

per annum ('per year,' or 'for each year,' p. 79);

Quod erat demonstrandum ('what was to be shown/demonstrated,' p. 114);

Homo sapiens ('sensible human being' or 'human species,' pp. 126, 191, 273);

memento mori ("Remember you must die." p. 136);

datum ('that which is given,' e.g., 'a piece of information,' p. 275);

donum ('gift,' p. 275).

A high school French teacher of Eric Blair (to become George Orwell) and a friend of D. H. Lawrence, Huxley supported Orwell's writing and predicted the validity of his visionary ideas in *Nineteen Eighty-Four*. He is unquestionably one of the most important authors of the twentieth century, but also a recognized patron of others and an influential thinker. The Latin references encountered in his superior prose—numerous, diverse and insightful—constitute a significant contribution to the thesis that Vergil's language is far from being dead. One enormously interesting thing about the case of *Island*, which can be considered paradoxical, significant or both, is the fact that, in its pages, several foreign languages, such as French, German and even Sanskrit, are mentioned and/or quoted by the same variety of characters whose Latin quotations show an impressive competence in the ancient language regardless of whether they are in favor of everything that Western culture stands for (e.g., the Rani) or against it (most of the other Palanese people).

The Latin motto of Huxley's alma mater, Balliol College, a constituent of the University of Oxford (whose other distinguished alumni include Adam Smith,

Matthew Arnold and Boris Johnson), is *Floreat Domus de Balliolo* ("May the house of Balliol flourish."). It is interesting from the grammatical standpoint as it contains a verb in the Present Active Subjunctive, third person singular form, *floreat* (from the second-conjugation verb *floreo florēre* – 'to bloom/flower/flourish'), meaning (based on the jussive application of the mood) 'may/let (it) flourish.'

3. Sinclair LEWIS (1885–1951)

Harry Sinclair Lewis was born on February 7, 1885, in Sauk Centre, Minnesota, and studied at Yale University (B.A. in 1908). He published his first short story, "The Passage in Isaiah," in 1907, his first novel, *Hike and the Aeroplane*, in 1912 and his first play, *Hobohemia*, in 1919. While his first novel, published under the pseudonym Tom Graham, was addressed to the juvenile reader, most of Lewis's subsequent novels are serious, occasionally satirical, works realistically depicting the American people along with their diverse and complex problems of everyday life. The most acclaimed of them include *Free Air* (1919), *Main Street: The Story of Carol Kennicott* (1920), *Babbitt* (1922), *Arrowsmith* (1925), *Mantrap* (1926), *Elmer Gantry* (1927), *Dodsworth* (1929), *Ann Vickers* (1933), *It Can't Happen Here* (1935), *Gideon Planish* (1943), *Cass Timberlane: A Novel of Husbands and Wives* (1945) and *Kingsblood Royal* (1947). In 1930, Lewis won the Nobel Prize in Literature as the first American writer to receive this distinction. He died on January 10, 1951, in Rome, Italy.

The assets of Lewis's works had been immediately recognized by filmmakers and, as a result, many of his books were adapted for the screen, quite a few, e.g., *Babbitt*, *Arrowsmith* and *Mantrap*, more than once. The most successful adaptations include John Ford's Oscar-nominated *Arrowsmith* (1931; starring Ronald Colman and Helen Hayes), John Cromwell's *Ann Vickers* (1933; featuring Irene Dunne, Walter Huston and Conrad Nagel), William Keighley's *Babbitt* (1934; starring Aline MacMahon and Guy Kibbee), William Wyler's Oscar-winning *Dodsworth* (1936; featuring Walter Huston, Ruth Chatterton, Mary Astor, Paul Lukas and David Niven), George Sidney's *Cass Timberlane* (1947; starring Spencer Tracy, Lana Turner and Zachary Scott) and Richard Brooks's Oscar-winning *Elmer Gantry* (1960; featuring Burt Lancaster, Jean Simmons, Arthur Kennedy and Dean Jagger).

Latin references have been discovered in four of Lewis's novels: *Babbitt*, *Elmer Gantry*, *Dodsworth* and *Kingsblood Royal*. In the first novel (1922), the only Latin expression appears in a paragraph where the narrator describes the intellectual assets of George F. Babbitt's neighbor, Howard Littlefield, Ph.D.:

> He could, on ten hours' notice, appear before the board of aldermen or the state legislature and prove, absolutely, with figures all in rows and with precedents from Poland and New Zealand, that the street-car company loved the Public and yearned over its employees; that all its stock was owned by Widows and Orphans; and that whatever it desired to do would benefit property-owners by increasing rental values, and

help the poor by lowering rents. All his acquaintances turned to Littlefield when they desired to know the date of the battle of Saragossa, the definition of the word "sabotage," the future of the German mark, the translation of "*hinc illae lacrimae*" ['hence these tears' or 'that is what the tears were for'], or the number of products of coal tar. He awed Babbitt by confessing that he often sat up till midnight reading the figures and footnotes in Government reports, or skimming (with amusement at the author's mistakes) the latest volumes of chemistry, archeology, and ichthyology. [p. 25]

The Latin reference comes from *Andria* (in English: *The Girl from Andros*), line 125, a Roman comedy by Terence (full name: Publius Terentius Afer; born in Carthage, died in Greece in 159 B.C.), based on *Samia* and *Perinthia*, two Greek plays by Menander. Originally understood literally, referring to the tears of Pamphilus shed at Chrysis's funeral, the words were subsequently used proverbially by other authors, including Horace.

Due to its extensive focus on religious content, as its titular character is a self-centered and money-hungry evangelist offering quackery for profit, *Elmer Gantry* ([1927]1960) has a substantial number of Latin references, probably more than any other book by Lewis.

A couple of religious terms in Latin come up early in the book, when Brother Gantry discusses theological issues with other students of Mizpah Theological Seminary:

> "I never preach about any such a doggone thing!" Elmer protested. "I just give 'em a good helpful sermon, with some jokes sprinkled in to make it interesting and some stuff about the theater or something that'll startle 'em a little and wake 'em and help 'em to lead better and fuller daily lives."
>
> "Oh, do you, dearie!" said Zenz. "My error. I thought you probably gave 'em a lot of helpful hints about the **innascibilitas** ('inability of being born' or 'self-existence') attribute and the **res sacramenti** ('the thing that was pledged'). Well, Frank, why did you become a theologue?" [p. 93]

The second Latin phrase is a part of a narrative paragraph describing Gantry's ideas on certain aspects of religion:

> Who the dickens cared whether Adoniram Judson became a Baptist by reading his Greek New Testament? Why all this fuss about a lot of prophesies in Revelation—he wasn't going to preach that highbrow stuff!

3. Sinclair LEWIS (1885-1951)

And expecting them to make something out of this *filioque* ['and the Son,' i.e., 'inclusion of Christ'] argument in theology! Foolish! [p. 124]

The next Latin reference, as a matter of fact, a phrase quite familiar to the English speakers, appears in a scene where the Reverend Dr. Gantry is contemplating about the merits of his new secretary, Miss Hettie Dowler:

> And she had such stimulating suggestions for sermons. In these many years, neither Cleo nor Lulu had ever made a sermon-suggestion worth anything but a groan, but Hettie—why, it was she who outlined the sermon on The Folly of Fame" which caused such a sensation at Terwillinger College when Elmer received his LL.D., got photographed laying a wreath on the grave of the late President Willoughby Quarles, and in general obtained publicity for himself and his dear old **Alma Mater**." [p. 429]

Before the phrase *alma mater* (literally: 'a nourishing mother') established its general meaning referring to a school, college or university from which one has graduated and/or the song or hymn of that school (which started with the University of Bologna adopting its motto *Alma Mater Studiorum* – 'nurturing mother of studies'), it was used as an honorific title for various Latin mother goddesses, especially Ceres or Cybele, and later also in the Catholic religion to refer to Virgin Mary.

The final excerpt worth quoting, for it unambiguously illustrates Gantry's untruthfulness and hypocrisy, has, in fact, a Latin phrase that helps make that point. The context is a telephone conversation between Gantry and Hettie, who, feeling lonely, invites the minister to her private place:

> "I'm so terribly lonely this evening. Is oo working hard?"

> "I've got to get up some sermons."

> "Listen! Bring your little Bible dictionary along and come and work at my place, and let me smoke a cigarette and look at you. Wouldn't you like to ... dear ... dearest?"

> "You bet. Be right along."

> He explained to Cleo and his mother that he had to go and comfort an old lady *in extremis* ['in an extremely difficult situation' or 'dying'], he accepted their congratulations on his martyrdom, and hasted out. [pp. 436-437]

The titular protagonist of *Dodsworth* ([1929] 1941) is a successful owner of an automobile business who, at the age of fifty, decides, finally, to take a vacation and spend it in Europe with his wife. And that is when the problems begin as Fran, who has been a devoted housewife until that point, all of a sudden realizes that she has some other, social and romantic, needs.

The first Latin phrase appears early in the book, when the narrator describes Sam's mood and reflections regarding the cosmopolitan people he has met on the **Ultima** (the ship bringing Sam and Fran to Europe; a Latin name, by the way, meaning 'last/final') during the pre-dinner cocktail and the dinner itself:

> He was excited by their merriment at first; then it seemed to him pitiful that all of them, and he himself, should so rarely cease thus their indignant assertion of the importance of their own little offices and homes and learnings, and let themselves rejoice in friendliness. They seem to him like children, excitedly playing now, but soon to be caught by weary maturity. He felt a little the **lacrimae rerum** ['tears of things'] of the whole world. He wanted to weep over the pride of the waiters as—the one moment on the voyage when they were important and beautiful and to be noticed—they bore in the platters of flaming ice cream. He wanted to weep over the bedraggled small-town bride who for the moment forgot that she had not found honeymooning quite so glorious, nor the sea so restful. And he saw as pitiful the fact that Fran expected to find youth again merely by changing skies. [pp. 56-57].

The additional significance of the quotation results from the fact that it comes from Book I, line 462, of the *Aeneid* by Vergil (full name: Publius Vergilius Maro, 70–19 B.C.), the foremost epic poem by one one of the greatest poets not only from the Augustan period, also the author of the *Eclogues* and the *Georgics*. It appears as a part of the scene where Aeneas and Achates contemplate the paintings depicting the Trojan War at the temple of Juno in Carthage, and Aeneas, moved by their content, expresses his sadness and compassion to his armor-bearer, finishing with the sentence *Sunt hic etiam sua praemia laudi; sunt lacrimae rerum et mentem mortalis tangent* ("Here, too, the praiseworthy has its rewards; there are tears for things and mortal things touch the mind.").

The second and final Latin reference comes later in the story, when Sam Dodsworth, back in the USA, and his friend, Ross Ireland, are trying to take a taxi in New York to get to the theater. Here is a part of Ross's extensive monologue, showing how the naked girls in the show business can lead to some extremely political comments:

3. Sinclair LEWIS (1885-1951)

> "Honestly, Sam, I don't get these United States. We let librarians censor all the books, and yet we have musical comedies like this—just as raw as Paris. We go around hollering that we're the only **bona fide** (literally: in good faith,' better in this context: 'genuine/real') friends of democracy and self-determination, and yet with Haiti and Nicaragua we're doing everything we accused Germany of doing in Belgium, and—you mark my word—within a year we'll be starting a Big Navy campaign for the purpose of bullying the world as Great Britain never thought of doing. We boast of scientific investigation, and yet we're the only supposedly civilized country where thousands of supposedly sane citizens will listen to an illiterate clodhopping preacher or politician setting himself up as an authority on biology and attacking evolution."
> [pp. 209-210]

Only one Latin expression was found in Lewis's *Kingsblood Royal* (1947), but because it contains quite a popular phrase, it is worth quoting within its extensive but self-explanatory context:

> More of the black workers were dismissed every day by Wargate's and the smaller firms. Every day the Mayo Street corners were more packed, the grumbling less amiable, and so the canny authorities sent in more policemen—and so the policemen were stoned now and then—and so they sent in still more policemen—and so one Negro was shot and four arrested—and so a two-by-four was dropped from a third story upon a policeman's head—and so Feathering said, "I told you so; join the Sant Tabac"—and so there were accelerated dismissals of Negroes from Wargate's, from the Aurora Coke Company, from the Kippery Knitting Works, from the grain-loading gangs at the elevators, from the railroad car-shops—and so the street-corner gangs became more ugly—and so more policemen were sent in **per omnia saecula saeculorum** ['through all ages and ages'].
>
> Among the white labor-union leaders, a third protested, a third said nothing, and a third rejoiced. [pp. 318-319]

Popular and appreciated in his own times, somewhat underrated in later years and eclipsed by some other American 20th-century writers—such as Hemingway, Faulkner, Steinbeck and Fitzgerald—Sinclair Lewis deserves high praise for his original and flowing prose, as well as for his deep and genuine engagement in moral, social and political issues. While his wisdom is confirmed by the unceasing relevance of his ideas long time after his death—even, in fact, as illustrated by the excerpts presented above, a hundred years after they were printed, the Latin scholars owe the distinguished author their gratitude for employing Vergil's language in accomplishing his honorable goals. Thus, it should not be considered unfitting to remind the reader about the Latin motto of Lewis's alma mater, Yale (or *Universitas Yalensis*): *Lux et Veritas* ("Light and Truth").

4. F. Scott FITZGERALD (1896–1940)

Francis Scott Key Fitzgerald was born on September 24, 1896, in St. Paul, Minnesota. He studied at Princeton University, but did not graduate. Instead, he joined the army and, afterwards, having married Zelda Sayre and published his first novel, *This Side of Paradise* (1920), he traveled in Europe, where he got influenced by the "Lost Generation" writers, Ernest Hemingway in particular. In addition to his numerous short stories, Fitzgerald's major works are the following novels: *The Beautiful and the Damned* (1922), *The Great Gatsby* (1925) and *Tender Is the Night* (1934). His last project, set in Hollywood, was the novel *The Last Tycoon*, which was finished after the author's death by Edmund Wilson and published in 1941. Fitzgerald died on December 21, 1940, in Hollywood, Los Angeles, California.

Fitzgerald's pivotal work, *The Great Gatsby*, has been filmed five times, including one TV production. The silent, relatively successful, adaptation (starring Warner Baxter, Lois Wilson, Neil Hamilton and William Powell) was made by director Herbert Brenon in 1926. All the three big-screen versions— Elliott Nugent's (1949; starring Alan Ladd, Betty Field and Macdonald Carey), Jack Clayton's (1974; featuring Robert Redford, Mia Farrow, Bruce Dern, Karen Black and Sam Waterston) and Bazz Luhrmann's (2013; featuring Leonardo DiCaprio, Carey Mulligan, Joel Edgerton and Jason Clarke)—are controversial, to say the least, more or less inaccurate and definitely disappointing, despite some redeeming assets in each. Sidney Franklin's silent version of *The Beautiful and the Damned* (1922; starring Marie Prevost and Kenneth Harlan) is by far superior to the 2009 Australian production directed by Richard Wolstencroft. The other movies derived from the author's works worth mentioning here are Henry King's *Tender Is the Night* (1962; starring Jennifer Jones, Jason Robards, Jr., and Joan Fontaine); Elia Kazan's *The Last Tycoon* (1976; featuring Robert De Niro, Tony Curtis, Robert Mitchum, Jeanne Moreau and Jack Nicholson); and David Fincher's *The Curious Case of Benjamin Button* (2008; starring Brad Pitt, Cate Blanchett and Julia Ormond)—based on Fitzgerald's short story.

Three extensive Latin references, all deeply rooted in the Catholic religion, have been discovered in Fitzgerald's short story "Absolution" ([1924] 1969). The two characters, Father Schwartz and eleven-year-old boy Rudolph Miller (who ends up confessing the biggest of his sins to the priest), are both struggling with temptations, a sense of guilt and the challenges of confession due to the embarrassment caused by their sins. The first two quotations appear in the excerpt related to Rudolph accepting communion despite the fact that he has lied at his last confession and thus expecting to be severely punished by God (Carl Miller is Rudolph's strict father):

> When the bell rang for communion, however, he quivered. There was no reason why God should not stop his heart. During the past twelve hours he had committed a series of mortal sins increasing in gravity, and he was now to crown them all with a blasphemous sacrilege.
>
> ***"Domine, non sum dignus; ut inters sub tectum meum; sed tantum dic verbo, et sanabitur anima mea. ..."*** ["Lord, I am not worthy that you should enter under my roof; but only say the word, and my soul shall be healed."]
>
> There was a rustle in the pews, and the communicants worked their ways into the aisle with downcast eyes and joined hands. Those of larger piety pressed together their finger-tips to form steeples. Among the latter was Carl Miller. Rudolph followed him toward the altar-rail and knelt down, automatically taking up the napkin under his chin.
>
> The bell rang sharply, and the priest turned from the altar with the white Host held above the chalice:
>
> ***"Corpus Domini nostri Jesu Christi custodiat animam tuam in vitam aeternam."*** ["May the body of Our Lord Jesus Christ preserve your soul until life everlasting."] [p. 195]

The third Latin quotation is used by the author as the title of the closing section of the story, where Father Schwartz's unusual reaction to Rudolph's confession unexpectedly or, rather, in an unexpected way, lifts the burden off the boy's soul:

> ***"Sagitta Volante in Dei"*** ["A Flying Arrow in God's Hands" [p. 196]

Three verbs within those quotations are worth addressing due to their grammatical forms: *dic* (from the third-conjugation verb *dico dicere* – 'to say/tell'), being an exception among the present imperative singular forms, as it ends in a consonant rather than a vowel; *sanabitur* (from the first-conjugation verb *sano sanare* – 'to heal/cure'), being an example of the third person singular, future passive indicative form; and *volante* (from the first-conjugation verb *volo volare* – 'to fly'), being a sample of the present active participle in the ablative singular form. Also interesting from the grammatical standpoint is the phrase *in vitam aeternam*, which illustrates the use of the preposition *in* in connection with a noun/adjective in the accusative form, thus invoking the destination rather than location connotation. Hence, it is correct to translate the preposition as 'until' rather than 'in' or 'at.'

It is also worth pointing out that the last quotation can be easily confused with another Latin expression, *Sagitta Volante in Die*, being a part of a complete sentence, *Non Timebis a Sagitta Volante in Die* ("You Shall Not Be Scared by an Arrow Flying by Day") which happens to be the title of Duncan G. Stroik's Editorial appearing in Volume 37 of *The Institute for Sacred Architecture*. (Nota bene: I have serious doubts about the grammaticality of Stroik's title as the ablative case of *Sagitta Volante* preceded by the preposition *a* implies that the phrase is used as the agent of a sentence in the passive voice, in which case the form of *Timebis* (from the second- conjugation verb *timeo timēre*) should rather be *Timeberis*.)

A legal term in Latin appears in Fitzgerald's short story "Financing Finnegan" ([1938] 1969). Finnegan is a writer who, despite his debts, intends to collect literary material on an expedition to the North Pole. However, to appease his creditors (Cannon and Jaggers) before he leaves, he makes most of his life insurance over to the two men. Here is the passage commenting on the situation after the news reaches New York that Finnegan's life was claimed by the Arctic:

> I was sorry for him, but practical enough to be glad that Cannon and Jaggers were well protected. Of course, with Finnegan scarcely cold—if such a simile is not too harrowing—they did not talk about it but I gathered that the insurance companies had waived **habeas corpus** [literally 'that you have the body,' usually a recourse allowing to report an unlawful detention] or whatever it is in their lingo, and it seemed quite sure that they would collect. [p. 520]

A couple more Latin references were found in two of the author's novels—**reductio ad absurdum** (literally 'reduction to the absurd,' a phrase referring to an argument or proof by contradiction) in *The Beautiful and the Damned* ([1922] 1986, p. 76) and **persona gratis**, most likely meant **persona grata** ('a welcome person,' which is really the reverse version of *persona non grata*) in *Tender Is the Night* ([1934] 1962, p. 277). The error in the latter quotation may have resulted from the fact that the author used it (after the negative phrase 'no longer') in reference to sick people visiting France or Italy and, most likely, tried to make the plural form of the well-known phrase, the correct version of which would have been *personae gratae* or, in the negative, *personae non gratae*.

The subject of several biographical movies—notably Henry King's *Beloved Infidel* (1959; starring Gregory Peck as the writer, and Deborah Kerr as Sheilah Graham, his one-time love interest and the author of the book the film is based upon) and Henry Bromell's *Last Call* (TV, 2002; featuring Jeremy Irons as Fitzgerald, Neve Campbell and Sissy Spacek)—F. Scott Fitzgerald is still a legend among American writers, idolized by many, including J. D. Salinger. Echoes of the writer's classical education are conspicuous in the Latin references with which he managed to embellish, so skillfully, some of his works—not only semantically rich and grammatically complex, but also drawn from three different fields: general, religious and legal. Even though he dropped out of Princeton (in 1917), the prestigious university is still proud of having him as one of its ex-students and storing some of his manuscripts in its archives. Thus, whether he is an alumnus or not, Princeton is Fitzgerald's alma mater, and it is appropriate to mention here its Latin motto: *Dei Sub Numine Viget* ("Under God's power, She flourishes").

5. James HILTON (1900–1954)

James Hilton was born on September 9, 1900, in Leigh, Lancaster, England, and was educated at Christ's College, Cambridge. He lived in London when he wrote his two most famous novels, *Lost Horizon* (1933) and *Goodbye, Mr. Chips* (1934). In 1938, Hilton settled in California, where he worked on a number of screenplays for some remarkable Hollywood productions, such as William Wyler's *Mrs. Miniver* (1942; starring Greer Garson, Walter Pidgeon and Teresa Wright), co-written with Arthur Wimperis, George Froeschel and Claudine West from the book by Jan Struthers, a movie that won six Academy Awards, including one for best writing. His other notable novels include *Rage in Heaven* (1932), *We Are Not Alone* (1937), *Random Harvest* (1941) and *So Well Remembered* (1945). His best-known nonfiction book is *The Story of Dr. Wassell* (1944). Hilton died on December 20, 1954, in Long Beach, California.

The general appeal of some of Hilton's works, possibly due to their overwhelming optimism, has been reflected in numerous film and TV productions. *Lost Horizon* has been filmed twice—by Frank Capra in 1937, with Ronald Colman, Jane Wyatt, Edward Everett Horton, Thomas Mitchell and John Howard; and by Charles Jarrott in 1973, with the cast including Peter Finch, Liv Ullmann, Sally Kellerman and George Kennedy. *Goodbye, Mr. Chips* has been adapted twice for the big screen—by Sam Wood in 1939, with Robert Donat winning an Oscar for the titular role and Greer Garson playing his wife; and by Herbert Ross in 1969, a musical with Peter O'Toole replacing Donat and the other members of the cast including Petula Clark, Michael Redgrave and George Baker—and several times for television. The other notable movies derived from Hilton's original works include W. S. Van Dyke, Robert B. Sinclair and Richard Thorpe's *Rage in Heaven* (1941; starring Robert Montgomery, Ingrid Bergman and George Sanders); Mervyn LeRoy's *Random Harvest* (1942; featuring Ronald Colman, Greer Garson, Philip Dorn and Susan Peters); Cecil B. DeMille's *The Story of Dr. Wassell* (1944; starring Gary Cooper, Laraine Day, Signe Hasso and Dennis O'Keefe); and Edward Dmytryk's *So Well Remembered* (1947; starring John Mills, Martha Scott, Patricia Roc and Trevor Howard).

Inspired by the characteristics cherished by Hilton partially in his own father and partially in his Latin teacher, *Goodbye, Mr. Chips* ([1934] 1986) is a story of Mr. Chipping, nicknamed 'Chips' by his students, a man who devoted all of his life to teaching Latin at Brookfield, an all-boys school in England. Out of the several references to the ancient language that the reader can enjoy in this fascinating book, the very first one is not a Latin word or phrase, but the problem of Latin pronunciation (based on the classical model) constituting the controversy between the headmaster and Chips. Here is an excerpt of their exchange:

> "This question of **Latin** pronunciation, for instance—I think I told you years ago that I wanted the new style used throughout the School. The other masters obeyed me; you prefer to stick to your old methods, and the result is simply chaos and inefficiency."
>
> At last Chips had something tangible that he could tackle. "Oh, *that*!" he answered scornfully. "Well, I—umph—I admit that I don't agree with the new pronunciation. I never did. Umph—a lot of nonsense, in my opinion. Making boys say "Kickero' at school when—umph—for the rest of their lives they'll say 'Cicero'—if they ever—umph—say it at all. And instead of 'vicissim'—God bless my soul—you'd make them say, 'We kiss 'im'! Umph—umph!" And he chuckled momentarily, forgetting that he was in Ralston's study and not in his own friendly form room. [pp. 65-66].

The next couple of passages do include Latin quotations. They are part of Chips's speech delivered in July 1913, at the end-of-term dinner after he received his farewell presentations. In the first excerpt, he talks about his forty-two years at Brookfield and how happy he had been there during all that time. In the second one, he confesses that his students never grow old and that he always remembers them the way they were:

> "It has been my life," he said, simply. "***O mihi praeteritos referat si Jupiter annos.*** ["O if Jupiter could bring back those forgotten years to me.—Psalm 46.9, The Treasury of David]... Umph—I need not—of course—translate. ..." Much laughter. [p. 75]
>
> Sometimes, for instance, when people talk to me about our respected Chairman of the Governors, I think to myself, 'Ah yes, a jolly little chap with hair that sticks up on top—and absolutely no idea whatever about the difference between a Gerund and a Gerundive.' [Loud laughter] Well, well, I mustn't go on—umph—all night. Think of me sometimes as I shall certainly think of you. ***Haec olim meminisse juvabit*** ["One day it will please us to remember these things."—The *Aeneid*: Book I, line 203] ... again I need not translate." [p. 77]

The context of the *Aeneid* reference is the scene where the Trojans, having endured a long series of misfortunes, losing many people and ships, finally land on the shore of Carthage, and the titular protagonist addresses his comrades, trying to give them comfort and encouragement.

Chips's tendency to joke is also illustrated in the next excerpt when he comments about the new item on the school menu:

> There was a mysterious kind of rissole that began to appear on the School menu on Mondays, and Chips called it **abhorrendum** [the gerundive of the second-conjugation verb *abhorreo abhorrēre* – 'to shrink back from' or 'to be disinclined' – in the accusative case]—"meat to be abhorred." [pp. 84-85]

In December of 1917, due to the headmaster's illness, Chips was asked for the second time to be Acting Head of Brookfield, and in the spring of the following year, when the headmaster died, he was requested to carry on "for the duration." Thus, during the last months of WW I, Chips had both a teaching and administrative position. The Latin classes were conducted on the ground floor regardless of air-raid warnings, and Chips kept teaching even with the loud crashes of the guns being clearly heard and forcing him to speak louder. The final Latin quotation is a part of a scene in the classroom, when Chips tries to convince the boys about the relevance of both the ancient history and certain wisdom that the Latin language can offer at any time in the world's history. There is no need to translate the Latin sentence (which comes from Julius Caesar's *The Gallic Wars*, Book I, Chapter 48) as it is done quite well by Maynard, the student who volunteered to read that particular passage (the only suggestion for improvement could be changing the tense of the second verb into Plusquamperfectum (Pluperfect), or, Past Perfect in English; thus, inserting the auxiliary verb 'had' in front of the main verb 'busied'):

> "**Genus hoc erat pugnae**—this was the kind of fight—***quo se Germani exercuerant***—in which the Germans busied themselves. [p. 91]

It seems appropriate to mention here that Julius Caesar (full name: Gaius Julius Caesar; 100–44 B.C.), in addition to being the author and the main "actor" of *The Gallic Wars* (*Commentarii de bello Gallico*—the complete Latin title, which has the singular form of the noun 'war'), was a Roman general, statesman, member of the First Triumvirate and, after the deaths of Marcus Licinius Crassus and Gnaeus Pompeius Magnus, better known as Pompey (the other two members), a dictator and, consequently, the victim of the famous assassination that took place on the Ides of March (*Idibus Martiis*), i.e., on March 15.

Though set far from a boys' school and lessons of Latin, *Random Harvest* (1941) also shows Hilton's classical background, however, to a significantly smaller degree. Narrated in flashbacks, the novel tells a story of a young Englishman, Charles Rainier, who, affected by a war injury, loses his memory (he does not even know his name) and is sent to a hospital for shell-shock cases. The interesting quotation appears in an extensive scene focused on the relationship between the protagonist, at that point using the name Smith, and parson Blampied, who, after marrying Smith to Paula (the woman who rescued him from the hospital), offers the young man a job. The two men are absorbed in a conversation about Blampied's many acquaintances in different parts of the world and switch at some point to a political issue. The parson then juxtaposes the opinion of Monsieur Gaston Auriac from Madagascar with his own:

> Just now, we're in the midst of an argument as to the right way to treat Germany now the war's over. Gaston thinks the Allied armies should have pushed on to Berlin, even at the cost of an extra year of fighting, and then have broken Germany into fragments, acting with ruthless severity on the lines of **delenda est Carthago**. ["Carthage must be destroyed."—Cato the Elder] ... I, on the other hand, would have offered terms of simply astounding generosity—lifting the blockade the day after the Armistice, forbearing to ask for meaningless and uncollectable reparations, and inviting all the defeated countries into an immediate conference on equal terms to discuss the disarmament and rehabilitation of Europe. As you can imagine, we're enjoying as violent a discussion as the somewhat intermittent mails to Madagascar will permit. [p. 278]

Cato the Elder (full name: Marcus Porcius Cato; 234–149 B.C.), also known as Cato the Censor or Cato the Wise, was a Roman soldier, senator and historian. A participant in the Second Punic War, as a senator he was the most persistent advocate of the total destruction of Carthage, which explains the meaning of the quoted reference, in fact abbreviated from *Ceterum autem censeo Carthaginem esse delendam* ("Moreover, I consider that Carthage must be destroyed.").

While the last quotation offers one more example of 'gerundive'—*delenda* (from the second-conjugation verb *deleo delēre* – 'to destroy/annihilate'), the other quotations are equally interesting because of some unusual grammatical forms: *praeteritos* (perfect passive participle in the accusative plural form from the verb *praetereo praeterire* – 'to go/pass by'), *referat* (present subjunctive third person singular form of the verb *refero referre* – 'to carry/bring back'—the subjunctive mood resulting from being a part of a conditional sentence) and *meminisse* (an unusual form of the present active infinitive, from the verb *memini meminisse* – 'to remember/recollect').

Relatively underrated by literary critics, popular among readers and sought after by filmmakers, James Hilton will always be remembered as the man that created Mr. Chips, possibly the most lovable character among educators and one that is cherished by teachers and students of Latin alike. Hilton's Latin references are definitely among those that illustrate the unceasing relevance of the ideas expressed in the language of Ovid and Vergil. While the motto of Hilton's alma mater, Christ's College (whose other notable alumni, by the way, include John Milton and Charles Darwin), is not in Latin, it is at least in Old French, a language directly derived from Latin, and it reads *Souvent me Souvient* ("I often remember").

6. Thomas WOLFE (1900–1938)

Thomas Clayton Wolfe was born in Asheville, North Carolina, on October 3, 1900, and was educated at the University of North Carolina at Chapel Hill (B.A. in 1920) and at Harvard University (M.A. in 1922), where several of his plays, including *Welcome to Our City* (1923), were subsequently produced. He taught at New York University and, only partially fulfilling his childhood urge to see the world, traveled to England and Germany. His major works include *Look Homeward, Angel* (his first novel, 1929), *Of Time and the River* (1935), *From Death to Morning* (1935), *The Web and the Rock* (1939) and *You Can't Go Home Again* (1940). The last two novels, just like most of the works by the author, were published posthumously. Wolfe died on September 15, 1938, in Baltimore, Maryland.

A theatrical movie based on a work by Wolfe does not exist yet. However, there are several TV productions worth mentioning here. *Of Time and the River* was turned into a TV movie in 1953 by director Albert McCleery, with Sara Haden, Thomas Mitchell and Lamont Johnson cast in the parts of Mrs. Gant, Mr. Gant and their son, respectively. *Look Homeward, Angel* was the basis for two TV movies: John Olden's *Schau heimwärts, Engel* (1961, made in West Germany), starring Inge Meysel (as Eliza Gant), Christoph Bantzer (Eugene), René Deltgen (Oliver), Dietmar Schönherr (Ben) and Gunnar Möller (Luke); and Paul Bogart's American adaptation (1972), featuring Timothy Bottoms (as Eugene), Barbara Colby (Miss Brown), Ronny Cox (Jake Clatt), Charles Durning (Will Pentland) and Barnard Hughes (Dr. McGuire). The Germans also filmed Wolfe's play *Welcome to Our City*, which, under Frank Wisbar's direction, became *Willkommen in Altamont* (1965), starring Wilhem Borchert (as William Rutledge), Albert Lieven (Reeves Jordan), Günther Schramm (Henry Sorrell) and Alexander Golling (Preston Carr). And *You Can't Go Home Again* was made into a TV movie by Ralph Nelson, and the cast includes Lee Grant (as Esther Jack), Chris Sarandon (George Webber), Hurd Hatfield (Foxhall Edwards) and Tammy Grimes (Amy Carlton).

While most of Wolfe's writing is filled with autobiographical elements, *Look Homeward, Angel* ([1929] 1957, the title derived from a poem by John Milton) is definitely most autobiographical. It depicts the life of his family from way before Thomas/Eugene Gant was born until one summer day when he, after graduating from Chapel Hill, makes a decision to leave Asheville and enroll at Harvard, with mixed blessings from his family. Most of the names are changed. Thomas was the youngest of eight children, but two of his siblings died before he was born. Ben, whose name is kept unchanged, died in 1918, with most of the family, including young Thomas, at his bedside. The key towns got also renamed by the author; thus, Asheville becomes Altamont and Chapel Hill gets the name Pulpit Hill.

Eugene, the most intellectual and studious of all the children, gets an opportunity to study at a small private high school, where, among other things, he is introduced to the classical languages. Consequently, most of the Latin references in *Look Homeward, Angel* can be found in the part of the novel where Eugene acquires his secondary education under the guidance of Mr. Leonard and his wife. The word 'Latin' itself, along with some Latin titles, starts to appear on p. 180, and soon the reader is bombarded with Latin quotations. Here are several excerpts of that category, all more or less self-explanatory, frequently referring to some ancient Roman classics, and beginning with the narrator's wise comment regarding advanced Latin grammar:

> **Cogitata**. Neut. Pl. of participle used as substantive. **Quo** used instead of **ut** to express purpose when comparative follows. [p. 180]

> They spent a weary age, two years, on that dull dog, Cicero. **De Senectute** [*On Old Age*]. **De Amicitia** ["On Friendship]. They skirted Virgil because John Dorsey Leonard was a bad sailor—he was not at all sure of Virgilian navigation, He hated exploration. He distrusted voyages. Next year, he said. And the great names of Ovid, lord of the elves and gnomes, the Bacchic piper of **Amores** ["Love Affairs"], or of Lucretius, full of the rhythm of tides. **Nox est perpetua** ["The night is endless"].

> "Huh?" drawled Mr. Leonard, vacantly beginning to laugh. He was fingermarked with chalk from chin to crouch. Stephen ("Pap") Rheinhart leaned forward gently and fleshed his penpoint in Eugene Gant's left rump. Eugene grunted painfully.

> "Why, no," said Mr. Leonard, stroking his chin. "A different sort of Latin."

> "What sort?" Tom Davis insisted. "Harder than Cicero?"

> 'Well," said Mr. Leonard, dubiously, "different. A little beyond you at present."

> "—**est perpetua. Una dormienda. Luna dies et nox.** ['—is endless. To be slept through. Moon day and night.']." [p. 181]

> **Odi et amo: quare id faciam ...** ["I hate and I love: why I do this ..."]

"Well, not altogether," said Mr. Leonard. "Some of them," he conceded. *... fortasse requires. Nescio, sed fieri sentio et excrucior* ["perhaps you ask. I do not know but I sense that it happens, and I am tortured." Catullus, Poem 85]." [p. 182]

"*Nulla potest mulier tantum se dicere amatam*

Vere, quantum a me Lesbia amata mea est."

["No woman can say that she has been loved truly so much as my Lesbia has been loved by me." Catullus, Poem 87] [p. 182]

The horse bent furiously to his work, like a bounding dog. With four-hooved thunder he drummed upon the sounding earth. ***Quadrupedante putrem sonitu quatit ungula campum.*** [Vergil's *Aeneid*, Book 8, line 596; translated in the preceding sentence] [p. 270]

The last excerpt is a part of a scene taking place at Mr. Leonard's school after the outburst of WW II, where Margaret Leonard, in her attempt at comforting the boys, is encouraging Eugene to keep reading books of the young men fighting in war:

With glistening eyes, he read his own epilogue, enjoyed his **post-mortem** glory, as his last words were recorded and explained by his editor. Then, witness of his own martyrdom, he dropped two smoking tears upon his young slain body. ***Dulce et decorum est pro patria mori*** ["It is sweet and honorable to die for one's country." Horace, *Odes*, III. 213]. [p. 291]

The numerous Latin references, rich in content derived from works by several Roman authors, are a true gem to the enthusiasts of classical studies. They include lines created by Cicero (full name: Marcus Tullius Cicero; 106 –7 B.C.), a statesman, lawyer and scholar who ended up beheaded by the Second Triumvirate; Vergil or Virgil (see the entry on Hilton); Ovid (see the entry on Adams); Lucretius (full name: Titus Lucretius Carus; c. 9 – c. 55 B.C.), a poet and philosopher best known for *De rerum natura* (*On the Nature of Things*); Catullus (see the entry on Huxley); and Horace (full name: Quintus Horatius Flaccus; 65–27 B.C.), the leading lyric poet of the Augustan Age.

There are some other Latin expressions encountered in *Look Homeward, Angel* that are worth quoting. Here is the list, including translations and page numbers:

Quod potui perfeci. ("I have done what I could." p. 151);

Fuimus fumus. ("We have been smoke." p. 244);

Amo, amas, amat ('I love, you love, he/she/it loves,' p. 278);

ante-bellum ('pre-war,' p. 303);

personae ('characters,' p. 309);

Et ego in Arcadia ('Even I in Arcadia,' p. 520).

Among the rich variety of Latin references incorporated by Wolfe in his first novel, there are some that are worth addressing due to their grammatical content. There are, for instance, examples of such linguistic phenomena (some of them truly unique) as the 'gerundive' – *dormienda* (meaning 'about to be asleep,' from *dormio dormire* – 'to sleep'), the 'deponent verb' – *mori* (from *morior mori* – 'to die'), the 'semi-deponent verb' – *fieri* (from *fio fieri* – 'to become/be made'), the subjunctive mood – *faciam* (from *facio facere* – 'to do/make,' as a result of being a part of an indirect question), the passive voice – *excrucior* (from *excrucio excruciare* – 'to torture/torment') and the 'Accusative & Infinitive Construction' – *Nulla potest mulier tantum se dicere amatam* (with the perfect passive participle *amatam* being the accusative, and the implied verb *esse*—represented by the present active indicative third person singular form *est* at the end of the quotation—meant to be the infinitive part of the construction).

Despite the name of the protagonist being George Webber and the name of the town frequently referred to being Libya Hill (rather than Asheville), *You Can't Go Home Again* ([1940] 1998), the other pivotal work by Wolfe, is also autobiographical to a large extent. However, the number of Latin references in it is by far less impressive. Instead, the novel incorporates a remarkable variety of German and French expressions. Furthermore, the Latin phrases in this book play neither a dramatic role nor are they an inherent part of the story; frequently used as chapter titles, they mostly serve a decorative purpose. Thus, here is the list of those lexical items—presented without their contexts, though furnished with literal translations and, in a couple of cases, also with their intended meaning:

ad infinitum ('again and again/forever', in the book translated as 'to world's end forever,' p. 465);

Delirium Tremens ('a fit of trembling,' a psychotic condition typical of withdrawal in chronic alcoholics, here used as a nickname of a student, p. 671);

Ecclesiasticus ('words of teaching,' here used as a chapter title, p. 693);

Credo (literally: 'I trust/believe,' here used as a chapter title and meant as 'a statement of one's belief,' p. 700).

One of the greatest American writers of the twentieth century, on a par with Sinclair Lewis, William Faulkner, Ernest Hemingway, John Steinbeck, Flannery O'Connor and a few others, Thomas Wolfe has an impressive literary heritage—especially considering his short life. His genius became conspicuous to his teachers in all stages of his education: at the age of nineteen, he graduated from the University of North Carolina at Chapel Hill (its motto: *Lux Libertas*—"Light and Liberty"); he was twenty-one when he acquired his degree from Harvard (its motto: *Veritas*—"Truth"). It is truly fortunate, but not accidental, that a writer of his caliber is included among those that collectively testify, indirectly but conclusively, through their writing, to the ubiquity of Latin and the unique role that it plays in modern intellectual life. The numerous and insightful Latin references (accompanied by some Greek and German quotations) found in his prose, in addition to illustrating the highly academic atmosphere in the author's (as well as Eugene's, his fictitious alter ego's) youth, give, on more than one occasion, precious input on classical culture and the enormous impact of ancient writers on people of his generation (as best illustrated on pp. 351-352 of *Look Homeward, Angel*).

7. John STEINBECK (1902–1968)

Born in Salinas, California, on February 27, 1902, John Ernst Steinbeck, Jr.— the last name was shortened from 'Großsteinbeck' by his paternal grandfather when he emigrated from Germany—studied English Literature at Stanford University near Palo Alto, but did not graduate. After many unsuccessful attempts to sell his writing, Steinbeck finally published his first novel, *Cup of Gold*, in 1929. His major works of fiction include novels *Tortilla Flat* (1935), *The Grapes of Wrath* (1939), *The Moon Is Down* (1942), *Cannery Row* (1945), *The Wayward Bus* (1947), *East of Eden* (1952), *Sweet Thursday* (1954) and *The Winter of Our Discontent* (1961); novellas *The Red Pony* (1933), *Of Mice and Men* (1937) and *The Pearl* (1947); and short story collections *The Pastures of Heaven* (1932) and *The Long Valley* (1938). His notable nonfiction books include *Travels with Charley: In Search of America* (1962), *Steinbeck: A Life in Letters* (1965), *Working Days: The Journals of The Grapes of Wrath* (1989) and *Steinbeck in Vietnam: Dispatches from the War* (2012)—the last two titles published, of course, posthumously. He won the Pulitzer Prize for Fiction in 1940 and received the Nobel Prize in Literature in 1962. He died on December 20, 1968, in New York City.

Steinbeck's filmography consists of many screen adaptations of his original works and some screenplays. The most successful items in the first group include Lewis Milestone's *Of Mice and Men* (1939; starring Burgess Meredith, Lon Chaney, Jr. and Betty Field), John Ford's Oscar-winning *The Grapes of Wrath* (1940; featuring Henry Fonda, Jane Darwell, John Carradine and Charley Grapewin), Victor Fleming's *Tortilla Flat* (1942; starring Spencer Tracy, John Garfield and Hedy Lamarr), Irving Pichel's *The Moon Is Down* (1943; featuring Cedric Hardwicke, Henry Travers and Lee J. Cobb), Emilio Fernández's *La Perla* (*The Pearl*, made in Mexico in 1947; featuring Pedro Armendáriz and Maria Elena Marqués), Lewis Milestone's *The Red Pony* (1949; starring Myrna Loy, Robert Mitchum and Louis Calhern), Elia Kazan's Oscar-winning *East of Eden* (1955; featuring James Dean, Raymond Massey, Julie Harris and Burl Ives), Victor Vicas's *The Wayward Bus* (1956; starring Joan Collins, Jayne Mansfield and Dan Dailey); Gary Sinise's *Of Mice and Men* (1992; featuring John Malkovich, Gary Sinise and Ray Walston) and Anna Shapiro's *Of Mice and Men* (2014; starring James Franco, Joel Marsh Garland and Ron Cephas Jones). Notable among the films for which Steinbeck wrote the screenplays are Alfred Hitchcock's *Lifeboat* (1944; featuring Tallulah Bankhead, John Hodiak, Hume Cronyn and William Bendix) and Elia Kazan's

Oscar-winning *Viva Zapata!* (1952; starring Marlon Brando, Anthony Quinn and Jean Peters).

Set in Monterey, California, *Tortilla Flat* ([1935] 1953) is an enormously enjoyable, humorous and uplifting, story about a group of *paisanos*, simple and fun-loving friends, led by Pilon, who differs from the rest due to his philosophical inclinations, or, rather, unusual skills to justify their behavior (idleness and using other people) and cravings (drinking cheap wine, above all). The other members of the gang include Danny (a tragic character, despite inheriting two houses, a victim of love), Sweets Ramirez (the object of Danny's affection), Pablo, Joe Portagee, The Pirate and Jesus Maria Corcoran. The Latin reference, the sign of the cross, appears in a scene where Pilon and Joe (who has just returned from army jail) seek mystic treasure in the woods on St. Andrew's Eve:

> Pilon laid his cross over the depression, and he said, "All that lies here is mine by discovery. Go away, all evil spirits. Go away, spirits of men who buried this treasure, **In Nomine Patris et Filii et Spiritus Sancti**" ['In the name of the Father, and of the Son and of the Holy Spirit'], and then he heaved a great sigh and sat down on the ground.
>
> "We have found it, oh my friend, Big Joe," he cried. "For many years I have looked, and now I have found it."
>
> "Let's dig," said Big Joe.
>
> But Pilon shook his head impatiently. "When all the spirits are free? When even to be here is dangerous? You are a fool, Big Joe. We will sit here until morning; and then we will mark the place, and tomorrow night we will dig. No one else can see the light now that we have covered it with the cross. Tomorrow night there will be no danger." [p. 41]

To satisfy the reader's curiosity, the two paisanos do go back to the woods the following night, uncover something with an official US label on it, decide it would be illegal to take it and, instead of celebrating the discovery, get drunk on the beach. And, to get back to the quoted Latin version of the sign of the cross (*signum cruscis*), it is an interesting phrase from the grammatical standpoint as it offers a cluster of three nouns in the genitive singular form, each, despite the same (masculine) gender, having a different ending due to representing a different declension: *pat*r*is* (from the-third declension noun *pater patris* – 'father'), *filii* (from the second-declension noun *filius filii* – 'son') and *spiritus* (from the fourth-declension noun *spiritus spiritūs* – 'breath of life/spirit'). The other words in the sentence (excluding the preposition *in* and the conjunction *et*) are *nomine*, which is the ablative singular form of the third-declension neuter noun *nomen nominis* ('name'), and *sancti* being the masculine genitive singular form of the first/second-declension adjective *sanctus sancta sanctum* ('holy/saint').

A couple of Latin sentences have been discovered in Steinbeck's novel *The Winter of Our Discontent* (1961), a morality tale set in Long Island. Its protagonist, Ethan Allen Halley, is forced to work in a grocery store because of the family's fortune lost by his father. Though honest and honorable at heart, Ethan gradually, under the influence of his friends and acquaintances, compromises his integrity to gain his family fortune back, along with power in the local community. The quoted scene depicts a conversation between Ethan and Alfio Marullo, the owner of the grocery store where Ethan works, regarding honesty and stealing:

"We work it out some way."

"Then I couldn't steal from you without robbing myself."

He laughed appreciatively. "You're smart, kid. But you don't steal."

"You didn't listen. Maybe I plan to take it all.

"You're honest, kid."

"That's what I'm telling you. When I'm most honest, nobody believes me. I tell you, Alfio, to conceal your motives, tell the truth."

"What kind of talk you do?"

"***Ars est celare artem*** ["It is art to conceal art." Or: "True art conceals the means by which it is achieved." Or still better: "True art is to conceal art."]."

He moved his lips over that and then broke into a laugh. "Ho," he cried. "Ho! Ho! **Hic erat demonstrandum.** ["This was to be demonstrated/ proven."]

"Want a cold Coke?"

"No good for here!" He flung his arms across his abdomen.

"You aren't old enough for a bad stomach, not over fifty."

"Fifty-two, and I got a bad stomach."

"Okay," I said. "Then you came over at twelve if it was 1920. I guess they started **Latin** early in Sicily."

"I was choirboy," he said.

"I used to carry the cross in the choir myself. I'm going to have a Coke. Alfio," I said, "you work out a way for me to buy in here and I'll look at it. But I warn you, I don't have money." [p. 141]

What is rather unusual about the two quotations—one of them being an anonymous Latin proverb and the other a paraphrase of the formula *Quod erat demonstrandum* ("What was to be demonstrated") derived from Greek and used at the end of a logical, mathematical or philosophical equation—is that each is delivered by another person, both men, however, familiar with Latin due to the same experience that took place on two sides of the Atlantic. Grammatically, the first one offers one (third-declension) noun – *ars artis* ('art') – in two forms: nominative singular (*ars*), used as the subject, and accusative singular (*artem*) used as the direct object of the first-conjugation verb *celo celare* ('to hide'). The construction of the second quotation is a combination of the irregular verb *esse* ('to be') in the third person singular of the Imperfect Tense (*erat*) and a gerundive of the first-conjugation verb *demonstro demonstrare* ('to show/demonstrate') used to express necessity or obligation. It is worth pointing out (as one more advantage of knowing Latin) that a given conjugation of the verb is frequently reflected in the spelling of English derivatives: it explains, for instance, why 'demonstrable' is spelled with an 'a' as opposed to 'i' (which is typical of derivatives from verbs of other conjugations) as in, e.g., 'edible' or 'legible,' other adjectives of the same type.

But, to get back to the storyline of Steinbeck's novel, Ethan comes up with an idea of tipping the Immigration about Alfio's illegal status, makes his boss (unaware of Ethan's trick and believing in his honesty) arrested and even gets from him the store, which is just one step in his immorally accomplished social and economic climb.

One of Steinbeck's foremost nonfiction works, *Travels with Charley* ([1962] 1963), follows the author's adventures, with French poodle Charley as his only companion, in the United States of the early 1960s. It is a beautiful, reflective, honest and insightful memoir. Even though it does not belong in the scope of this book, the two Latin references found in its pages justify making an exception of the rule and including them here, especially because the book is, after all, a good example of a narrative work. The first one is the motto of the essays by John Addison that the narrator comes across in *The Spectator*, Edited by Henry Morley, Volume 1—Thursday, March 1, 1711, and reads while enjoying the sunshine in the White Mountains:

*"Non fumum ex fulgore, sed ex fumo dare lucem
Cogitat, et speciosa dehinc miracula promat."*

["He does not lavish at a blaze of his fire,
Sudden to glare, and in a smoke expire;
But rises from a cloud of smoke to light,
And pours his specious miracles to sight."] – Horace. [p. 38]

While the motto itself comes from *Ars Poetica* ("The Art of Poetry), a poem written by Horace (see the entry on Wolfe) in 19 B.C., in which the author offers advice to other poets on the art of writing poetry and drama—its translation presented above (within brackets) is copied from that done by Philip Francis himself.

The other reference, which has been already quoted in this entry (and thus needs no translation), becomes a part of a conversation between the narrator and a Filipino man that worked for him on a little ranch in the Santa Cruz Mountains of California. When asked by Steinbeck if he is afraid of the haunting place, the Filipino man replies he is not because of a charm he received from a witch doctor some years ago.

"Let me see the charm," I asked.

"It's words," he said. "It's a word charm."

"Can you say them to me?"

"Sure," he said and he droned, "***In nomine Patris et Filii et Spiritus Sancti.***"

"What does it mean?" I asked.

He raised his shoulders. "I don't know," he said. It's a charm against evil spirits so I am not afraid of them." [p. 61]

Despite the controversy around his Nobel Prize at the time it was granted, John Steinbeck indisputably belongs among the foremost American writers of the twentieth century. Deeply involved in the most crucial issues related to the condition of mankind, depicting life in a sensitive, compassionate and realistic way, Steinbeck's best works—such as *Of Mice and Men*, *The Grapes of Wrath* (possibly the most powerful and moving tale of dignity unaffected by poverty) and *East of Eden*—do not seem to age, and some of them, due to their unsurpassed values and universal appeal—are selected as required reading not only in American and British high schools. The Latin references encountered in his prose (including the sign of the cross, which illustrates his religious consciousness often reflected in his themes; he was Episcopalian), though relatively innumerous, contribute to the belief that the assets of Vergil's language should not be overlooked despite the false assumption of its uselessness. To conclude the entry on this great author, let me present the motto of his alma mater, Stanford—*Semper virens* ("Ever flourishing")—which had been preceded by a German version (*Die Luft der Freiheit weht*, meaning "The winds of freedom blow").

8. Irwin SHAW (1913–1984)

Irwin Shaw was born Irwin Gilbert Shamforoff on February 27, 1913, in South Bronx, New York, to a family of Jewish immigrants from Russia. He graduated from Brooklyn College (B.A. 1934), and, after establishing his career in writing, he served in the army during World War II, for some time attached (eventually as a warrant officer) to George Stevens's film unit. In addition to a host of short stories, he wrote novels—notably *The Young Lions* (1948, cashing on his war experience), *Lucy Crown* (1956), *Two Weeks in Another Town* (1960), *Rich Man, Poor Man* (1970), its sequel, *Beggarman, Thief* (1977; both titles exemplifying a poetic device known as 'asyndeton') and *Acceptable Losses* (1982)—and plays, the most successful being *Bury the Dead* (1936) and *Quiet City* (1939). A winner of the O. Henry Award (1944, 1945), the National Institute of Arts and Letters Grant (1946) and the Playboy Award (1964, 1970, 1979), he also received an Honorary Doctorate from Brooklyn College. He died on May 16, 1984, in Davos, Switzerland.

Shaw's filmography includes over a dozen screenplays, written between 1936 and 1968, and several screen adaptations of his novels and short stories. Among the films scripted by Shaw (usually in collaboration), the ones that stand out include George Stevens's *The Talk of the Town* (1942; starring Cary Grant, Jean Arthur and Ronald Colman), John Farrow's *Commandos Strike at Dawn* (1942; featuring Paul Muni, Anna Lee, Lillian Gish and Cedric Hardwicke) and Delbert Mann's *Desire Under the Elms* (1958; from Eugene O'Neill's play; starring Sophia Loren, Anthony Perkins and Burl Ives). The best adaptations of his original works are Edward Dmytryk's *The Young Lions* (1958; featuring Marlon Brando, Montgomery Clift and Dean Martin), Vincente Minnelli's *Two Weeks in Another Town* (1962; starring Kirk Douglas, Edward G. Robinson and Cyd Charisse) and Robert Parrish's *In the French Style* (1963; featuring Jean Seberg, Stanley Baker and Philippe Forquet), based on the short stories "In the French Style" and "A Year to Learn the Language." Also notable is the TV series based on the novel *Rich Man, Poor Man*, which was made in the years 1976-1977 with Peter Strauss (as Rudy Jordache), Nick Nolte (Tom Jordache) and Susan Blakely (Julie Prescott) in the leading roles. It was followed by Lawrence Doheny's TV movie *Beggarman, Thief* (1979), starring Jean Simmons (as Gretchen Jordache Burke), Glenn Ford (David Donnelly) and Lynn Redgrave (Kate Jordache).

One Latin reference (used twice) was found in Shaw's novel *Beggarman, Thief* (1977), which picks up the story of *Rich Man, Poor Man* in 1968, after the murder of Tom Jordache, and the main characters here are Tom's widow, Kate, their son, Wesley (who grew up without really knowing his father), and Tom's siblings, Rudy and Gretchen Burke. Another character that appears in the quoted scene is Alice Larkin, a *Time* Magazine reporter and aspiring novelist helping Wesley find information regarding his father's murder. She shares with Wesley her new, quite accidental, findings of a woman who might have intimately known his father when he was just sixteen:

> "It seems that there was a juicy divorce in Elysium quite a few years ago." Alice said, "a respected burgher named Harold Jordache—the name's familiar to you, I imagine ...?" She smiled at him over the platter of cold cuts.
>
> "Oh, come on," he said.
>
> "His wife sued him for divorce because she found him in bed with the maid. It was big news in Elysium, Ohio, and our stringer, his name is Farrell, you might look him up if you have time, covered it for the local sheet. Farrell said the wife walked away with a bundle, the house, half the business, alimony, a woman publicly scorned and all that in a small, God-fearing town. Anyway, can you guess the name of the lady taken ***in flagrante delicto*** ['in the act of wrongdoing']?"
>
> "You tell me," Wesley said, although he could guess the name and even guess what ***in flagrante delicto*** meant.
>
> "Clothilde," Alice said triumphantly. "Clothilde Devereaux. She runs a Laundromat just down the street from Farrell's paper. I have the address in my pocketbook. How does that grab you?"
>
> "I'll leave for Ohio tomorrow," Wesley said. [p. 206]

To satisfy the reader's curiosity, it has to be added that Wesley does find the mysterious lady in Elysium, they have a nice chat and, among other things, she learns from Wesley about the yacht his father owned on the Mediterranean, which he happened, for an apparent reason as of now, to name the *Clothilde*. As for the Latin phrase, it consists of a preposition (rather obvious), a present participle of the first-conjugation verb *flagro flagrare* ('to blaze/glow/flame') in the ablative singular case and the second-declension neuter noun *delictum* ('fault/offense/crime'). Thus, the literal meaning of the phrase is something like 'in blazing offense/crime,' with 'blazing,' naturally, used metaphorically. While in many other instances, the phrase *in flagrante delicto* is used in the legal sense, where it emphasizes the unquestioned guilt of a criminal, its implications in the above excerpt are purely moral.

Two Latin references have been discovered in *Acceptable Losses* ([1982] 1983), a thriller whose protagonist, literary agent Roger Damon, is exasperated due to a mysterious phone call involving threats and forcing him to look back into his past. The first quotation appears in the dialogue between Damon's wife, Sheila, and his friend and associate, Oliver Gabrielsen, shortly after they accidentally find out about a Mozart concert that Roger went to secretly:

> "Now," said Oliver, "why would he do anything like that, do you think?"
>
> "It might be because of Mozart," Sheila said.
>
> "What would that have to do with his making up a story to tell you? A concert isn't like having an assignation with another woman."
>
> "This particular concert," Sheila said, speaking slowly, "might be like having an assignation. Mozart's last work, the Requiem, contracted for by Count von Walsegg-Stupach to be sung for a Mass for his dead wife." Sheila's voice sank to a whisper. "***Dies Irae. Lacrimosa*** ['Day of Wrath. The Weeping One']. Another kind of assignation. Remember, Roger was born a Catholic, even if he hasn't done much about it since. [p. 159]

Since the origin of the Latin reference is only partially explained in the excerpt itself, it seems appropriate to add that *Lacrimosa* stands for The Virgin Mary, which emphasizes the dual, musical and religious significance of the whole reference.

The other reference, much longer, appears some twenty pages later, when Roger Damon, alone, goes from New York to the cemetery near Ford's Junction, where his parents and brother are buried.

> Yes, it had been a good idea to drive up from New York to his boyhood home to commune with his only family and to see for himself that their modest tombs had remained proper and fitting receptacles for those irreproachable and beloved souls.
>
> The day after he had heard the Mozart Requiem he had looked up the words of the Mass. His memory was good and his schoolboy **Latin** served well enough so that he could remember the first section. He said it to himself above the tombstones.

Requiem aeternam dona eis, Domine, et lux perpetua luceat eis.
Te decet hymnus, Deus, in Sion, et tibi reddetur votum in Jerusalem.
Exaudi orationem meam, as te omnis caro veniet.

["Eternal rest grant unto them, O Lord, and let perpetual light shine upon them.
To Thee is due the hymn, O God, in Sion, and to Thee shall the vow be paid in Jerusalem.
Oh, hear my prayer: unto Thee all flesh shall come."].

He skipped the repetition of the first three lines of the Mass and whispered the last two somber resounding phrases—"Kyrie eleison, Christe eleison" [Greek: "God, have mercy; Christ, have mercy."].

Honor thy father and thy mother, as the Lord God hath commanded thee, that thy days may be prolonged and that it may go well with thee ...
[pp. 191-192]

The above quotation offers four verb forms worth addressing: two present active subjunctive (jussive) forms in the third person singular – *luceat* (from the second-conjugation verb *luceo lucēre* – 'to shine') and *veniet* (from the fourth-conjugation verb *venio venire* – 'to come'), one verb, *reddetur* (from the third-conjugation verb *redo reddĕre* – 'to give back'), in the Future Passive Indicative, and one verb, *exaudi* (from the fourth-conjugation verb *exaudio* – 'to hear plainly'), in the Present Active Imperative singular form. The reference is of interest also because it illustrates the correlation between Latin and classical music.

Somewhat forgotten today and relatively underrated, Irwin Shaw, with some bestselling novels, such as *The Young Lions* (1948) and *Night Work* (1975), to his credit, is nevertheless one of the major American writers of the mid-twentieth century. Even though Latin references were found only in two of Shaw's works and, admittedly, not the author's top achievements, his contribution to the popularization of Vergil's language is relatively significant. The Latin motto of Brooklyn College, his alma mater, is *Nil sine magno labore* ("Nothing without great effort").

9. Julio CORTÁZAR (1914–1984)

Born on August 16, 1914, in Ixelles, Belgium, Julio Cortázar studied philosophy and languages at the University of Buenos Aires, which he did not graduate from due to financial problems, and worked as a teacher in a couple of schools. He was an Argentine writer of novels, short stories, poetry and essays. His major works include novels *Final Exam* (1950, published in 1985), *The Winners* (1960), *Hopscotch* (1963) and *A Manual for Manuel* (1973), and short story collections *Cronopios and Famas* (1962) and *Blow-up and Other Stories* (1968). Closely associated with a literary movement known as "Latin American Boom" and a winner of Prix Médicis (France, 1974) and Rubén Darío Order of Cultural Independence (Nicaragua, 1983), Cortázar died on February 12, 1984, in Paris, France.

Cortázar's published works inspired about a dozen short or feature films. Those that stand out include Manuel Antin's *Odd Number* (1962; starring Lautaro Murúa and María Rosa Gallo)—from the short story "Cartas de mama," and *Circe* (1964; featuring Graciela Borges, Raúl Aubel and Alberto Argibay)—from the story of the same name; Michelangelo Antonioni's *Blow-Up* (1966; starring David Hemmings, Vanessa Redgrave and Sarah Miles)—from the short story "Las babas de diablo," Jean-Luc Godard's *Weekend* (1967; featuring Mireille Darc, Jean Yanne and Jean-Pierre Kalfon)—from the short story "La autopista del Sur," Jana Bokova's *Diary for a Tale* (1998; starring Germán Palacios, Silke and Inés Estéves)—from the short story "Diario para un cuento," and Berenika (Maciejewicz) Bailey's *Mucha* (*The Fly*, 2010; featuring Tomek Danko, Piotr Waliszewski and Berenika Bailey).

One of Cortázar's prime novels, *The Winners* ([1960] 1965, originally published in Spanish as *Los Premios*), is a story of an unusual (metaphorical) ocean journey offered as a prize to some lottery winners, a diverse group of individuals including dentist Gabriel Medrano (who, toward the end of the book, gets killed with three bullets), secondary school teachers Carlos Lopez and Dr. Restelli, the Trejo family, Don Galo Porriño, Claudia Freire and her son Jorge, a couple known to the reader as Paula and Raul, Doña Pepa, Doña Rosita, the Presutti family, Captain Smith and several others. The novel brims with Latin references, most of them, however, relatively short and quite well-known to both Spanish and English speakers.

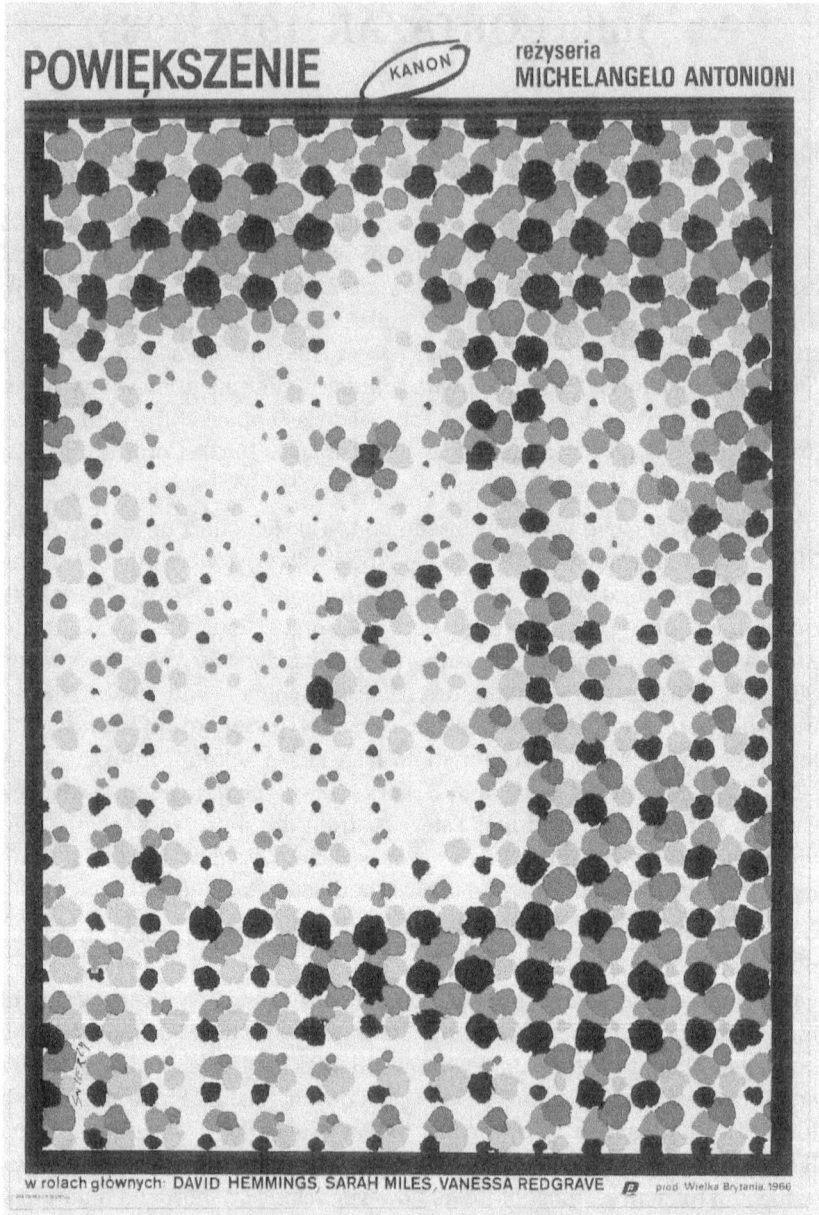

Figure 1.1. Polish poster, designed by Waldemar Świerzy (1968), for Michelangelo Antonioni's *Blow-Up* (1966, based on the short story by Julio Cortázar). Courtesy of the "Ikonosfera" Gallery and Transart Collection.

The person responsible for the first Latin expression is Persio, a proofreader at Kraft Publishing who travels with Claudia as her distant relative. The quoted excerpt shows Persio's reaction to Jorge's public recitation, which was encouraged by Claudia as a response to Persio's comment regarding amusement and spectacle.

> "Recite the verse about Garrick for Persio," said Claudia to Jorge. "A good illustration of your theory."
>
> "*When the public saw Mr. Garrick, an actor from England ...*" Jorge declaimed at a shout. Persio listened attentively and then applauded. There was applause from other tables, and Jorge blushed.
>
> "***Quod erat demonstrandum***" ['What was to be shown/demonstrated'], Persio said. "Of course, I was alluding to a more ontological plane, to the fact that all amusement is like the consciousness of a mask, which animates and finally supplants the real face." [p. 20]

Another Latin reference worth quoting in its context appears in the conversation between Lopez and Paula:

> The orange blouse got to Lopez too, as he was coming on deck after having arranged his things. Paula was reading, facing the sun, and he leaned up against the railing and waited until she looked up.
>
> "Hello," said Paula. "How are you, professor?"
>
> "***Horresco referens***," Lopez murmured. "Don't call me professor or I'll throw you overboard, book and all."
>
> "Françoise Sagan, and she doesn't merit that kind of treatment. I see the river air awakens piratelike instincts in you. Walk the plank or something like that, no?" [p. 106]

While there are two literary references in the above excerpt (Françoise Sagan was a well-known French playwright, novelist and screenwriter; 1935 – 2004), the bold-printed Latin quotation comes from Vergil's *Aeneid* (Book II, line 204), and the sentence—composed of a first person singular form of the third-conjugation verb *horresco horrescĕre* ('to dread/become terrified/shudder') in the Present Active Indicative Tense and a present active participle of the irregular verb *rĕfĕro rĕferre* ('to carry back/bring back/restore/repeat/answer')— means "I shudder as I relate" and offers an example of a poetic device known as 'aposiopesis' (breaking off in speech or a story to address something outside of it). While in the above excerpt the quotation is used to allow a Cortázar's character to shine in a small talk with a fellow passenger, when used originally by Vergil (see the entry on Lewis), it shows Aeneas's feelings as he relates (to queen Dido and her court people) the scene where two huge serpents emerge unexpectedly from the sea and are about to devour Laocoön and his sons, thus preventing the Trojan priest from revealing the real truth behind "the Trojan horse" abandoned by the Greeks.

One more Latin reference, appearing toward the end of the book, after the unusual events on the ship make the passengers behave in strange ways, deserves a special treatment due to its historical significance. *Vox populi, vox Dei*, meaning "The voice of the people (is) the voice of God," happens to be the title of a Whig tract of 1709, eventually becoming *The Judgment of Whole Kingdoms and Nations, Concerning the Rights, Power, and Prerogative of Kings, and the Rights, Privileges and Properties of the People*, a historical book containing texts by Baron John Somers Somers, Daniel Defoe and John Dunton.

> He was choking, he was too upset to go on. Taking him by the arm Lopez tried to sit him down, but Pelusa resisted. Then Lopez stood up and looked Señor Trejo straight in the eye.
>
> "***Vox populi, vox Dei***," he said. "Go have breakfast, sir. And as for you, Señor Porriño, keep your comments to yourself. And that goes for the ladies, too."
>
> "Unbelievable!" Don Galo vociferated, to a background of feminine groans and exclamations. "It's an abuse of power!" [p. 350]

The remaining Latin references encountered in the book are listed below, without the contexts in which they appear, along with the English translations and page numbers:

curriculum vitae ('a detailed account of one's educational background, professional training and work experience,' pp. 72, 182);

ad infinitum ('eternally/forever,' p. 95);

ad libitum ('as much or as often as necessary or desired, p. 107);

sanctum sanctorum ('the holy of holies,' humorously: 'a private or secret place,' p. 113);

9. Julio CORTÁZAR (1914–1984)

ipso facto ('by the very fact or act,' p. 149);

pervigilium veneris ('the vigil of Venus,' it also happens to be the title of a poem written between the second and fifth centuries, attributed to either Publius Annius Florus or Tiberianus, p. 240);

illo tempore ('in/at that time,' p. 257).

The first item on the list is a phrase commonly used in English and other (probably not only) European languages; while *curriculum* by itself is usually associated with a school syllabus, a list of course components or simply what is being taught, the second element is the genitive singular form of the feminine noun *vita* ('life'); thus, if one insists on receiving the literal translation of the pair of words, it should be something like 'the course of life.' Among the other phrases, there are two composed of the preposition *ad* and a noun in the accusative case (a normal sequence, something to be expected), two more phrases – *sanctum sanctorum* and *pervigilium veneris* – being a combination of two nouns, one in the nominative case and the other in the genitive case (plural and singular, respectively), and two phrases in the ablative case (the most common and most versatile of the cases), the first one being an example of an ablative of manner and the second one an ablative of time.

Julio Cortázar, whose impact was acknowledged, among others, by Chilean novelist Roberto Bolaño and Puerto Rican novelist Giannina Braschi, is unquestionably one of the greatest, most innovative, most influential and most popular international writers of the twentieth century. Due to the unusual blend of realism and fantasy in the content of his prose, the genres he is usually placed within include magical realism and surrealism. Based solely on the Latin references found in *The Winners*, the writer's contribution to the thesis of the immortality of Vergil's language is enormous and can be surpassed only by a few. The Latin motto of the University of Buenos Aires, which the author attended, is *Argentum virtus robur et studium* ("Argentine virtue is strength and study.").

10. Saul BELLOW (1915–2005)

Saul Bellow was born Solomon Bellows on June 10, 1915, in Lachine, Quebec, Canada, to a family of Lithuanian-Jewish immigrants. A dedicated lover of the Bible and a big fan of Shakespeare and the Russian novelists of the nineteenth century, Bellow was educated at the University of Chicago, from which he transferred to Northwestern University (B.A. in Anthropology and Sociology, 1937, with honors) and then did graduate work at the University of Wisconsin. He contributed his fiction and criticism to several prestigious magazines and taught at Yale University, the University of Minnesota, New York University, Princeton University, the University of Puerto Rico, the University of Chicago, Boston University and others. In addition to four short story collections, one play and a few nonfiction books, he wrote fourteen novels, including *Dangling Man* (1944, his debut), *The Victim* (1947), *The Adventures of Augie March* (1953, National Book Award), *Seize the Day* (1956), *Henderson the Rain King* (1959), *Herzog* (1964, National Book Award), *Mr. Sammler's Planet* (1970; National Book Award), *Humboldt's Gift* (1975, Pulitzer Prize), *More Die of Heartbreak* (1987), *A Theft* (1989), *The Actual* (1997) and *Ravelstein* (2000, his last). Besides the already mentioned literary recognitions, Bellow received the *Croix de Chevalier des Arts et Lettres* in 1968, the Nobel Prize in Literature in 1976 and the National Medal of Arts in 1988. He died on April 5, 2005, in Brookline, Massachusetts.

Bellow's highly intellectual prose, full of references, symbolism and philosophical questions and dilemmas, is not easy to translate into images. Consequently, there is only one theatrical movie based on his writing, Fielder Cook's *Seize the Day* (1986; starring Robin Williams, Glenne Headley, Richard B. Shull and David Bickford), which received mixed reviews despite some good performances. Other than that, his filmography consists of some episodes of minor TV series, including one based on *Humboldt's Gift*, made in 1975 as a part of the talk show *2nd House*.

The protagonist of *Mr. Sammler's Planet* (1970) is a somewhat eccentric but highly educated, enormously experienced and unusually contemplative man, Arthur Sammler, who was born in Krakow, survived the Holocaust and, having lived for some time in England, eventually found safety and education in America. He looks at life in a way much different from anyone's around him, worries about the future of the world and tries to find answers to a lot of crucial questions. Sammler's erudition is instrumental in providing all of the Latin words and phrases that one can find in the book.

The first Latin reference, absolutely self-explanatory, appears in an extensive narrative passage regarding Sammler's sessions with the university students that Shula-Slawa, his daughter, hired to read to him due to his blindness:

> He found after they had read to him for a few hours that he had to teach them the subject, explain the terms, do etymologies for them as though they were twelve-year-olds. "*Janua*—a door. Janitor—one who minds the door." "*Lapis*, a stone. Dilapidate, take apart the stones. One cannot say it of a person. [p. 40]

The next reference is again the narrator's description of Sammler's thoughts; this time, the scholar analyzes more general philosophical ideas which he is confronting with those of Dr. Lal:

> So many false starts, blind alleys, postulates which decayed before the end of the argument. Even the ablest thinkers groping as they approached their limits, running out of evidence, running out of certainties. But whether they were optimists or pessimists, whether the final vision was dark or bright, it was generally **terra cognita** ['familiar territory'] to old Sammler. So Dr. Lal had a certain value. He brought news. [p. 58]

The Latin phrase quoted in the above paragraph is the reverse of the popular expression *terra incognita*, which has its genesis in the times when Roman mapmakers drew a land area not yet explored and, consequently, labeled it in this way, which meant the "Unknown Territory." Consequently, the land that was discovered by Columbus and his followers, *terra incognita* by that time, came to be known as the "New World."

The next two quotations refer to Walter Bruch, an old acquaintance whom Sammler and his cousin Angela come across at a Rouault exhibition. Both quoted passages testify to the man's eccentricity:

> In a black raincoat, in a cap, gray hair bunched before the ears; his reddish-swarthy teapot cheeks; his big mulberry-tinted lips—well, imagine the Old World; imagine souls there by the barrelful; imagine them sent to incarnation and birth with dominant qualities **ab initio** ['from the beginning']. [p. 60]

> Bruch might very suddenly begin to sing like the blind man on Seventy-second Street, pulling along the seeing-eye dog, shaking pennies in his cup: "What a friend we have in Jesus—God bless you, sir." He also enjoyed mock funerals with **Latin** and music, Monteverdi,

Pergolesi, the Mozart C Minor Mass; he sang *"Et incarnatus est"* ["And he was incarnate."] in falsetto. [p. 61]

Sammler's deep thoughts regarding the condition of Humankind, the terror related to living and dying, are the context of the following passage, including a few Latin phrases or sentences:

> The planet was our mother and our burial ground. No wonder the human spirit wished to leave. Leave the prolific belly. Leave also this great tomb. Passion for the infinite caused by the terror, by *timor mortis* ['fear of death'], needed material appeasement. *Timor mortis conturbat me* ["Fear of death disturbs me."]. *Dies irae* ['Day of wrath']. *Quid sum miser tunc dicturus* ["What shall I, frail man, be pleading at that time?"]. [p. 185]

The above passage consists of two references. The sentence referring to the fear of death comes from a responsory of the Catholic Office of the Dead, in the third Nocturn of Matins (as arranged in the Roman Breviary by Pope Pius V); the remaining part comes from the Georgian Chant *Dies Irae*, based on the prophecy of *Sophonias 1:14-16* and used in the *Requiem Mass*. An item interesting from the grammatical standpoint is the combination of *sum* (present tense, first person singular of the irregular verb *esse* – 'to be') and *dicturus* (future participle of the third-conjugation verb *dico dicĕre dixi dictum* – 'to say/speak/tell'), together meaning 'I am about to speak' or 'I shall speak/plead' (the future progressive translation, 'I shall be pleading,' obviously possible as well).

The other Latin references discovered in the pages of *Mr. Sammler's Planet* are **Quod erat demonstrandum** ('That which had to be shown/demonstrated," p. 54) and **pro bono publico** ('for the public good,' p. 202).

The narrator/protagonist of Bellow's novel *More Die of Heartbreak* (1987) is Kenneth Trachtenberg, also an immigrant to the USA, this one giving up France in favor of the Middle West as his new domicile. Just like Sammler, Kenneth is an intellectual with philosophical inclinations, and the book itself, just like the previous one, is more a character development study than an exciting, action-packed story. The only Latin reference was discovered in a passage illustrating Kenneth's current deliberations during his cab ride with his uncle, Professor Benn Chlorophyll, to the Miami Airport:

> During Uncle's silent interval I had time to consider poor Aunt Lena's principle, adapted Swedenborg or Blake. Suppose that what he saw was the measure of a man. Then what was Uncle now? A person like Benn

can't be compartmentalized: a visionary with plants, a dub with the women. If you have peculiar talents you must be prepared to defend them. How many people in this (humanly underdeveloped) world have such distinguished abilities (a credit to **Homo sapiens**) [literally: 'sensible human being,' technically: 'human species']? But this is what befalls talent when one tenth of the person makes galactic calculations, while his human remainder is still counting on its fingers. [p. 306]

One of the greatest thinkers among the writers of the twentieth century, the author of deeply sophisticated novels addressing, boldly and realistically, the problems of modern civilization with protagonists that stand out for their bravery, sensitivity and thoughtfulness, Saul Bellow is also, just like his heroes, a scholar of the highest caliber, well educated in every respect including the classical studies. While one of his novels is a translation of a very well-known Latin saying, *Carpe diem*, he also embellished his other novels with rare Latin references, giving an indirect testimony to the significance and immortality of the language of Vergil, Ovid and Julius Caesar. It is appropriate, thus, to cite the Latin mottos of the universities where he was educated. They are *Crescat scientia; vita excolatur* ("Let knowledge grow from more to more, and so be human life enriched")—the University of Chicago; and *Quaecumque sunt vera* ("Whatsoever things are true.")—Northwestern University's motto originating from the New Testament book of Philippians (4:8).

11. Morris L. WEST (1916–1999)

Morris Langlo West was born on April 26, 1916, in St. Kilda, Victoria, Australia, and educated at the University of Melbourne. A novelist and a playwright, he is best known as the author of such novels as *Gallows of the Sand* (1955), *The Big Story* (1957), *The Devil's Advocate* (1959), *The Naked Country* (1960), *The Shoes of the Fisherman* (1963), *The Ambassador* (1965), *The Tower of Babel* (1968), *The Salamander* (1973), *The Navigator* (1976) and *The Clowns of God* (1981). The Vatican correspondent for the *Daily Mail* in the years 1956-1963 and a winner of the James Tait Black memorial prize (1959), West, who also used pen names Michael East and Julian Morris, died on October 9, 1990, in Clareville, New South Wales, Australia.

Among West's relatively numerous film credits, there are five major theatrical productions based on his novels—Don Chaffey's *The Crooked Road* (1965; starring Robert Ryan, Stewart Granger and Nadia Gray; from *The Big Story*), Michael Anderson's *The Shoes of the Fisherman* (1968; featuring Anthony Quinn, Laurence Olivier, Oskar Werner, David Janssen, Vittorio De Sica and John Gielgud), Guy Green's *The Devil's Advocate* (1977; starring John Mills, Stéphane Audran and Jason Miller), Peter Zinner's *The Salamander* (1981; featuring Franco Nero, Anthony Quinn, Martin Balsam, Sybil Danning and Christopher Lee) and Tim Burstall's *The Naked Country* (1985; starring John Stanton, Rebecca Gilling and Ivar Kants).

Focused on Vatican politics as the background of the fictitious election of a Ukrainian pope, *The Shoes of the Fisherman* ([1963] 1968) was published (ironically and unforeseeably) on June 3, 1963, the day of the death of Pope John XXIII, and about fifteen years before the real and historically significant election of Slav Karol Wojtyła as Pope John Paul II. Needless to say, the book abounds in Latin references.

The very first Latin phrase deserves to be presented in its context as the excerpt offers some interesting historical information:

> Every coin new-minted in the Vatican City, every stamp now issued, bore the words **sede vacante**, which even those without Latinity might understand as "while the Chair is vacant." The Vatican newspaper carried the same sign on its front page, and would wear a black band of mourning until the new Pontiff was named. [p. 6]

The next quoted excerpt, relating just one part of the electoral procedures, focuses on Cardinal Leone of the Holy Office, who is also the Dean of the Sacred College.

> The lector was reading from the Acts of the Apostles. "'In those days, Peter began and said, Men, Brethren, the Lord charged us to preach to the people and to testify that He is the one who has been appointed by God to be judge of the living and of the dead. ...'" The choir sang, "***Veni, Sancte Spiritus ...*** Come, Holy Spirit, and fill the hearts of the faithful." Then Leone began to read in his strong stubborn voice the Gospel for the day of the conclave ... [p. 14]

The unexpected turning point in the story is when Ukrainian Kiril Cardinal Lakota is elected to be the Pope. Here is an extensive excerpt relating the pivotal moment in the history of the Church:

> In a loud voice Leone challenged him:
>
> "***Acceptasne electionem*** [Do you accept election]?"
>
> All eyes were turned on the tall, lean stranger with his scarred face and his dark beard and his distant, haunted eyes. Seconds ticked away slowly, and then they heard him answer in a dead flat voice:
>
> "***Accepto ... Miserere mei Deus. ...*** I accept. ... God have mercy on me!" [p. 29]

A good and vigilant Latin grammarian could wonder whether the form of the noun *Deus* ('God') is correct in the quoted excerpt. Since the usual ending of the second declension, masculine singular nouns ending in '-us' in the nominative singular case is '-e' in the vocative singular case, one can expect the form to be *Dee* rather than *Deus*, just like *serve*, *amice* or *Brute*. However, there is no consensus about that particular form: according to some, the classic Latin form was *Dee*; according to others, it did not exist, and, according to still others, both forms coexisted. In any case, though, *Deus* was considered to be an acceptable vocative form in the Vulgate, i.e., the common or colloquial version of the language.

A Latin reference that is definitely worth quoting here appears in the novel for the first time when the newly elected Pope concludes his extensive address to the cardinals with a brief question. The Latin expression, apparently revealing the Pope's insecurity, uncertainty or need to be accepted, is clearly one of his favorite ones, as it also appears on pp. 45 and 286, both times used by the Ukrainian Pontiff.

Then he handed them like a challenge the formal Latin question:

Quid vobis videtur ... "How does it seem to you?" [p. 43]

There are several more Latin expressions used throughout the book, all, as it is easy to guess, referring to the religious or Catholic theme. Here is the list with the English translations, all of which, except the penultimate one, are offered by the author himself:

Ex oriente lux ... ('A light out of the East,' p. 40);

Appello ad Petrum ("I appeal to Peter." p. 44);

Cor ad cor loquitur ("Heart speaks to heart." pp. 49, 105);

Deinde ego te absolvo a peccatis tuis ("I absolve you from your sins." p. 71);

In manus tuas, Domine ('Into your hands, O God,' p. 80);

Opus Dei ('Work of God,' p. 242);

Placetne, fratres ("What say you, my brothers? Does that please you or not?" p. 286).

Two of the quotations on the list use verbs in the Present Active Indicative, first person singular form – *Appello* (from the third-conjugation verb *appello appellĕre* – 'to drive to/direct the mind to something') and *absolvo* (from the third-conjugation verb *absolvo absolĕre* – 'to loosen/relate/complete'); one in the Present Active Indicative, third person singular form – *loquitur* (from the third-conjugation deponent verb *loquor loqui* – 'to speak'), and one in the Present Active Indicative, second person singular form – *Placetne* (from the second-conjugation verb *placeo placēre* – 'to please/be agreeable to') plus the enclitic particle '-ne' used to make a 'yes/no' question. Based on the information provided in the last clause, the correct translation of the last quotation on the list is "Does that/it please (you), brothers?" (with the third person singular subject implied by the ending '-t' of the verb). Hence, the author's version of the translation is not only unnecessarily longer, but also incorrect since the particle '-ne' does not introduce or imply any negative connotation or expectation.

Among the other interesting grammatical aspects within the quotations, it is worth pointing out *ad Petrum* and *In manus tuas* – two examples of the accusative of destination (or 'the place to which'), the first one (singular) preceded by the preposition *ad* ('to/toward/against') and the second (plural) by the preposition *in* (here meaning 'into'). Finally, *a peccatis tuis* is a sample of the ablative of separation (both the noun and the possessive pronoun being ablative plural forms), illustrating, at the same time, the correct choice (in front of a consonant) between the two forms of the preposition *a/ab* ('from/away from').

Morris L. West is the first out of two Australasian writers discussed in this book, the other one being C. K. Stead. West is a popular and well-respected writer of the twentieth century, and his recurrent theme, religion, is something that he enriches his prose with due to his precious experience as a Vatican correspondent. It is rather to be expected that his other novels also brim with Latin references, but, even without that assumption, the author's contribution to the promotion of various aspects of the ancient language is absolutely impressive. Quite suitably, the Latin motto of West's alma mater, the University of Melbourne, is *Postera Crescam Laude* ("I will grow in the esteem of future generations.")

12. Flannery O'CONNOR (1925–1964)

Born on March 25, 1925, in Savannah, Georgia, Mary Flannery O'Connor studied writing at the University of Iowa. She started her writing career in 1946 with a shorty story, "The Geranium," which was followed by thirty-one more short stories—published in collections *A Good Man Is Hard to Find and Other Stories* (1955), *Everything That Rises Must Converge* (1965) and *The Complete Stories* (1971, posthumously recognized with the 1972 U.S. National Book Award for Fiction); two novels—*Wise Blood* (1952) and *The Violent Bear It Away* (1960); and numerous essays. She died on August 3, 1964, in Navicent Health Baldwin, Milledgeville, Georgia.

While O'Connor's film credits include several television productions—shorts, segments of TV series and TV movies— the only feature film based on her prose is John Huston's *Wise Blood* (1979; starring Brad Dourif, John Huston, Harry Dean Stanton and Dan Shor).

Abundant in Latin words, most of which appear on two consecutive pages, is O'Connor's short story "A Temple of the Holy Ghost" ([c. 1954] 1979). While the story has no narrator among the characters, the most obvious protagonist is a twelve-year-old girl, consistently referred to by the author as "the child." When two fourteen-year-old girls, Joanne and Susan (calling each other Temple One and Temple Two), who are schooled at a local convent, spend a weekend with the child and her mother, it becomes an opportunity for the child first to exhibit some of her worst behavior and then carry out her moral self-analysis. In order to entertain their guests, the hosts invite two boys, Wendell and Cory Wilkins, who occasionally help old lady Buchell out on her farm. While the boys try to impress the girls with some hillbilly songs performed to a guitar accompaniment, Joanne and Susan respond with their own performance:

> The singer frowned and for a few seconds only strummed the guitar. Then he began "The Old Rugged Cross," and they listened politely but when he had finished they said, "Let us sing one!" and before he could start another, they began to sing with their convent-trained voices,
>
> > *"Tantum ergo Sacramentum*
> > *Veneremur Cernui:*
> > *Et antiquam documentum*
> > *Novo cedat ritui;"*

The child watched the boys' solemn faces turn with perplexed frowning stares at each other as if they were uncertain whether they were being made fun of.

> *"Praestet fides supplementum*
> *Sensuum defectui.*
> *Genitori, Genitoque*
> *Laus et jubilatio*
> *Salus, honor, virtus quoque ..."*

The boys' faces were dark red in the gray-purple light. They looked fierce and startled.

> *"Sit et benedictio;*
> *Procedenti ab utroque*
> *Compar sit laudatio.*
> *Amen."*

["Down in adoration falling,
Lo! the sacred Host we hail;
Lo! o'er ancient forms departing,
newer rites of grace prevail;
faith for all defects supplying
where the feeble senses fail.
To the everlasting Father,
and the Son who reigns on high,
with the Holy Ghost proceeding
forth from Each eternally,
be salvation, honor, blessing,
might and endless majesty.
Amen."]

The girls dragged out the Amen and then there was a silence.

"That must be Jew singing," Wendell said and began to tune the guitar.

The girls giggled idiotically but the child stamped her foot on the barrel. "You big dumb ox!" she shouted. "You big dumb Church of God ox!" she roared and fell off the barrel and scrambled up and shot around the corner of the house as they jumped from the banister to see who was shouting. [pp. 88-89]

When, after the weekend, the two girls are brought back to the convent by the child, her mother and the chauffeur, some of them go to the chapel, where the child has a special opportunity to continue her moral self-analysis. The following excerpt, extracted from that scene, once more refers to the already quoted hymn "*Tantum Ergo Sacramentum*," written in 1264, for the Feast of Corpus Christi, by Thomas Aquinas (the English translation by Scott P. Richert).

> The child knelt down between her mother and the nun and they were well into "*Tantum Ergo*" before her ugly thoughts stopped and she began to realize that she was in the presence of God." [p. 96]

The extensive Latin references in O'Connor's short story play manifold purposes. They emphasize the differences in the background and personality between the girls educated at the convent and the local boys, they show the impact of the girls' education on their behavior outside of the school environment, and—most importantly to the reader's advantage—they create a humorous situation resulting from the encounter of the two significantly different cultures.

Flannery O'Connor was closely associated with a literary movement known as Christian realism. Her prose, usually set in rural American South, strongly reflected her Roman Catholic faith, and ethical questions were always at the forefront of her stories. Her Latin references, predictable and purely religious as a result of her upbringing and sensitivity, constitute one more example of how the ancient language remains vivid, at least in some circles and cultures, within the modern version of both written and spoken English.

13. Gore VIDAL (1925–2012)

Gore Vidal was born on October 3, 1925, in West Point, New York, and was educated at Sidwell Friends School (1934-1936), St. Albans School (1936-1939), Los Alamos Ranch School (1939-1940) and Phillips Exeter Academy (1940-1943). A popular novelist and playwright, he was openly bisexual, genuinely interested in history and deeply engaged in politics, all of which is reflected in his writing. His major fiction publications include novels *The City and the Pillar* (1948), *Julian* (1964), *Myra Breckenridge* (1968), *Burr* (1973), *Empire* (1987) and *Hollywood* (1990); and plays *A Visit to a Small Planet* (1957), *The Best Man* (1960), *An Evening with Richard Nixon* (1972) and *Weekend* (1968). Gore died on July 31, 2012, in Hollywood, Los Angeles, California.

In the 1950s, Gore wrote scripts for numerous episodes of a variety of television series, including two episodes for *The Philco Television Playhouse*, the latter of which, "The Death of Billy the Kid" (1955), was subsequently used as the basis for Martin Ritt's feature film *The Left Handed Gun* (1958; starring Paul Newman, Lita Milan, John Dehner and Hurd Hatfield). While the author's other notable credits as a screenwriter (both in collaboration with other writers) are Joseph L. Mankiewicz's screen version of Tennessee Williams's *Suddenly, Last Summer* (1959; featuring Elizabeth Taylor, Katharine Hepburn, Montgomery Clift, Albert Dekker and Mercedes McCambridge) and René Clément's French-American co-production *Is Paris Burning?* (1966; featuring Jean-Paul Belmondo, Alain Delon, Charles Boyer, Kirk Douglas, Yves Montand, Leslie Caron, Orson Welles and Glenn Ford); the major feature films based on his published prose include Norman Taurog's *Visit to a Small Planet* (1960; starring Jerry Lewis, Joan Blackman and Earl Holliman), Franklin J. Schaffner's *The Best Man* (1964; featuring Henry Fonda, Cliff Robertson, Edi Adams, Margaret Leighton and Lee Tracy) and Michael Sarne's *Myra Breckenridge* (1970; starring Raquel Welch, John Huston, Mae West and Farrah Fawcett).

Two Latin references have been found in Gore's outstanding play *The Best Man* ([1960] 2001). Set in Philadelphia of 1960, it relates the background politics and tricks of fictitious presidential primaries, in which the major competitors for the Democratic Party's nomination are Secretary of State William Russell and Senator Joseph Cantwell.

The first Latin expression comes up in a scene where Joe Cantwell, his wife, Senator Clyde Carlin and members of his campaign staff discuss the release of some medical records (indirectly revealing Russell's promiscuity) that may hurt the opponent and help Cantwell win the nomination:

BLADES. All neatly bound. Six hundred copies to be released to the delegates at three-thirty P.M. Russell's doctor is in town. That means there's going to be some kind of a statement.

CANTWELL. *(Nods.)* He's going to fight.

CARLIN. Aren't you fellows afraid of getting into trouble? Stealing medical records?

BLADES. *(Quickly.)* We didn't steal them.

CANTWELL. They were given to us. **Pro bono publico** ['For the public good']. Now just look at this ... *(Cantwell shows Carlin the file. The phone rings in the living room. Mabel answers it.)* [p. 53]

The second Latin reference appears in a scene related to a trick pulled, ineffectively (as it turns out), by the other side. Marcus, a man who served in the army with Cantwell during World War II, tries to insinuate the candidate's sexual misconduct, but his theory falls through when he is confronted by Cantwell in front of Russell:

MARCUS. Just the two of them. Like I told you. It's in the record there ... they were, you know ... they were ...

CANTWELL. *(Inexorably.)* Fenn was caught with an enlisted man ***in flagrante delicto*** ['in the act of wrongdoing'] on the afternoon of 14 June 1944 in the back of the post church. The M.P.s caught him ...

MARCUS. *(Rapidly.)* That's right. And that's when he broke down and told about everything and everybody ... the M.P.s laid this trap for him ... they'd been tipped off ...

CANTWELL. By the Advocate General ...

MARCUS. That's right. By Colonel Conyers, he was the one finally broke up this whole ring of degenerates ... And Fenn when he was caught gave, oh, maybe twenty, thirty names and one of those names was Joe Cantwell, his roommate ...

CANTWELL. Correct. Now: What happened to those twenty-eight officers and men who were named at the court-martial?

MARCUS. They were all separated from the service ... Section Eight we called it ... for the good of the service, they were all kicked out ...

CANTWELL. All except one.

MARCUS. That's right ... all except you.

CANTWELL. *(Smiles at Russell.)* And why wasn't I?

MARCUS. I ... well ... I don't know. I suppose it's in the records or something. [p. 69]

The role of the two Latin quotations, both embellishing the lines spoken by Senator Joseph Cantwell, is probably to point out the politician's inclination to show off his superior education—unless it is to be assumed that they appear there as a natural part (considering the class of people involved in the scene) of legal and/or ordinary everyday English.

Three Latin references have been encountered in Gore's other novel, *Myra Breckenridge* (1968), a controversial, satirical and audacious account, in the form of a diary, of an unusual individual who, having undergone a gender reassignment surgery, decides to pursue a Hollywood career and his/her uncle's wealth.

The first expression, derived from Classical Latin through Medieval Latin and used, without any spelling change, in everyday English (hence, there is almost no need to translate it), is a part of a long paragraph in which the narrator/protagonist, Myron/Myra, reveals to Uncle Ted, better known as singing cowboy Buck Loner, Myron's mother's last words regarding the inheritance:

"Gertrude," I positively *rasped* through a Niagara of tears unshed, "with her dying breath, or one of her dying breaths—we missed a lot of what she said toward the end because of the oxygen tent and the fact she could not wear her teeth—Gertrude said, 'Myron—and you too, angel girl—if anything happens to me and you ever need help, go to your Uncle Ted, go to Buck Loner and remind that son-of-a-bitch'—I am now quoting **verbatim** ['word by word']—that the property in Westwood just outside of Hollywood where he has his Academy of Drama and Modeling was left to us jointly by our father whose orange grove it was in the Twenties, and you tell that bastard'...—'that I have a copy of the will and I want my share to go to you, Myron, because that property must be worth a good million bucks by now!'" I stopped, as though too moved by my own recital to continue. [p. 15]

The next two Latin references appear in conversations between Myra and Letitia, two women of identical backgrounds and similar profiles. In the first excerpt, including a phrase which literally means 'without which not,' Letitia addresses Myra; in the second one, offering a phrase with an unusual mixture of Latin and English, the roles are reversed, Myra speaks to Letitia:

> "You seem particularly well equipped to give the course in Posture. I couldn't help but notice how you looked when you entered the room, you carry yourself like a veritable queen. As for Empathy, it is the Sign Kwa Known [*sine qua non*] ['prerequisite/fundamentals'] of the art of film acting." [p. 19]

> Women like ourselves owe it to one another to present a united front to the enemy. Meanwhile, as **quid** for my **quo**, she will try to find work for Mary-Ann. All in all, as satisfying an encounter as I have had since Dr. Montag first introduced himself to us at the Blue Owl Grill. [pp. 141-142]

The two Latin references, both used in a funny manner (emphasizing Myra's pretentiousness) and in rather unusual circumstances, significantly add to the satirical tone of the whole novel. The bold-printed words in the last excerpt are extracted from the Latin expression *quid pro quo* ('this for that,' or 'one thing for another'); thus the whole phrase where the two Latin words are inserted between English words can be translated as 'as her favor for my previous favor to her.'

Praised for his elegant language, versatility and originality, Gore Vidal is unquestionably one of the major American writers of the second half of the twentieth century. The Latin references discovered in his works, even though they do not carry any special grammatical or cultural significance, testify to his erudition, profoundly illustrate the context for some popular expressions and, indirectly, support the thesis that Latin is still far from being dead.

14. Herman RAUCHER (1928–)

Born on April 13, 1928, in Brooklyn, New York, and educated at New York University, Herman Raucher is a novelist, playwright and screenwriter. He wrote six novels—*The Night the Sun Came Out on Happy Hollow Lane* (1969), *Summer of '42* (1971), *A Glimpse of Tiger* (1971), *Ode to Billy Joe* (1976), *There Should Have Been Castles* (1978) and *Maynard's House* (1980); and three plays including *Harold* (1962) and *Kitty Hawk: The Musical* (2000). The films based on his novels (for which he wrote his own screenplays)—in some cases, the movie, made first, was followed by a novelization—include Melvin Van Peebles's *Watermelon Man* (1970; starring Godfrey Cambridge, Estelle Parsons and Howard Caine; from *The Night the Sun Came Out on Happy Hollow Lane*), Robert Mulligan's *Summer of '42* (1971; featuring Jennifer O'Neill, Gary Grimes and Jerry Houser), Max Baer, Jr.'s *Ode to Billy Joe* (1976; starring Robby Benson, Glynis O'Connor and Joan Hotchkis) and Kelly Reichardt's *Ode* (1999; featuring Heather Gottlieb, Kevin Poole and Jon Wurster). Other notable movies that Raucher wrote the screenplays for include Robert Ellis Miller's *Sweet November* (1968; starring Sandy Dennis, Anthony Newley and Theodore Bikel) and Charles Jarrott's *The Other Side of Midnight* (1977; featuring Marie-France Pisier, John Beck, Susan Sarandon and Raf Vallone), the latter based on the novel by Sidney Sheldon, with whom Raucher shares the screenplay credits.

A couple of Latin references have been discovered in Raucher's popular autobiographical novel *Summer of '42* (1971), which, set in 1942 on Nantucket Island, relates the teenage protagonist's first sexual experiences during his vacation. The first reference, being a famous quotation of Julius Caesar's most laconic report to the Roman Senate of his victory at the Battle of Zela against Pharnaces II of Pontus. Oscy is Hermie's buddy, and the notes the narrator refers to clearly offer educational information in more than one area.

> Hermie went to bed that night with a steamroller named Oscy barreling around in his dreams. And yet, it wasn't all that bad. For after the preliminary there'd be a clean shot at the green-eyed champion. In the middle of deeper night, Hermie switched on his bed lamp and began heavy training by carefully studying his "notes." So what if it was in **Latin**? By applying himself he could become a fucking whiz in **Latin**. He might even become a **Latin** whiz at fucking. ***Veni, vidi, vici*** ("I came, I saw, I conquered.). Yaaaaaaaa, Sheena. [p. 174]

The second Latin phrase appears much later in the book, when Hermie is getting ready for his life-changing experience with Dorothy, a married woman several years older:

> He felt so good that he didn't hear the croaking harmonica outside. Life was falling marvelously in place for him. He was shedding the agonizing skin of youth, and an irresistible fellow was emerging, smiling at him in the mirror. And when he left the room, it was with the knowledge that when he returned he'd be a man. He was, from head to toe, a waling erection that radiated sex and confidence and maturity. He disdained bringing along his notes because that suddenly seemed ugly. But in his pocket he placed the last of hos red-hot rubbers because, as the Coast Guard so aptly put it, **Semper Paratus** ['Always Prepared']. [pp. 239-240]

While the Latin quotation in the first excerpt offers an interesting triplet of verbs—all being the third principal parts (Perfect Active Indicative, first person singular) of *venio venire veni ventum* ('to come/arrive' – fourth conjugation), *video vidēre vidi visum* ('to see' – second conjugation) and *vinco vincĕre vici victum* ('to win/conquer/defeat' – third conjugation) and all, together, exemplifying two poetic devices, alliteration and asyndeton. The historical significance of the quotation results from the fact that it is attributed to Julius Caesar (see the entry on Hilton), as used by him in the letter sent to the Senate in 46 B.C. after his quick victory at the Battle of Zela against Pharnaces II of Pontus. The quotation in the second excerpt, occasionally shortened to 'Semper Par,' is used as the official motto of the United States Coast Guard.

Raucher's novel *A Glimpse of Tiger* ([1971] 1975) is definitely a love story, this one set in Manhattan and focused on the rather unusual, and thus clearly doomed, romantic relationship between two young people of quite different profiles, Tiger and Luther, both living, temporarily, in a fantasy world.

Three Latin references have been found in the book, the first one (just a single word) appearing in a scene where Leon and Fat, two controversial characters, present their crazy idea of founding some kind of an obscene club to the young couple. The following excerpt depicts a part of their discussion of the logistical details:

> So Luther ended the discussion. "No phone."
>
> Fat looked up, undaunted, even reborn. "Well, I was afraid you might take that attitude so—" He shuffled about some papers and came up

14. Herman RAUCHER (1928–)

with a new batch. "I have an alternate idea. We teach dancing at people's homes. All the latest stuff. Leon's the master at it. Anyway, the gig is, though it *looks* like we're teaching dancing, what we're *actually* doing is booking orgies and—" He stopped abruptly and lapsed into pitiful apologia. "We'll need a phone. I'm sorry."

Luther stood up, signaling ***finis*** ['boundary/limit/border']. "Well, I tell you, Fat—you better figure out a way to make it work with carrier pigeons, 'cause Poppa don't allow no dancin' in here." He became very threatening. [p. 88]

The second Latin reference comes up in a scene rather unrelated to the main story, where Tiger, job hunting in the lobby of a Madison Avenue building, overhears a dialogue between two females:

"Well, he didn't call again last night, but I expected that."

"He's playing it cute. Him with his new semi-executive status."

"Anyway, my hair is set for eight o'clock tonight, just in case." ***Semper Paratus,***

shall we say?"

"Mine too. I'm streaked."

"I noticed. How much?"

"Thirty. Mr. Horatio."

"Thirty? Jesus."

"But it's Mr. Horatio."

"For thirty you should get Liberace." [p. 112]

There is a grammatical inconsequence in the Latin reference. Since both interlocutors of the dialogue are females, the gender of the participle 'prepared' should have been feminine (*parata*), not masculine (*paratus*). Even though the reader does not know much about the two absolutely anonymous characters, and the kind of job they are talking about can only be guessed, the

Latin quotation does sound funny and out of place—especially based on the kind of language within which it clearly stands out.

And the last Latin reference, a self-explanatory religious quotation, is a part of a scene toward the end of the novel, where Tiger, having broken up with Luther, comes to the Y after work, and he, absolutely unexpected, is waiting for his ex-girlfriend in the room:

> A pious Luther was standing before her, like a priest calling at the home of an unfortunate parishioner. His collar was turned around, and he was a curly-topped Pat O'Brien to talk the men out of a prison riot. What a soul-searing sight. Luther before the cross. God's emissary. "Hi," he said. "***Pax vobiscum*** ["May peace be with you."] and all that shit." The anger and power of J. Christ were certainly being put to the test. [p. 181]

While Herman Raucher's position in literature is admittedly not on a par with such writers as F. Scott Fitzgerald, Sinclair Lewis, Aldous Huxley or John Updike, his novels, including one definite nationwide bestseller (*Summer of '42*), have been extremely popular among not exclusively young readers and also recognized by critics for their unique assets in the area of humor, compassion, realism and understanding of the human soul. The Latin references encountered in his works, even though not overly numerous or insightful, offer one more argument in support of the statement that the ancient language does not deserve to be discarded or forgotten.

The Latin motto of Raucher's alma mater, New York University, is *Perstare et Praestare* ("To persevere and to excel").

15. Umberto ECO (1932–2016)

Born on January 5, 1932, in Alessandria, Piedmont, Italy, and educated at the University of Turin, Umberto Eco Omri was a versatile scholar whose research ranged from history and literature to political and social sciences to literary and film semiotics to popular culture. In addition to being a philosopher, literary critic and aesthetician, Eco taught semiotics at the University of Bologna and authored seven novels, including *The Name of the Rose* (1980), *Foucault's Pendulum* (1988), *The Island of the Day Before* (1994), *Baudolino* (2000) and *The Prague Cemetery* (2010). He died on February 19, 2016, in Milan, Lombardy, Italy.

Especially popular and critically acclaimed among his novels were the first two, *The Name of the Rose* and *Foucault's Pendulum* ([1988] 1989). The former, despite its abundance of Latin references, is outside of this project's scope as it is set in the fourteenth century. The latter, equally rich in Latin quotations—all skillfully used to create the impression of authenticity—tells a story that spans over centuries (in flashbacks), but it starts and ends in modern times. Consequently, it does deserve to be included here. The enormously complex and absolutely extraordinary mystery, expertly and cunningly enhanced with historical facts and documents, is tackled by Casaubon (the narrator), Diotallevi and Jacopo Belbo, three editors of Garamond Press/Manutius (a publishing company located in Milan), who, triggered by Colonel Ardenti's discovery of a coded message, get obsessed with "The Plan," a conspiracy allegedly originated by the Templars. The conspiracy, eventually, seems to be destroyed by its own forces, represented anonymously by a mysterious man calling himself Aglié, but not until many people, including Colonel Ardenti and two of the editors (the third one, Casaubon, is awaiting to be killed while concluding his narration), disappear in mysterious circumstances.

There are so many Latin references in the book that it is absolutely impossible to present all, let alone in their contexts, within the 300-word limit. Consequently, only a selection is listed below with as much explanatory information as possible. The criteria of the choice include frequency of appearance, originality and insightfulness. Phrases and sentences that appear in other entries are definitely avoided unless they are used by the author more than once. The priority has also been given to those references that are translated by Eco himself, which constitute the first of the two lists, presented below:

in posteriori parte spine dorsi (kissed 'on the behind, then on the navel and the mouth,' pp. 98, 451);

in humane dignitatis opprobrium (engaged 'in mutual fornication,' p. 98);

Steganographia, hoc est ars per occultam scripturam animi sui voluntatem absentibus certa, Trithenius, Frankfurt, 1606 ("The art of using secret writing in order to bare your soul to distant persons." p. 133);

lapis exillis ('stone from exile,' pp. 141, 395, 437);

post hoc ergo ante hoc ("What follows causes what came before." p. 339);

facies hermetica ('stiff smile of condescension on his lips, pp. 339, 341);

miranda sextae aetatis ('the wonders of the sixth and final appointment,' p. 395);

terra foetida ('stinking sepulcher,' p. 437);

Ego sum qui sum. – Exodus 3:14 ("I am that I am." p. 495).

The second list includes most of all the other references encountered in the book, and their translations are provided by the author of this volume—not infrequently with the help of special resources:

In hanc utilitatem angeli saepe figuras, characteres, formas et voces invenerunt ... – Johannes Reuchlin, ***De arte cabalistica***, 1517 ("To this advantage, angels have discovered designs, symbols, shapes and voices ..., *On the Art of Kabbalah*, p. 21);

amor fati ('love of one's fate,' 45);

impotentia coeundi ('erectile dysfunction,' p. 51);

Sub umbra alarum tuarum, Jehova. – ***Fama Fraternitatis***, in *Allgemeine und general Reformation*, Cassel, Wessel, 1514, conclusion ('Under the Shadow of Thy Wings, Jehovah – *A Discovery of the Fraternity*, pp. 72, 190, 193);

*Taxpayer's **Vade Mecum*** (literally: 'with me,' in reality: 'handbook/guide,' p. 74);

Cur, quomodo, quando ('Why, how, when,' p. 94);

De insolentia Templariorum ('On the usurpations of the Templars,' p. 96);

Crede firmiter et pecca fortiter. ('Believe strongly, sin boldly,' p. 107);

Thomas Burnet, *Telluris Theoria Sacra*, Amsterdam, Wolters, 1694 (*The Sacred Theory of the Earth*, p. 125);

post CXX annos patebo ("In 120 years I shall come forth." pp. 170, 192, 396, 535);

Corpus Hermeticus, Stobaeus, **excerptum** VI (*The Body of Mystic Wisdom*, 'excerpt,' p. 184);

Confessio fraternitatis Roseae Crucis, ad aruditos Europae (*The Confession of the Fraternity of the Order of the Rosy Cross to All the Learned of Europe*, p. 190);

Heinrich Khunrath' ***Amphitheatrum sapientiae aeternae*** (*Amphitheater of Eternal Wisdom*, p. 196);

Maier's ***Arcana arcanissima*** (*The Most Mysterious Secrets*, p. 196);

Fama (here: *A Discovery*, pp. 197, 470)

Robert Fludd's ***Apologia compendiaria Fraternitatem de Rosea Cruce suspicionis et infamiis maculis aspersam, veritatem quasi Fluctibus abluens et abstergens*** ('The Defense of the Fraternity of the Rosy Cross regarding the disgraced distrust spread as if the truth were being washed by the Waves and wiped off,' p. 197);

Fludd's ***Tractatus apologeticus integritatem societatis de Rosea Cruce defendens*** ('A treaty defending the integrity of the society of the Rosy Cross,' p. 197);

Fludd's ***Utriusque cosmi historia*** (*Brief Remarks on the Universe*, pp. 197, 284);

De Naturae Secretis (*On the Secrets of Nature*, p. 197);

Maier's ***Silentium post clamores*** (*Silence After Shouts*, pp. 197, 201);

Johann Valentin Andreae's ***Turris Babel*** ('The Tower of Babel,' pp. 198, 202);

Theatrum Chemicum (*Chemical Theater*, p. 203);

vis movendi ('the power of moving,' p. 222);

sic transit gloria mundi ('Thus passes the glory of the world,' p. 250);

Ordo Templi Orientis ('Order of the Temple of the East,' pp. 269, 340);

Liber AL vel legis, 1904 (*The Book of the Law*, pp. 269, 270);

Quid est veritas ('what is the truth,' p. 288);

Nequaquam vacui/vacuum ('No way, emptiness,' pp. 339, 396);

Quod ubique, quod ab omnibus et quod semper ('What is everywhere, what is believed by everyone, what is always, p. 340);

CONDOLEO ET CONGRATULATOR ('Condolences and congratulations,' p. 340);

(Latino) **sine flexione** (Latin 'without inflections,' p. 375);

Omnia Movens ('All Moving,' 378);

Quantum mortalia pectora ceacae noctis habent ('How dark the night that shrouds the hearts of men! – Ovid, p. 380);

Qualis Artifex Pereo ('What an artist the world is losing in me.' p. 414);

Humanum Genus ("Mankind," Pope Leo XIII's encyclical, p. 425);

Templi Resurgentes Equites Synarchici ('the Risen again Synarchic Knights of the Temple,' p. 426);

Umbilicus Telluris ('the Navel of the World,' p. 453);

Claudicat ingenium, delirat lingua, labat mens. – Lucretius, *De Rerum Natura*, iii 453 ('... genius breaks down, tongue slips, mind fails,' *On the Nature of Things*, p. 528).

An overwhelming richness of Latin references in the book, probably unsurpassed by any work of fiction, offers one more reason for admiring and praising Umberto Eco, a twenty/twenty-first-century scholar and writer whose brilliance in so many fields is hard to imagine. The quotations constitute an unusual basis for additional studies in history, culture and Latin itself. One can find here a lot of verbs, mostly in the Present Tense but occasionally in other tenses, e.g., in the Future (*patebo*, from the second-conjugation verb *pateo patēre* – 'to be/stand open'); there are a couple of examples of gerund, both in the genitive case: *coeundi* (from the fourth-conjugation verb *coeo coire* – 'to go/come together' or 'to unite') and *movendi* (from the second-conjugation verb *moveo movēre* – 'to move'); there are samples of the present participle, three in the nominative singular and one in the nominative plural form: *abluens* (from the third-conjugation verb *abluo abluĕre* – 'to wash away'), *abstergens* (from the second-conjugation verb *abstergeo abstergēre* – 'to dry off'), *movens* (from the verb already mentioned) and *resurgentes* (from the third-conjugation verb *resurgo resurgĕre* – 'to rose again').

16. John UPDIKE (1932–2009)

One of the most distinguished modern American writers, John Updike was born in Reading, Pennsylvania, on March 18, 1932. He graduated from Harvard University (1954) and, for a year on the Knox Fellowship, studied at Ruskin School of Drawing and Fine Art at the University of Oxford, England. Before he became a full-fledged novelist, he was a member of the staff of *The New Yorker*, where his first short works were published. He is best known for his Rabbit Angstrom tetralogy—*Rabbit, Run* (1960), *Rabbit Redux* (1971), *Rabbit Is Rich* (1981) and *Rabbit at Rest* (1990)—concluded with an epilogue novella *Rabbit Remembered* (2001), and for his three Bech books—*Bech, a Book* (1970), *Bech Is Back* (1982) and *Bech at Bay* (1998). His other significant works include *The Centaur* (1963), *Couples* (1968), *The Witches of Eastwick* (1984), *Roger's Version* (1986), *Brazil* (1994), *In the Beauty of the Lilies* (1996) and *Terrorist* (2006). Updike also wrote poetry, short stories and essays. His multitude of awards include two Pulitzer Prizes (1982, 1991), two O. Henry Prizes (1966, 1991), Honorary Doctor of Letters from Harvard University (1992) and the American Academy of Arts and Letters Gold Medal for Fiction (2007). Updike died on January 27, 2009, in Danvers, Massachusetts.

Since Updike's assets as a writer go far beyond providing an engaging story, his works are not among those that easily translate into movies. Consequently, there are not many screen adaptations derived from his fiction. While several of his novels and short stories were turned into television productions, there are only two theatrical pictures based on his books: Jack Smight's *Rabbit, Run* (1970; starring James Caan, Anjanette Comer and Carrie Snodgress), written for the screen by Howard B. Keitsek, and George Miller's *The Witches of Eastwick* (1987; featuring Jack Nicholson, Cher, Susan Sarandon, Michelle Pfeiffer and Veronica Cartwright), scripted by Michael Cristofer.

Set in Pennsylvania (where Updike was born), the novel *The Centaur* ([1963] 1964) focuses on the relationship between two men, George Caldwell, a disillusioned fifty-year-old teacher, and his enthusiastic teenage son, Peter, the narrator of most of the book. Here is a scene where Peter's high school teacher tests his knowledge of Latin, quoting lines 402-409 from Book I of *The Aeneid* and expecting him to translate and analyze but offering quite a lot of guidance:

Miss Appleton seemed rather flustered and out of breath, probably from the long climb. "Peter, translate," she said, and then she read aloud with her impeccable quantities,

"Dixit, et avertens rosea cervice refulsit,
mbrosiaque comae divinum vertice odorem
spiravere, pedes vestis defluxit ad imos,
et vera incessu patuit dea."

...

"What glowed? Nor *she* glowed. **Cervice** glowed."

"She spoke, and, turning, her, uh, rosy crevice—" Laughter from the others. I blushed.

"*No!* **Cervice, cervice**. Neck. You've heard of the cervix. Surely you've heard of the cervical vertebrae."

...

"Oh, no. Dear child, no. **Vertice** here is the noun, *vertex*, *verticis*. Vortex. A vortex, a whirl, a *crown* of hair, of what kind of hair? What agrees?"

"Ambrosial."

...

"I don't understand **ad imos**."

"**Imus**, a rather archaic word. The superlative of **inferus**, below, down below. **Ad imos**, to the lowest extremity. Here, literally, to the lowest extremity of her feet, which makes little sense in English. It is used as emphasis; the poet is astounded."

...

"Down, down to her feet, and in truth opened—"

"*Was* opened, *was* exposed, made manifest as **vera**. **Vera dea**."

"As a true goddess."

"Quite so. What does *incessu* have to do with the sentence?"

"I don't know."

"Really, Peter, this is disappointing. College material like yourself. *Incessu*, in stride, in gait. She was in gait a true goddess. Gait in the sense of carriage, of physical style; there is a *style* to divinity. These lines brim with a sense of that radiance, breaking in upon the unknowing Aeneas. ***Ille ubi matrem agnovit***; he recognized his mother. Venus, Venus with her ambrosial fragrance, her swirling hair, her flowing robe, her rosy skin. Yet he sees only as she is ***avertens***, as she is turning away." [pp. 139-141]

Updike's novel *Couples* (1968) depicts the struggles of a few married couples—Piet and Angela Haneman, Matt and Terry Gallagher, Freddy and Georgene Thorne, Ken and "Foxy" (Elizabeth) Whitman and Frank and Janet Appleby—to stay happy and together (not always successfully) in the era of the sexual revolution, the 1960s. It has a few Latin words and phrases scattered all over the book. Two of the instances—***Ulmis hollandicis***, a name of a tree (p. 391), and ***per diem***, a phrase used in reference to the total cost of 'daily' meals in a guest house (p. 467)—are rather insignificant. The first one of those that are worth quoting appears early in the book during one of the parties:

Frank Appleby was given two bottles to uncork, local-liquor-store Bordeaux, and went around the table twice, pouring once for the ladies, and then for the men. In Cambridge the Chianti was passed from hand to hand without ceremony.

Freddy Thorne proposed a toast. "For our gallant boys in the *Thresher*."

"Freddy, that's ghoulish!" Marcia little-Smith cried.

"Freddy, really," Janet said.

Freddy shrugged and said, "It came from the heart. Take it or leave it. ***Mea culpa, mea culpa.***" ['My fault'] [p. 37]

The other Latin reference was found in a paragraph where Foxy, married to Ken (a scientist) but having a love affair with Piet (a construction man), makes a casual comment about divorce which is triggered by the company's discussion about John and Jacqueline Kennedy. Her comment is unexpectedly interrupted by the narrator's non-sequitur information about what she sees when she intentionally turns her head. What she is looking at is the banner headline of the newspaper mentioning the fate of the deposed and assassinated President of South Vietnam, whose last name in English happens to be spelled the same way as the accusative singular form of the Latin word for 'day,' unexpectedly followed by the noun's declension (at least the first four cases singular)—an unusual and bilingual sample of the stream of consciousness.

> Foxy said, "I'm curious about divorce." In turning her head to mute this admission she read the banner headline of the newspaper left neatly folded at Ken's empty place: **DIEM** OVERTHROWN. **Diem.** *Dies, diei, diei, diem.* "I wonder sometimes if Ken and I shouldn't get one." [p. 293]

The third part of Updike's "Rabbit" tetralogy, *Rabbit Is Rich* ([1981] 1982), continues narrating the story of Harry "Rabbit" Angstrom's unusual life in his fictitious city in Pennsylvania after his financial status considerably improves due to an inherited car dealership business. A winner of the Pulitzer Prize and the National Book Award, the book also happens to have a couple of Latin phrases in it. The first passage depicts a discussion on Catholicism and Pope John Paul II:

> Cindy Murkett unexpectedly speaks. "He's been a priest in a Communist country; he's used to taking a stand. The American liberals in the church talk about this ***sensus fidelium*** ['sense of the faithful'] but I never heard of it; it's been ***magisterium*** ['teaching authority of the Roman Catholic Church'] for two thousand years. What is it that offends you, Peggy, if you're not Catholic and don't have to listen?" [p. 268]

The other Latin quotation is a part of a passage related to Harry's pregnant daughter-in-law Pru's stay in a hospital after her fall down the stairs. The characters mentioned are Nelson, Harry's son, and Soupy, the clergyman who married Nelson and Pru:

> At the hospital, he [Nelson] asks Soupy, "How'd you get here so soon?" genuinely admiring. Snicker all you want, the guy *is* magical somehow.
>
> "The lady herself," the clergyman gaily announces, doing a little sidestep that knocks a magazine to the floor from a low table where too many are stacked. *Woman's Day. Field and Stream.* A hospital of course wouldn't get *Consumer Reports*. A killing article in there a while ago about medical costs and the fantastic mark-up on things like aspirin and cold pills. Soupy stoops to retrieve the magazine and comes up slightly breathless. He tells them, "Evidently, after they calmed the dear

16. John UPDIKE (1932–2009)

> girl down and set her arm and reassured her that the fetus appeared unaffected she still felt such concern that she woke up at seven a.m. and knew Nelson would be asleep and didn't know who to call. So she thought of *me.*" Soupy beams. "I of course was still deep in the arms of Morpheus but got my act together and told her I'd rush over between Holy Communion and the ten o'clock service and, behold, here I am. ***Ecce homo*** ["Behold: a man"]. She wanted to pray with me to keep the baby, she'd been praying co*n*stantly, and at least to this point in time as they used to say it seems to have *worked!*" [p. 317]

The fact that it is used by a man of God, the reference *Ecce homo* may appear in the given context to be either accidental or inappropriate since the two Latin words were originally used by Pontius Pilate (as quoted in the Vulgate translation in the Gospel of John) as he presents Jesus Christ, about to be crucified on his order, to the hostile and mocking crowd. However, based on Soupy's jovial, outgoing and humorous personality, the religious interpretation of the quotation, drawing a parallel between the purpose of Jesus Christ's sacrifice (salvation of mankind) and the purpose of Soupy's timely arrival at the hospital (to help Pru in her predicament) is quite likely even if it seems presumptuous and immodest (on the user's part).

Especially rich in Latin quotations is Updike's book *The Witches of Eastwick* ([1984] 1985), an extraordinary novel telling the story of three women possessing special powers—Alexandra Spofford, Jane Smart and Sukie Rougemont—and their complex relationship with mysterious seducer Darryl Van Horne in a fictitious (titular) Rhode Island town. The first couple of quoted below paragraphs refer to the victim of Sukie's seduction, Clyde Gabriel, her intellectual but helpless (under her spell) boss. First, we are given a quotation from an old poem by Lucretius that Clyde feels sentimental about, and, then, in the continuation of the description of his mental state, before he ends up killing his wife, Felicia, and hanging himself, we are given the title of the poem:

> In his solitary daze of booze and longing he had pulled down from a high dusty shelf his college Lucretius, scribbled throughout with the interlinear translations of his studious, hopeful college self. ***Nil igitur mors est ad nos neque pertinent hilium, quandoquidem natura animi mortalis habetur.*** ["Therefore, death is nothing to us nor concerns us in the least.] He leafed through the delicate little book, its Oxford-blue spine worn white where his youthful moist hands had held it over and over. He looked in vain for that passage where the swerve of atoms is described, that accidental undermined swerve whereby matter complicates, and all things are thus, through accumulating collisions, including men in their miraculous freedom, brought into being; for

without this swerve all atoms would fall ever downwards through the ***inane profundum*** ['empty profound'] like drops of rain. [p. 159]

Tonight his old college ***De Rerum Natura*** ["About the Nature of Things"] folded its youthfully annotated pages and slipped between his knees. He was thinking of going out for his ritual stargaze when Felicia barged into his study. [p. 160]

The next quotation is focused on Alexandra's problems and her unexpected encounter with a squirrel:

The spark of life inside the tiny skull wanted to flee, to twitch away to safety, but Alexandra's sudden focus froze the spark even through glass. A dim little spirit, programmed for feeding and evasion and seasonal copulation, was meeting a greater. ***Morte, morte, morte*** ['death' in ablative case], Alexandra said firmly in her mind, and the squirrel dropped like an instantly emptied sack. [p. 246]

The last passage has all the four protagonists:

Alexandra got the prick—tribute of a sort. Darryl mumbled "***Hoc est enim corpus meum***" ["For this is my body"] as he did the distribution; over the champagne he intoned, "***Hic est enim calix sanguinis mei***" ["For this is a chalice of my blood"]. Across from Alexandra, Jenny's face had turned a radiant pink; she was allowing her joy to show, she was dyed clear through by the blood of triumph. [p. 260]

An overwhelming abundance of Latin references has been found in Updike's *Roger's Version* (1986), as the novel addresses a number of religious and philosophical issues. The narrator/protagonist, Roger Lambert, is a professor at a Divinity School, married, after divorcing his first wife (which caused his loss of a minister's job), to Esther, a woman fourteen years younger, with whom he has a twelve-year-old son, Richie. Approached by a young scientist, Dale Kohler, whose passion is to prove the existence of God by means of math and computer, Lambert, despite being aware of Dale's subsequent love affair with Esther, eventually helps the young man get a grant for his controversial project, which, unfortunately, leads to Dale's despair and loss of faith. Dale is a good friend of Verna's, Lambert's half-sister's nineteen-year-old daughter, who struggles with many challenges, the raising, as a single mother, of a one-and-a-half-year-old half-black girl, Paula, being one of them. Estranged from her parents, Verna accepts help from her uncle, both financial aid and moral support; he guides her through the process of getting an abortion and saves her from losing Paula, who gets seriously injured as a result of being physically abused by her mother; eventually, he arranges Verna's reunion with her mother and finances her trip to Ohio. In the meantime, however, Lambert yields to Verna's invitation to join her in bed, possibly in her gesture to express gratitude, the incestuous character of the act notwithstanding.

Two comparatively brief Latin references appear early in the book when Lambert, analyzing his first conversation with Dale, tries to sum up what he already knows and thinks about the problem at hand:

> Barth had been right: **totaliter aliter** ['totally other']. Only by placing God totally on the other side of the humanly understandable can any final safety for Him be secured. [p. 32]

> Rather than follow her, I seized the moment to look up the Barth quote. It involved, I remembered, a series of **vias** ['roads'], each discounted as a path to God. [p. 40]

Though Dale does not know Latin, he does include a Latin phrase in one of his arguments during another debate with Lambert:

> "To pump blood eight feet up to the head the giraffe has to have such high blood pressure that when he bends down to take a drink he would black out, except there's a special pressure-reducing mechanism, a network of veins, called the **rete mirabile** ['wonderful net']. [p. 86]

During a Thanksgiving dinner party at the Lamberts,' to which Dale was invited along with Verna, Roger, influenced by a couple of glasses of white wine, carries on about his studies, injecting numerous Latin phrases and elaborating about Tertullian, his idol:

> He claimed, for instance, that the soul is naturally Christian: **anima naturaliter christiana**. And—you mathematicians—he did some of the basic Christian calculations. He invented the Trinity; at least he used the word **trinitas** for the first time in ecclesiastical **Latin**. And he put forward the formulation **una substantia, tres personae** ['one substance, three persons'] for God, and for Christ the notion of a double essence, **duplex status**, rather nicely, **non confusus sed conjunctus in una persona—deus et homo** ['not fused but connected in one person—God and Man']. [p. 119]

The longest and most meaningful series of Latin quotations appear at the very beginning of Chapter III of the novel, where Lambert, without any warning or announcement, shares his further deliberations with the reader. Due to the copyright restriction, only the first several lines are cited below:

> ***Quem enim naturae usum, quem mundi fructum, quem elementorum saporem non per carnem anima depascitur?*** For what use of Nature, what enjoyment of the world, what taste of the elements is not consumed by the soul ***per carnem***—by the agency of the flesh? Tertullian wrote these words in ***De resurrectione carnis*** [*About the Resurrection of the Flesh*] around 208, well after he had fallen away from orthodoxy into Montanism. [p. 149]

About twenty pages later, there is another scene of Dale's visit to Lambert's office where the two men's theological debate is resumed, and the professor/narrator embellishes his report with more Latin quotations. Here is a select part of their conversation:

> ***"Certum est,"*** I murmured, ***"quia impossibile est."***
>
> "What's that?" the young man asked. He did not know **Latin**. ...
>
> "'It is certain,'" I translated, "because it is impossible.' Tertullian." [p. 168]

Since *Roger's Version* is practically an unusual course in advanced Latin and an extensive discourse on philosophy (carried on, primarily, in the ancient language), a presentation of many excerpts had to be given up here. However, some of the Latin expressions are worth quoting outside of their context. Here is the list of such lexical items, along with their translations and page numbers:

ineptum ('out of place, in poor taste,' p. 169);

pudibundus ('shamefaced,' p. 171);

Natura veneranda est, non erubescenda. ("Nature should be revered, not to be ashamed of." p. 175);

in carnem ('in the flesh,' p. 183);

Esse est percipi. ("To be is to be perceived." p. 210);

Deus absconditus ('hidden God,' p. 219);

esse ('to be,' p. 220);

de facto ('in fact/in effect,' p. 287);

persona non grata ('an unwelcome person,' p. 290);

Id, Ego, Superego ('Ego, Id, 'Superego,' p. 301).

The above list includes a few interesting items from the point of view of their grammatical content. There are, for instance, two examples of the 'gerundive' – *veneranda* and *erubescenda* – both used as parts of phrases (including a form of the verb *esse* – 'to be') exemplifying the 'gerundive of obligation/necessity,' and one example of a (third conjugation) verb in the present passive infinitive form – *percipi* (from 'percipio percipere' – 'to feel/take in/sense/perceive'), meaning 'to be perceived.'

Other Latin phrases incorporated by John Updike in his works include ***homo sapiens*** ('wise human being' or 'human species')—found in his novels *S.* ([1988], 1989, p. 121) and *Bech Is Back* (1982, p. 150)—and ***sui generis*** ('of his/her own kind/in a class by itself/unique') and ***in absentia*** ('while not present') both found in *Bech Is Back* (p. 109 and p. 155, respectively). Additionally, in *Roger's Version*, the author makes a reference to Roman numerals (p. 99).

While John Updike's superior education, erudition, wit and originality shine through all of his prose and poetry, his knowledge of Latin is conspicuous in a bigger number of works than in any other mainstream fiction writer's, at least American. Whether consciously or accidentally, directly or indirectly, Updike does support the study of the so-called "dead" language and the classical culture much more convincingly and extensively than any other novelist ever has on this side of the Atlantic Ocean. His competence in Latin is more than obvious in his works, so it is not presumptuous to guess that he, probably more than other Harvard students, appreciated its mottos—both the original one (*Christo et Ecclesiae* – "For Christ and Church") and the current one (*Veritas* – "Truth")—and, when his graduation diploma was accompanied by the *summa cum laude* phrase, not only did he know exactly what the distinction meant, but he was also aware of the ablative case of both the adjective *summa* ('highest') and the noun *laude* ('praise'), as well as of the meaning of the preposition *cum* ('with'). He was neither surprised to see the preposition inserted between the modifier and the noun, nor unaware that in the correct Latin spelling of the letter *ā* in *summa* should carry a macron not only to imply it represented a long vowel, but also to distinguish the case of the adjective (ablative) from the nominative (spelled without a macron). It is worth adding here that the motto of the University of Oxford is *Dominus illuminatio mea* ("The Lord is my light."), with the verb implied.

17. John Gregory DUNNE (1932–2003)

Born on May 25, 1932, in Hartford, Connecticut, as the fifth of six children of a prominent surgeon, and educated at Princeton University, John Gregory Dunne was a novelist, screenwriter and critic. His major novels include *Vegas: A Memoir of a Dark Season* (1974), *True Confessions* (1977), *Dutch Shea, Jr.* (1982), *The Red, White and Blue* (1987), *Playland* (1994) and *Nothing Lost* (2004). His notable nonfiction books are *The Studio* (1969), *E. P. Dutton* (1977), *Quintana and Friends* (1978) and *Crooning* (1990). A younger brother of writer Dominick Dunne and the husband of writer Joan Didion, John Gregory Dunne died on December 30, 2003, in Manhattan, New York.

Dunne's major accomplishments as a screenwriter include Jerry Schatzberg's *The Panic in Needle Park* (1971; starring Al Pacino, Kitty Winn and Alan Vint), co-written with Joan Didion from the book by James Mills; Frank Perry's *Play It as It Lays* (1972; featuring Tuesday Weld, Anthony Perkins and Tammy Grimes), co-written with Didion from her novel; Frank Pierson's *A Star Is Born* (1976; starring Barbra Streisand, Kris Kristofferson and Gary Busey), co-written with Didion, based on the original story by William A. Wellman and Robert Carson (filmed in 1937); and Jon Avnet's *Up Close & Personal* (1996; featuring Michelle Pfeiffer, Robert Redford and Stockard Channing), co-written with Didion from a book by Alanna Nash. The married couple John and Joan also wrote the screenplay for Ulu Grosbard's *True Confessions* (1981; starring Robert De Niro, Robert Duvall and Charles Durning), the screen adaptation of Dunne's prime novel.

Set in Los Angeles just after World War II, Dunne's *True Confessions* ([1977] 1978) is a powerful and multidimensional murder mystery. The protagonists are two brothers, Tom and Des Spellacy, a policeman and a priest, whose involvement in the case further influences and defines their complex relationship. The unidentified murder victim is given an unusual nickname, "The Virgin Tramp." Because of the Irish-Catholic background of the main story, numerous Latin references, all related to religious rituals, can be found in the book. The first few are a part of a long scene relating the sumptuous funeral of Chester (Chet) Hanrahan, a major supporter of the Church:

> "***Credo in unum Deum ...***" ["I believe in one God."] Augustine O'Dea sang. The vicar general's rich bass rolled through the cathedral. Desmond Spellacy was originally supposed the sing the funeral mass, but Mrs. Chester Hanrahan had vetoed that. "All he's done for Holy Mother the Church," she had sobbed after the coronary, "Chet deserves

a bishop at least." It was the Cardinal she wanted, but His Eminence was indisposed. A touch of the flu. Although Desmond Spellacy suspected that the real reason His Eminence was absent was because he had never been able to stand Chester Hanrahan.

"***Patrem omnipotentem ...***" ['Almighty Father'] The men's choir took up the refrain.

...

"***Oremus ...***" ["Let us pray."]

...

"***Lavabo inter innocentes ...***" ["I will wash (*manus meas* – my hands) in innocence."] Bishop O'Dea intoned.

Appearances. They were very much on Desmond Spellacy's mind today. Augustine O'Dea, for example. (pp. 46-47);

"***Orate fratres ...***" ["Pray, brothers."]

In the front pew, Mrs. Chester Hanrahan leaned toward her husband's casket and keened loudly. The organist from Immaculate Conception High School began to play "Lovely Lady Dressed in Blue." It was Chet's favorite "number," according to Mrs. Chester Hanrahan. [p. 50]

Three lexical items, each in a different form, are worth commenting on here. *Oremus* is the Future Active Subjunctive Tense, first person plural form of the first-conjugation verb *oro orare* ('to pray/beg'); *lavabo* is the Future Active Indicative Tense, first person singular form of the first-conjugation verb *lavo lavare* ('to wash/bathe'); and *orate* is the Present Active Imperative, second person plural form of the verb already mentioned.

The second series of Latin references come up in the passage where the narrator reveals Des Spellacy's thoughts regarding Sonny McDonough, the only Catholic member of the county Board of Supervisors and President of the Planning Commission:

Desmond Spellacy noted Sonny McDonough's liabilities. Sonny sang "***Tantum Ergo***" in the shower. Or to be specific, Sonny sang "***Tantum Ergo***" in the shower after playing golf with Desmond Spellacy. You couldn't outwait Sonny. You couldn't stay in the locker room until he finished his shower. Not if you minded catching a cold or smelling bad. So into the shower. And there would be Sonny, all lathered up. "***Tantum ergo, Sacramentum, Veneremur cernui; et antiquam documentum ...***" The memory made Desmond Spellacy flinch. [p. 60]

The easiest way to show the meaning of the bold-printed references is to translate all as a whole: "Therefore, so great a sacrament, let us venerate with heads bowed; and the ancient document ..."—an excerpt from the Medieval Latin Hymn (c. 1264) attributed to St. Thomas Aquinas.

The remaining Latin references that appear in the book are presented in the following list, along with their translations and page numbers:

Sanctus ('Holy,' p. 18);

Agnus Dei ('Lamb of God,' p. 18);

Credo ("I believe." p. 18);

In principio erat verbum ... ("In the beginning was the Word." p. 54);

Et verbum caro factum est ... ("And the Word became flesh." p. 58);

mons veneris (literally: 'mount of Venus,' in anatomy: female's 'mons pubis,' p.146);

Ego te absolvo ... ("I forgive/absolve you." p. 208);

Confiteor. ("I Confess." p. 210);

Mea culpa. Mea maxima culpa. ('Through my own fault. Through my most grievous fault.' p. 358).

Even though *True Confessions* appears to be a classic example of murder mystery, the novel is much more than that; it offers an insightful study of character and human relations. Furthermore, Dunne's other works, both fiction and nonfiction, revealing a rich versatility in content and style, definitely demand that his writing be classified as the mainstream. Despite the narrow thematic range of his Latin references, Dunne deserves to be praised for offering an extensive illustration of the perseverance (against all odds) of the ancient language in modern fiction.

The motto of his alma mater, Princeton University, is *Dei Sub Numine Viget* ("Under God's power, She flourishes").

18. C. K. STEAD (1932–)

Christian Karson Stead, or Karl Stead, was born on October 17, 1932, in Auckland, New Zealand. In addition to studying at the University of Auckland (where he received his B.A. and M.A. degrees and was subsequently employed as Professor of English), Stead got his Ph.D. from the University of Bristol. He is a highly acclaimed poet, literary critic, short-story writer and novelist, most famous for his novel *Smith's Dream* (1971), which, in 1977, was turned by director Roger Donaldson into a film entitled *Sleeping Dogs* (featuring Sam Neill, Nevan Rowe, Ian Mune and Warren Oates), the first movie production from New Zealand to be shown in the United States. Stead was honored with the CBE order of chivalry, the Commander of the British Empire.

The book by Stead where three significant Latin quotations have been found is *Sister Hollywood* ([1989] 1990), a novel set in New Zealand and the USA (mostly Los Angeles), primarily in the 1940s and early 1950s. The narrator/protagonist is Bill Harper, a boy growing up in Auckland with his family of movie fans—including a sentimental grandmother, demanding parents (father being an ambitious local politician) and three diverse sisters—all enjoying films in the local theaters. The major episode of the novel is the story that Bill tells us of his oldest sister, Edi, who leaves the family without any warning and ends up in Hollywood, where, having married an aspiring but unsuccessful actor from Australia, she becomes (under the name Arlene Tamworth) first a movie producer's secretary (with an inevitable love affair between the two of them) and then a screenwriter.

The first Latin quotation appears in a passage where the narrator describes the responses to letters that the mother had written to Hollywood with inquiries about her daughter after the whole family saw her playing a small part in a Hollywood picture.

> Mother must have been uncertain which studio had made the picture, *Out on a Limb*, so she'd written to ones whose names she knew, asking whether they could give her the address of an actress called Edith Harper. MGM and Paramount had written back saying they knew of no actress of that name. I still have those letters. One is headed 'Paramount Productions Ltd / 5451 Marathon Street, Hollywood, Calif / Telephone Hollywood 2411 / Cable Address Famfilms.' The other is headed '**Ars Gratia Artis**' in a curve over the head of the MGM lion. Below that it reads simply 'Metro-Goldwyn-Mayer Studios / Culver City / California.' [p. 57]

The famous phrase, known in English as "Art for art's sake," expressing a philosophy that art's intrinsic value should be deprived of any political or didactic ideas or messages, even though quoted in Latin in the MGM logo, is historically credited to French poet, playwright and novelist Théophile Gautier (1811-1872) and is thus more widely known in the French version as *l'art pour l'art*. Regardless of that, however, the slogan or its paraphrase or interpretation has been used or addressed even before Gautier by others, including French philosopher Victor Cousin or American writer/critic Edgar Allan Poe. Subsequently, it was strongly advocated (and practiced) by other writers, Oscar Wilde in particular. And, Hollywood studio Metro-Goldwyn-Mayer, consistently trying to live up to the slogan of its logo, has definitely built up a reputation for itself as a producer of enormously artistic, financially ambitious and aesthetically pleasing pictures, leaving, however, films that address serious political, social and moral issues to other studios, such as Warner Bros. and 20th Century-Fox.

The second reference to Latin takes place in a paragraph narrating one of Bill's memorable evening events of 1948, going with his class to see a movie with their English teacher, Mr. Pearl, by the students called Pansy Pearl:

> We were to meet at the Embassy Theatre in town, which stood where the Auckland City Library is now, and I remember getting off the tram and running down Wellseley Street, a few minutes late, conscious of my grey flannel trousers and my blue and gold school blazer with its rep. pocket and school monogram – a gold lion rampant over a scroll that read '**Per Angusta, Ad Augusta**' – through hardship to glory [or, literally, 'through difficulties to honors']. [p. 96]

The non-sequitur reference is an old Latin saying which is more or less synonymous with the more widely known *Ad astra per aspera* or *Per aspera ad astra*, both meaning "Through hardships to the stars."

The third and last Latin quotation, or rather just a Latin word adopted by the English language without any spelling changes, appears only a few pages later. It is used in the narrative part regarding Bill's father campaign speech. While the speech is not quoted verbatim, Bill's paraphrase is quite accurate and comprehensive:

> There were some pretty strong winds being whipped up against Labour just now. He didn't deny that. And he didn't deny their principal source was the United States of America. The question was this: was the Labour Party going to stand monolithic and inflexible like an oak, and risk being snapped and broken? Or was it going to show a little flexibility, a little

18. C. K. STEAD (1932–)

adaptability? Wasn't politics the art of the possible? Of course that **dictum** ['a formal and short statement expressing a general principle'] could be used to argue in favour of any and every compromise. It could be the rationale for a sellout of principles. [p. 104]

The word 'dictum' is a substantive derived from the third-conjugation verb '*dico dicĕre dixi dictum*' ('to say/indicate'), or, to be exact, from its fourth principal part or supine (thus, implying passivity), and, consequently, though rather hard to be represented by a single English word, it can be literally translated as 'something that has been said/indicated.'

It is rather obvious that the examples of Latin quotations in Stead's novel do not seem to be purposefully selected by the author and incorporated in his work to show the significance of the language. Though rather marginal, they constitute a natural part of his prose, illustrating, once again, that modern English-language literature cannot exist without admitting the Latin heritage or, at least, it cannot escape some of its predominant traces. While the main character/author's high school motto has been quoted in his (autobiographical, to some extent) novel and above, the mottos of his colleges, The University of Auckland and the University of Bristol, can be looked up in outside sources. They are, respectively, *Ingenio et labore* ("By natural ability and hard work") and *Vim promovet insitam* (usually translated as "Learning promotes one's innate power"), the latter extracted from Horace's *Ode 4. 4*. From the grammatical standpoint, the first quotation offers another, double in this case, example of the 'ablative of means' with an implied preposition; the second one is a statement in the present tense with the subject missing (because, in fact, the complete version begins with *Doctrina sed* ..., meaning "But instruction ...") and the direct object (naturally, in the accusative case) preceding the verb.

19. Jerzy KOSINSKI (1933–1991)

Jerzy Kosiński, in English Kosinski (real name: Józef Lewinkopf), was born on June 14, 1933, in Łódź, Poland, and was educated at the University of Łódź (M.A. in history and sociology). He was a teaching assistant at the Polish Academy of Sciences and was a sharpshooter in the Polish Army before, in 1957, he migrated to the United States, where he graduated from Columbia University and received grants from the Guggenheim Fellowship (1967) and the Ford Foundation (1968). His major novels, published in English under the simplified name of Jerzy Kosinski, include *The Painted Bird* (1965, his most acclaimed and largely autobiographical work), *Steps* (1968), *Being There* (1970), *The Devil Tree* (1973, revised in 1982), *Blind Date* (1977), *Passion Play* (1977) and *The Hermit of 69th Street* (1988). Having met Roman Polanski at the National Film School in Łódź, they have been friends ever since, and Kosinski narrowly missed attending the tragic party at his friend's in Los Angeles, where Sharon Tate and others were killed by Charles Manson's followers in 1969. A National Book Award winner, Kosinski committed suicide on May 3, 1991, in Manhattan, after suffering from multiple illnesses.

Two feature films have been based on Kosinski's works—Hal Ashby's *Being There* (1979; featuring Peter Sellers, Shirley MacLaine, Melvyn Douglas, Jack Warden, Richard Dysart and Richard Basehart), which brought an Oscar for Douglas and an Oscar nomination for Sellers; and Václav Marhoul's Czech production of *The Painted Bird* (2019; starring Petr Kotlár, Nina Sunevic and Alla Sokolova). The author himself appeared as an actor in Warren Beatty's *Reds* (1981; featuring Warren Beatty, Diane Keaton, Edward Herrmann and Jack Nicholson) and in Daniel Adams's *A Fool and His Money* (1989; starring Jonathan Penner, Gerald Orange and Sandra Bullock), and he provided his voice in Alan Adelson and Kate Taverna's documentary *Łódź Ghetto* (1988).

Kosinski's book *The Hermit of 69th Street* ([1988] 1991) is not a typical novel; it is rather an enormously extensive monologue with the writer (represented by the fictitious protagonist named Kosky) sharing his notes, opinions, reflections and observations on a number of topics covering, in the stream-of-consciousness mode, almost every aspect of life. It also includes several Latin references that are scattered all over the volume. The first two references are parts of passages relating the protagonist's deliberation about word formation and an experience with a prostitute, respectively:

Spiritual is his favorite word and for a reason: it contains the word spirit, as well as ritual. Just think of the scribe who first invented this word! And speaking of inventive words, how about the word sexton? Imagine having, in one bell-ringing word, sex, sexton (a book – and at that one formed by folding sheets into his favorite number six!) and a bon-ton of professions too: a warden, a caretaker and a janitor! A bell ringing word which, for him also evokes **sexta hora** ['the sixth hour'], that is a *siesta*; a well deserved nap in the afternoon, adapted from **Latin** sp. for 6th hour. [p. 19]

Jefferson, himself a champion of Polish liberty seeking champions, called Kosciuszko "the purest son of liberty of all." … Now, he takes another look at her. Her cheeks are naturally rosy. She is full of *Ros*, of **liquor vitae** ['liquid of life'], life's subtle inner dew. No wonder. She is young. Awfully young. How young is she? [p. 31]

The next excerpt catches the protagonist after he takes a shower and is disturbed by the discovery of his hair loss:

He examines the clump again, this time under the light and through the magnifier: THE HAIR LOSS CAUSES PSYCHIC SHOCK, says his inner mordant examiner. He goes over it with a fine tooth comb. The hair is his. **Sic transit Gloria mundi** ["Thus passes the Glory of the world."]. Enough said. [p. 105]

The reference, the complete version of which is *Pater Sancte, sic transit Gloria mundi*, had been used in the years 1409–1963 in the ritual of papal coronation ceremonies; the formula was said three times by the papal master of ceremonies as, kneeling in front of the pope, he held a silver or brass reed with a tow of smoldering flax.

The final excerpt is in quotation marks because it is a letter that the protagonist receives from the head of Thanatos Institute in Yama, California, regarding a hypothetical suicide note. This passage is just one of a few that antecede or signal the author's own suicide a few years after the book is published.

"An ordinary suicide note is the least understood genre of undistinguished penmanship (as distinguished from distinguished literary creation), and we hope, my dear Mr. Kosky, to understand its nature better by asking you – as well as some other six hundred distinguished American fictional pen-masters, to write for us, **pro bono publico** ['for the public good'], one quasicide: a simulated suicide note –

such as you would write if one of your fictional protagonists was suicide-bound, and for yourself were you ever to voluntarily dispose of your physical Self by means of suicide," writes Dr. Sam Hill, Jr., ... " [p. 181]

The other two Latin references that appear in the book but do not need to be presented in their contexts are *congressus subtilis* (a form of sexual intercourse, p. 324) and Friedrich Nietzsche's *Ecce Homo* (meaning "Behold the Man," p. 406), a book expressing the author's humility as a philosopher.

While the Latin references discovered in Kosinski's prose are rather innumerous (that is all I have found even though I have read most of his works), his contribution to the thesis of this book is still precious as it increases the diversity of the voices by adding one more ethnicity. The Latin motto of his major alma mater, the University of Łódź, is *Veritas et Libertas* ("Truth and Freedom), and that of Columbia University is *In lumine Tuo videbimus lumen* ("In Thy light shall we see light"). The latter motto, in addition to illustrating a verb in the Future Active Indicative Tense, first person plural – *videbimus* (from the second-conjugation verb *video vidēre* – 'to see'), is of grammatical interest because of the two different cases of the same neuter noun – *lumine* (ablative singular) and *lumen* (accusative singular, a form identical to nominative only because of the noun's neuter gender) – both from *lumen, luminis* ('light').

20. John IRVING (1942–)

Born John Wallace Blunt, Jr., on March 2, 1942, in Exeter, New Hampshire, John Winslow Irving was educated at Phillips Exeter Academy, a boarding school where his stepfather, Colin Franklin Newell Irving, and his uncle were employed as faculty. His biological father was a WW II hero. Irving studied in Vienna under the program of the Institute for the International Education of Students and took a summer course in German at Harvard. He received his B.A. from the University of New Hampshire (1965) and his MFA from the University of Iowa (1967). His first novel was *Setting Free the Bears* (1968). His other notable works include *The World According to Garp* (1978), *The Hotel New Hampshire* (1981), *The Cider House Rules* (1985), *A Prayer for Owen Meany* (1989), *A Widow for One Year* (1998) and *Until I Find You* (2005). Irving has received several distinctions, notably from the Rockefeller Foundation, the National Endowment for the Arts and the Guggenheim Foundation. He is also a winner of an O. Henry Award.

As many as five films have been made from Irving's works. They are George Roy Hill's *The World According to Garp* (1982; featuring Robin Williams, Mary Beth Hurt, Glenn Close, John Lithgow and Hume Cronyn); Tony Richardson's *The Hotel New Hampshire* (1984; starring Rob Lowe, Jodie Foster, Paul McCrane and Beau Bridges); Mark Steven Johnson's *Simon Birch* (1998; featuring Joseph Mazzello, Ashley Judd, Oliver Platt and David Strathairn), based on *A Prayer for Owen Meany*; Lasse Hallström's Academy Award-winning *The Cider House Rules* (1999; starring Tobey Maguire, Charlize Theron, Delroy Lindo, Paul Rudd and Michael Caine); and Tod Williams's *The Door in the Floor* (2004; featuring Elle Fanning, Jeff Bridges, Kim Basinger and Jon Foster), based on *A Widow for One Year*. Irving wrote his own screenplay for *The Cider House Rules*, winning one of the two Oscars for the film; the other one went to Michael Caine as Best Supporting Actor.

Set in New Hampshire, like most of Irving's novel, *A Prayer for Owen Meany* ([1989] 1990) is a comic and moving story of a physically underdeveloped boy, the titular character, who believes he is God's instrument, even though his best friend, Johnny Wheelwright, is the narrator and the protagonist. The author incorporates six minor Latin references in this novel. The first passage, including a well-known phrase, is rather self-explanatory:

> Owen Meany used to say that we residents of Gravesend were sitting over a **bona fide** ['genuine/real'] outcrop of intrusive igneous rock; he would say this with an implied reverence—as if the consensus of the

Gravesend community was that the Exeter Pluton was as valuable as a mother lode of gold. [p. 12]

The second Latin phrase is also quite well known in English, even though its original meaning referred to a part of the Italian mainland owned by Venice. It is used twice by the narrator in the description of a partly comic, partly disastrous Christmas season performance as Owen, in the role of Baby Jesus, experiences an unexpected but conspicuous erection, apparently triggered by Barb Wiggin's (the rector's wife) kiss on the mouth "for good luck," as he is being carried to the manger on the stage (Johnny, playing Joseph, is in the midst of it all; Harold Crosby is one of the other "actors"):

> Hidden from the congregation's view, but ominously visible to us, Barb Wiggin seized the controls of the angel-lowering apparatus like a heavy-equipment operator about to attack the **terra firma** ['dry/firm land'] with a backhoe. When Owen caught her eye, she appeared to lose her confidence and her poise; the look he gave her was both challenging and lascivious. A shudder coursed through Barb Wiggin's body; she gave a corresponding jerk of her shoulders, distracting her from her task. Harold Crosby's meant-to-be-stately descent to earth was momentarily suspended. [pp. 215-216]

> Harold Crosby, who thought both God and Barb Wiggin had abandoned him forever, swung like a victim of a vigilante killing among the mock flying buttresses; Dan, an accomplished mechanic of all theatrical equipment, eventually mastered the angel-lowering apparatus and returned the banished angel to **terra firma**, where Harold collapsed in relief and gratitude. [p. 230]

The final Latin phrase in the book, again one that is commonly used in English (mostly by educational institutions to signify one of the three honors (the other two being *summa cum laude* – with highest praise, and *magna cum laude* – 'with great praise') awarded to their graduates, appears in a passage where Johnny, years later, in the context of his move to Canada, describes his educational assets:

> In 1968, you needed fifty points to become a landed immigrant; landed immigrants could apply for Canadian citizenship, for which they'd be eligible in five years. Earning my fifty "points" was easy for me; I had a B.A. ***cum laude*** ['with praise'], and a Master's degree in English—with Owen Meany's help, I'd written my Master's thesis on Thomas Hardy. [p. 453]

20. John IRVING (1942–)

A passage regarding Latin, without using any Latin lexicon, is worth quoting here as it addresses the fate of the ancient language as a school course and, at the same time, illustrates Owen's mature and open mind, as well as his uncompromising audacity, which antecedes the heroic climax. Here are Owen's thoughts, expressed in the school magazine, *The Voice*, regarding the new headmaster's decision:

> It was the *way* he had scrapped the **Latin** that was wrong, Owen pointed out.
>
> "IT IS SHREWD OF THE NEW HEADMASTER TO MAKE SUCH A POPULAR DECISION—AND WHAT COULD BE MORE POPULAR WITH STUDENTS THAN ABOLISHING A REQUIREMENT? *LATIN*, ESPECIALLY! BUT THIS SHOULD HAVE BEEN ACCOMPLISHED BY A VOTE—IN FACULTY MEETING." [P. 329]

Irving's powerful novel *A Widow for One Year* ([1998] 2001) is abundant with Latin quotations. The first group appears in the first part of the book, the year is 1958, and is triggered by the relationship of Marion Cole, an unhappy wife unable to recover from the tragic loss of her two sons, with Eddie O'Hare, a sixteen-year-old boy tied to her sons through attending the same school. The unusual situation has been intentionally orchestrated by Marion's unfaithful husband Ted (a writer and illustrator for children's books), in the hope of winning custody over their four-year-old daughter, Ruth, now the only child. Here is a passage related to Marion's obsession with her sons' photographs, eagerly shared with Eddie, starting with the boy arriving at Exeter and having no problem recognizing its landmark sign:

> **HVC VENITE PVERI**
> **VT VIRI SITIS**
>
> ["Come hither, boys, that you may become men"]
>
> (The U's in **HUC** and **PUERI** and **UT** had all been carved like V's, of course.) [pp. 74-75]

The ironic punchline of the quotation is presented a couple of pages later, in the dialogue between Eddie and Marion, the scene taking place in bed:

> "Do you know Latin?" Marion whispered to him.
>
> "Yes," he whispered back.

> She rolled her eyes upward, above the bed, to indicate the photograph of that important message, which her sons had not navigated. "Say it in Latin for me," Marion whispered.
>
> "*Huc venite pueri ...*" Eddie began, still whispering.
>
> "Come hither boys ..." Marion translated in a whisper.
>
> "*... ut viri sitis*," Eddie concluded; he'd noticed that Marion had his hand again and placed it against the crotch of her panties.
>
> "... and become men," Marion whispered. Again she gripped the back of his neck and pulled his face against her breasts. "But you *still* haven't had sex, have you?" she asked. "I mean not *really*."
>
> Eddie closed his eyes against her fragrant bosom. "No, not really," he muttered. [p. 77]

The next quoted passage takes place years later, in 1990, when Ruth travels in Europe as a successful novelist. While researching in Amsterdam red district, she unexpectedly witnesses a murder and anonymously provides the details of the crime to the police, information that turned out instrumental in catching the murderer.

> Ruth Cole left Amsterdam for New York on a late-morning flight the following day, having had the taxi take her to the nearest post office en route to the airport. At the post office, she mailed the envelope to Harry Hoekstra, who was almost a sergeant in the Amsterdam police force— District 2. It might have surprised Ruth to know the motto of the 2nd District, which was inscribed in Latin on the police officers' key rings.
>
> ***ERRARE***
> ***HUMANUM***
> ***EST***
>
> To err is human, Ruth Cole knew. Her message, together with the Polaroid print coater, would tell Harry Hoekstra much more than Ruth had meant to say. [pp. 417-418]

The popular quotation, the complete version of which is *Errare humanum est, persevere autem diabolicum* ("It is human to err, but diabolical to persist [in error]"), is frequently, without evidence in his works, attested to Seneca (full name: Lucius Annaeus Seneca the Younger; 4 B.C.–65 A.D.), a Hispano-Roman Stoic philosopher, statesman and playwright.

The final Latin reference, derived from William Thackeray's *Vanity Fair*, is again related to Eddie, or rather, his unexpected discovery:

> Eddie was glad to have found, among his father's uncountable underlinings, a passage that seemed to please Minty's former students. Eddie chose the last paragraph from *Vanity Fair*, for Minty had always been a Thackeray man. "Ah! **Vanitas Vanitatum!** ['Vanity of Vanities']" [p. 524]

Unlike most of Irving's novels, *A Son of the Circus* (1995) is not set in the author's familiar New Hampshire area; instead, it is set partially in Canada and partially in India, where the protagonist, Dr. Farrokh Daruwalla, was born and which country, after settling in Canada, he visits periodically. The Latin references incorporated in this book are neither numerous nor unique, but worth quoting anyway. The first Latin word, meaning 'guilt' but used as a modifier of a rosary, appears in a paragraph related to the robbery of Jesuit missionary Martin Mills:

> "They took only my **culpa** beads and my casual clothes," Martin remarked. "I'll have to buy some cheap local wear—it would be ostentatious to show up at St. Ignatius looking like this!" Whereupon he laughed and plucked at his startlingly white collar. [p. 330]

The other reference, a complete sentence (translated within the dialogue), is a part of a scene where Mills and Dr. Daruwalla run into a begging crippled boy and are wondering how they can help him:

> "Wouldn't you like your foot to be *cleaner-looking*?" Martin Mills asked the cripple. "Wouldn't you like to look less like a *hoe* or *club*?" As he spoke, he cupped his hand near the bony fusion of ankle and foot, which the beggar awkwardly rested on the heel. Close up, the doctor could confirm his earlier suspicion: he would have to saw through bone. There would be little chance of success, a greater chance of risk.
>
> "**Primum non nocere**," Farrokh said to Martin Mills. "I presume you know **Latin**."
>
> "'Above all, do no harm,'" the Jesuit replied. [p. 332]

Irving's eleventh novel, *Until I Find You* (2005), tells the story of Jack Burns who, born in Toronto and educated in Canada and New England, becomes a Hollywood actor, but long before that, when he is just a boy, he travels with his mother to remote places looking for his missing father, a church organist. The first quotation appears in a scene where Jack's mother (Alice) is confronting her son about the push-up bra he has received from Emma Oastler (it belonged to her mother) and slept with—even when it took place in his mother's bed:

> "What's this, Jack?" she asked, holding up the stinking bra. The way she looked at her son—well, he would never forget it. It was as if she'd discovered Emma's *mother* in the bed between them; it was as if she'd caught Jack ***in flagrante delicto*** ['in the act of wrongdoing'], the little guy in intimate contact with that hairy, private place.
>
> "It's a push-up bra," he explained. [p. 173]

The next three Latin references are related to Jack attending church, first in relation to hymns and then to a Latin inscription on the altar:

> Jack struggled to hear the Lord's noise in the music. But even when Vogel played the ***Sanctus*** ["Holy"] and the ***Agnus Dei*** ["The Lamb of God"], the Lord wasn't speaking to Jack. [p. 590]
>
> ...
>
> Heather saw Jack looking at the **Latin** inscription on the altar. As Mr. Ramsey had observed, Jack struggled with **Latin**.
>
>
>
> **VENITE**
> **EXULTEMUS**
> **DOMINO**
>
>
>
> "'Come let us praise the Lord,'" his sister said. [p. 739]

The same quotation appears three times on pp. 818-819. The scene takes place in Zurich, and the person that sings it is Jack's father, William Burns.

Even though there is no Latin version among the mottos of Irving's almae matres, the author, somewhere in his education, has acquired an impressive knowledge of the classical culture, which is evident in several of his works. The quotations that have been discovered in his prose constitute a nice mixture of some phrases adapted in the English language, some popular Latin expressions usually associated with law or Christian liturgy and a few Latin quotations of a general character. Thus, it would not be presumptuous to conclude that the high position that Irving holds among the modern American writers can indirectly testify to the important role that Latin plays in modern Western culture in general.

A matter not directly related to Latin, but significant in Irving's life and thus appropriate to be mentioned in the conclusion of his entry, is the fact that the distinguished author, for political reasons, officially became a Canadian citizen in December 2019.

21. Dermot McEVOY (1950–)

Born in Dublin, Ireland, Dermot McEvoy immigrated to the USA in 1954. He graduated from Hunter College and was a writer and editor for *Publishers Weekly* magazine before he published his first novel, *Terrible Angel: A Novel of Michael Collins in New York*, in 2004. His other two novels are *Our Lady of Greenwich Village* (2008) and *The 13th Apostle: A Novel of Michael Collins and the Irish Uprising* (2014).

A significant number of Latin references have been found in McEvoy's second novel, *Our Lady of Greenwich Village* (2008), focused on political races in New York City between GOP congressman Jackie Swift and democrat Wolfe Tone O'Rourke, both candidates inspired by an unusual vision, an appearance of Virgin Mary. The first Latin expression appears in a passage where O'Rourke goes to a bar, Hogan's Moat or, simply, the Moat, and runs into some interesting characters, one of them being Nuncio Baroody:

> Nuncio—no one remembered his real first name—had come by his sobriquet (if you could believe the mendacious Nuncio) through scandal. He had once been a priest, and he served as the secretary to the Papal Nuncio in Paris. His downfall had been the whiskey and Pernod and the occasion when the real Nuncio caught him in the confessional in a pederastic act with an 11-year-old boy. The Church had suspended him ***a divinis*** [literally, 'far from the divine,' or, better, 'canonical suspension'], banning him from celebrating mass and other sacraments. [p. 26]

The Latin phrase is an example of the ablative of separation with the form of the preposition 'ab' deprived of the consonant as a result of preceding a word beginning with a consonant.

Another example of Latin was found in a relatively funny scene, where O'Rourke has a meeting with agents of the American Express, and, rather unprepared, tells them a story involving Paul VI, whose name here is presented in the Latin form:

> The gentlemen were beginning to shift uncomfortably in their chairs, but O'Rourke couldn't stop. "So we go into the whole spiel about where the American Express Card is accepted by everybody all over the universe and then we shift back to Pope Paul and the Sistine Chapel. This time he has a blank card in his hand and at this point we print his

name, in **Latin**—***PAULUS PP VI***—on the card with a real zap, zap, zap kind of special effect. Then the Pope ends it with the tag-line: 'The American Express Card. Don't leave *Rome* without it!'" [p. 62]

The Latin phrase "Opus Dei," used as a name of an organization, is mentioned in the book many times in a variety of contexts. Below is an extract from Cyclops Reilly's column published in the *Daily News* on May 24, 2000 (Reilly is a columnist supporting O'Rourke in his campaign), which explains what it really is. The other pages where the phrase is mentioned are 111, 193, 205, 207, 209, 226, 233 and 240.

> But these folks don't do these weird things—so they say—to get a sexual kick. They do it for the love of God.
>
> I ain't lying.
>
> They belong to an extreme right-wing organization of the Catholic Church called ***Opus Dei***. ***Opus Dei*** is **Latin** for "the Work of God." They think of themselves as being elite. Kind of like the marines of the Church.
>
> There are a lot of rumors swirling around New York and Washington, D.C. right now and they involve an ***Opus Dei*** priest named John Costello. When last seen, he was going into the papal nunciate in Washington for a meeting. [pp. 231-232]

The other Latin references in McEvoy's novel that are worth mentioning without getting into detail about their context are **A.D.** (a commonly used abbreviation for *Anno Domini*, meaning 'in the year of the Lord'—p. 248—one noun in the 'ablative of time when' case, with the preposition implied, and the other in genitive), ***Mater Dolorosa*** (translated as 'Christ's sorrowful mother'— pp. 274 and 275) and ***Siemper Fi*** (a shorted variety of *Semper Fidelis*, 'Always Faithful/Loyal'—p. 296), the motto of the United States Marine Corps, with the first word, for some unknown reason, spelled in the book in the Spanish way.

Considering McEvoy's background, it is rather understandable why his writing is quite abundant with Latin expressions. The motto of his alma mater, Hunter College, is *Mihi cura futuri* ("The care of the future is mine"), with the verb in the original version implied and the personal pronoun in the dative rather than the genitive (possessive) case.

II.
Latin in Crime and Detective Fiction

1. Raymond CHANDLER (1888-1959)

Born on July 23, 1888, in Chicago, Illinois, Raymond Thornton Chandler, abandoned in childhood by his alcoholic father, moved with his mother, originally from Ireland, to England and was educated at Dulwich College, London. He started writing in the early 1930s, published his first short story, "Blackmailers Don't Shoot," in *Black Mask* Magazine in 1933 and his first novel, *The Big Sleep*, in 1939. A British citizen between 1907 and 1956, Chandler won the Best Novel Edgar Award from the Mystery Writers of America in 1955 (for *The Long Goodbye*). He died on March 26, 1959, in La Jolla, California, while serving as the President of the Mystery Writers of America.

An author of seven and a half novels and a bunch of short stories, Raymond Chandler is arguably the most acclaimed of all American detective fiction writers. Praised for his unique style and tone that reveal an original compromise between romanticism and cynicism, he created the most charismatic private eye, Philip Marlowe, whose name (possibly modeled after Joseph Conrad's Marlow) appeared for the first time in Chandler's first novel, thus becoming the final version of the protagonist's former (and latter) names—Carmady, John Dalmas and John Evans—used throughout the author's short stories. Marlowe—who is as much an observer and commentator of the corrupted reality as he is a modern knight errant frequently interfering in the course of events, consistently defending the weak and the poor—was played on the big screen by a number of first-rate actors—Dick Powell in Edward Dmytryk's *Murder, My Sweet* (1945), based on *Farewell, My Lovely* (1940); Humphrey Bogart in Howard Hawks's *The Big Sleep* (1946), from the novel of the same title (1939); Robert Montgomery in *The Lady in the Lake* (1946), a movie version of the 1943 novel, directed by the star himself; George Montgomery in John Brahm's *The Brasher Doubloon* (1947), a screen adaptation of *The High Window* (1942); James Garner in Paul Bogart's *Marlowe* (1960), which was based on *The Little Sister* (1949); Elliott Gould in Robert Altman's screen version (1973) of *The Long Goodbye* (1953); and Robert Mitchum in two late adaptations: Dick Richards's *Farewell, My Lovely* (1975) and Michael Winner's *The Big Sleep* (1977). In the TV series *Philip Marlowe, Private Eye* (1983-1986), the charismatic detective is portrayed by Powers Boothe. Chandler's last novel, *Playback* (1958), originally conceived as a screenplay, was never filmed, while his unfinished novel was completed by Robert B. Parker, published as *Poodle Springs* in 1989 and made into a TV film by Bob Rafelson in 1998.

Chandler's filmography also includes several screenplays; in addition to adapting other writers' works for the screen, including James M. Cain's *Double*

Indemnity (filmed by Billy Wilder in 1944) and Patricia Highsmith's *Strangers on a Train* (filmed by Alfred Hitchcock in 1951), he wrote the original script for George Marshall's *The Blue Dahlia* (1946; starring Alan Ladd, Veronica Lake and William Bendix).

One of many tokens of the writer's rank and the popularity of his protagonist is the collection *Raymond Chandler's Philip Marlowe: A Centennial Celebration* (1988), which consists of twenty-six Marlowe short stories, each by a different author, including one, "The Pencil," by Chandler himself.

A Latin-related simile, rather than a Latin quotation, has been found in Chandler's short story "The Man Who Liked Dogs" ([1934] 1977). The pertinent sentence is uttered by the narrator/protagonist, private detective Carmady, in a conversation with Chief of Police Fulwider and a cop named Galbraith. Fulwider is about to fire Galbraith for incompetence; Galbraith, though, has some valid arguments in his defense, information somewhat embarrassing to his boss:

> The fat chief jumped as though a bee had stung the end of his nose. Then he doubled a meaty fist and hit Galbraith's jaw with what looked like a lot of power. Galbraith's head moved about half an inch.
>
> "Don't do that," he said. "You'll bust a gut and then where would the department be?" He shot a look at me, looked back at Fulwider. "Should I tell him?"
>
> Fulwider looked at me, to see how the show was going over. I had my mouth open and a blank expression on my face, like a farm boy at a **Latin** class. [p. 64]

A Latin quotation appears in another short story by Chandler, "Mandarin's Jade" ([1937] 1977), this one featuring private eye John Dalmas (the narrator). It is a part of the final conversation between Police Lieutenant Reavis and the detective, who has been seriously injured during his confrontation with the crooks. They talk about the criminals that need to be arrested (psychic Soukesian referred to first) and Dalmas's condition:

> "I was there," I said. "At his house. He knows something. I don't know what. He was afraid of me—yet he didn't knock me off. Funny."
>
> "Amateur," Reavis said dryly. "He left that for Moose Magoon. Moose Magoon was tough—up till lately. A record from here to Pittsburgh. ... Here. But take it easy. This is **ante mortem** ['before death'] confession liquor. Too damn good for you." [pp. 213-214]

1. Raymond CHANDLER (1888–1959) 113

Figure 2.1. The image of Humphrey Bogart (as Philip Marlowe) in the poster "The Cinema According to Chandler," designed by Waldemar Świerzy (1988) for the retrospective organized by the Film Society "Kinematograf 75" (Poznan, Poland). Courtesy of the "Ikonosfera" Gallery and Transart Collection.

The phrase *ante mortem* is the reverse of the expression *post mortem* often used in the context of a medical examination, which is one of the cases where the Latin-English phrase (here: 'post-mortem examination') is simplified and shortened to a monolingual version,

Two Latin references have been discovered in Chandler's possibly most complex novel, *The Long Goodbye* ([1953] 1981). While (chronologically) the second one, **Tegenaria domestica** (p. 142), is just a Latin name of a spider species, known in North America as the 'barn funnel weaver' and in Europe as the 'house/drain spider,' the first one is a relatively well-known phrase (adapted in English as either an adverb or an adjective) used by the narrator in a descriptive paragraph:

> The whole thing was just window-dressing. The clients of The Carne Organization were charged a minimum of one hundred fish **per diem** ['per day'] and they expected service in their homes. They didn't go sit in no waiting rooms. Carne was an ex-colonel of military police, a big pink and white guy as hard as a board. [p. 111]

Appreciated equally by mystery and mainstream fiction readers, Raymond Chandler is indisputably one of the top few crime fiction authors writing in the English language. He is revered by his peers (references to his name and books appear in dozens of novels, mysteries in particular, more than once in works by Ed McBain, Sara Paretsky, Andrew J. Fenady and Greg Iles) and highly acclaimed by the critics. Three of his novels—*The Big Sleep, Farewell, My Lovely* and *The Long Goodbye*—are included in the publication *1001 Books You Must Read Before You Die* (Universe, 2007). Even though the Latin references found in his prose are neither numerous nor overly insightful, his inclusion in this publication is significant by the mere prestige of his name. The Latin motto of Dulwich College, the alma mater of Chandler (and, also, P. G. Wodehouse) is *Detur gloria soli Deo* ("Let glory be given to God alone"), including a verb in the Present Passive Subjunctive form, *detur* (from the first-conjugation verb *do dare* – 'to give'), and the dative case, *Deo*, of the second-declension masculine noun *Deus* ('God'), which explains why the preposition 'to' (only implied in Latin) is physically present in the English translation.

2. S. S. VAN DINE (1888–1939)

S. S. Van Dine (real name: Willard Huntington Wright) was born on October 15, 1888, in Charlottesville, Virginia. He was educated at St. Vincent College, Pomona College and Harvard University (without graduating). His first novel, *The Benson Murder Case*, was published in 1926, and was followed by eleven others, most, just like the first one, featuring art connoisseur and amateur detective Philo Vance. The last one, *The Winter Murder Case*, came out in 1939. The author resided in Santa Monica, California, but died in New York City on April 11, 1939.

About a dozen feature films based on Van Dine's works, all using the original titles of the novels, were made between 1929 and 1947. The best, by far, are the ones starring William Powell in the role of Philo Vance—Malcolm St. Clair's *The Canary Murder Case* (1929; co-starring Jean Arthur, James Hall and Louise Brooks), Frank Tuttle's *The Greene Murder Case* (1929; co-starring Florence Eldridge and Jean Arthur) and *The Benson Murder Case* (1930; co-starring William 'Stage' Boyd and Eugene Pallette), and Michael Curtiz's *The Kennel Murder Case* (1933; co-starring Mary Astor and Eugene Pallette). The other impersonators of the gifted but rather snobbish sleuth include Basil Rathbone (in David Burton and Nick Grinde's *The Bishop Murder Case*, 1929), Warren William (in H. Bruce Humberstone's *The Dragon Murder Case*, 1934, and in Alfred E. Green's *The Gracie Allen Murder Case*, 1939), Paul Lukas (in Edwin L. Marin's *The Casino Murder Case*, 1935), Edmund Lowe (in Edwin L. Marin's *The Garden Murder Case*, 1936) and others.

The narrator of all Van Dine's novels is the author himself, who claims to have been Philo Vance's personal attorney and constant companion. John F.-V. Markham, New York's District Attorney and Vance's close friend, also appears in the books as one of the main characters. Numerous Latin references have been found in Van Dine's *The Canary Murder Case* ([1927] 1945), a novel in which Philo Vance "helps" Markham solve the mystery of Broadway beauty Margaret Odell's murder in her apartment. Because of the abundance of the quotations, they will be selectively presented, the more interesting and relatively lengthy ones first and in their contexts.

Most of the philosophical references in the book are related to Vance either criticizing Markham's modus operandi, giving him advice or both. In the following quotation, Vance offers advice to the DA about how to read people's faces. The individual serving as an example is Dr. Ambroise Lindquist, a fashionable neurologist:

"Really, y'know, Markham, old thing," he added, "you should study the cranial indications of your fellow man more carefully—***vultus est index animi*** ["The face is the index of the mind."] Did you, by any chance, note the gentleman's wide rectangular forehead, his irregular eyebrows, the pale luminous eyes, and his outstanding ears with their upper rims, their pointed tragi and split lobes?" [p. 95]

The proverb quoted in the above excerpt has several versions in the English translation, including one that sounds quite nice: "The eyes are the mirror of the soul." While the genesis of the aphorism is not definitely known, a synonymous sentence has been attributed to Cicero (see the entry on Wolfe).

In the next quotation, Vance warns Markham about the danger of jumping to conclusions when the DA is anxious to arrest a suspect:

"You're always in such a haste," Vance lamented. "Why leap and run? The wisdom of the world's philosophers is against it. ***Festina lente*** ["Hurry up slowly."], says Caesar; or, as Rufus has it, ***Festinatio tarda est*** ["Speed is slow-paced."]. [p. 131]

Even though Vance (or the author) attributes the first of the pretty well-known maxims to Julius Caesar and the other one to Rufus (probably referring to the Christian whose father helped to carry the cross used in Jesus Christ's crucifixion), both sayings are rather anonymous, and the first one was originally known in Greek.

The next three Latin references are, again, parts of Vance's responses to the DA's way of thinking and directly triggered by Markham's inability to see things in the right way:

"You're so deficient in imagination, old thing."

"I take it that you would have me close my eyes and picture Spotswoode sitting up-stairs here in the Stuyvesant Club and extending his arms to 71st Street. But I simply couldn't do it. I'm a commonplace chap. Such a vision would strike me as ludicrous; it would smack of a hasheesh dream. ... You yourself don't use ***Cannabis indica*** [name of an annual plant in the genus Cannabis, or, simply, marijuana], do you?"

"Put that way, the idea does sound a bit supernatural. And yet: ***Certum est quia impossible est*** ["It is certain because it is impossible."]. I rather like that maxim, don't y' know; for, in the present case, the impossible is true. Oh Spotswoode's guilty—no doubt about it." [pp. 246-247]

"To-morrow I'll apply for an order of exhumation."

Vance looked at him with waggish reproachfulness, and sighed.

"Recognition of my transcendent genius, I see, is destined to be posthumous. *Omnia post obitum fingit majora vetustas* ["Time magnifies everything after death."]. In the meantime I bear the taunts and jeers of the multitude with a stout heart. My head is bloody, but unbowed." [p. 253]

The first of the two references is a paradoxically sounding axiom which was originally used by Tertullian (full name: Quintus Septimus Florens Tertullianus; c. 160–c. 220 A.D.), an author from Carthage of Berber and Phoenician origin, called "the father of Latin Christianity" and the "founder of Western theology, in Chapter 5 of his *De Carne Christi* (*On the Flesh of Christ*). The second reference, offering another insightful line, comes from *Elegiae*, III. 1. 23. 65, by Sextus Propertius (c. 50–15 B.C.), a Latin elegiac poet of the Augustan Age.

The last quotation offers a good example of a Latin sentence structure, where the subject, *vetustas* (a third-declension feminine abstract noun meaning 'past time'), is positioned at the end; the main part of the predicate, *fingit* (the Present Active Indicative, third person singular form of the third-conjugation verb *fingo fingĕre* – 'to form/mold'), is in the middle; the direct object, *omnia* (the neuter accusative plural form of the third-declension adjective *omnis omnis omne* – 'all/each,' here meaning 'everything'), at the very beginning; and the predicate accusative part (obviously, matching the direct object also in number), *majora*, (derived from the first/second-declension adjective *magnus magna magnum* and providing an example of the comparative form, switching to the third declension), inserted between the verb and the subject. Hence, an alternative translation of that line, more literal but less polished, could be "After death the past time makes everything bigger."

The other Latin references discovered in *The Canary Murder Case* are also worth presenting; their contexts, however, are not as important. Thus, here is the list of such lexical items, along with their translations and page numbers:

amicus curiae ('friend of the court,' p. 5);

in statu quo ('in the existing state of affairs,' p. 58, a rare, ablative, version of the common expression);

corpus delicti ('the dead body of the victim,' p. 68);

arbiter elegantarum ('a judge of artistic taste and etiquette,' p. 79);

prima facie (literally, 'at first face,' or, better, based 'on the first impression,' pp. 102, 161);

ipso facto ('by the very fact/act,' p. 112);

personae gratae ('people acceptable/welcome,' p. 126);

eheu ('alas' or 'bummer!,' p. 132);

Vae misero mihi ('Oh, poor me!' p. 147);

locus standi ('the right/ability to bring a legal action or to appear in a court,' p. 194);

modus operandi ('a particular way/method of doing something,' p. 224);

magnus Apollo! ('great Apollo!' p. 252).

Equally abundant with Latin references is Van Dine's novel *The Kennel Murder Case* ([1933] 1980). While the challenge of the murder case consists in the fact that the (first) victim, dog breeder Archie Coe, was found in the locked room of his townhouse (the technical trick explaining the mystery revealed at the very end), the main characters are basically the same as in the previous novel: amateur detective Philo Vance, District Attorney John F.-X. Markham and Homicide Bureau Sergeant Ernest Heath.

Once again, the pretext for quoting any foreign language proverbs is the diametrically opposite way of thinking and acting represented by the DA and the detective. Here is a colorful and trilingual example of the two men's sarcastic exchange:

> "That's about all," Markham confessed. "What would you have suggested?"
>
> "Really, Markham, I hadn't a suggestion today." Vance leaned back in his chair. "But tomorrow—"
>
> "You're so helpful and satisfying," Markham snapped. "'*Morgen, morgen, nur nicht heute; sagen immer träge Leute.*' [a translation from German: "Tomorrow, tomorrow, but not today; that's what lazy people say."]."

"Markham—my very dear Markham!" Vance protested reprovingly. "Really, don't y' know, I'm not lazy. I give you Cicero: '*Aliquod crastinus dies ad cogitandum dabit.*' ["Tomorrow will give some food for thought."]" [p. 253]

Unfortunately, the rest of the Latin expressions in the novel (most quoted several times) are commonly-used legal, medical or general terms, which, for practical and comparative reasons, are listed below, again along with their translations and page numbers:

De mortuis ('About the dead ones,' p. 48, the beginning of a well-known proverb *De mortuis nihil nisi bonum*, meaning 'Of the dead (say) nothing but good.");

post mortem ('after death,' pp. 51, 57, 126);

rigor mortis (literally 'stiffness of death,' or, better, 'postmortem rigidity,' p. 56, 57, 67, 124, 193, 197);

terrarius ('of land,' mentioned here as the origin of the name of the dog breed 'terrier,' meaning 'ground dog,' p. 175);

modus operandi ('a particular way/method of doing something,' p. 289).

The third and last of Van Dine's novels researched for the project, *The Bishop Murder Case*, 1929), with the same trio of men involved in the investigation, was read in its Polish translation; its title, *Piosenka śmierci* (1991), meaning '*The Song of Death*.' Since the context of any of the references is rather difficult or even impossible to present without taking the liberty of translating the author's prose back to English, the best solution is simply, once again, to make a list of the Latin lexical items encountered in the Polish version, along with their English translations. Here is the list:

Quod erat demonstrandum ('what had to be shown/demonstrated,' p. 72);

modus operandi ('a particular way/method of doing something,' p. 72);

ex post facto ('having retroactive effect/force,' p. 73);

reductio ad absurdum (literally: 'reduction to absurdity,' meaning 'form of refutation showing contradictory or absurd consequences following upon premises as a matter of logical necessity,' p. 73);

ecce homo ("behold the man," p. 80);

pro tempore ('for the time being,' p. 85);

non sequitur ('a conclusion or statement that does not logically follow from the previous argument or statement,' p. 86);

post mortem ('after death,' p. 91);

prima facie (literally: 'at first face,' p. 93);

Eheu ('Alas,' p. 95);

Nil quam difficile est, quin quaerendo investigari possit. ("Nothing is so difficult but that it may be found out." p. 117);

dramatis personae ('the characters of a play/narrative,' p. 133);

Sursum corda ("Lift up your hearts." p. 206);

Sic transit ('Thus passes,' p. 217, the beginning of the famous quotation *Sic transit gloria mundi*, meaning "Thus passes the glory of the world.");

Hic jacet ('here lies,' words often beginning an epitaph, p. 241).

One of the most popular American writers of the first half of the twentieth century, S. S. Van Dine is also one of the most dedicated Latin fans, which shows probably in all of his works. What is more, his Latin references— inevitably recurring due to their unmatched multitude— constitute an impressive mixture of legal terms, everyday expressions and, most importantly, cultural epigrams, which provide additional flavor to the dialogues. In addition to testifying to the author's impressive educational background, the references carry that particular characteristic over to the author's protagonist, also adding more substance to two of his other traits, arrogance and pomposity—all revealed in apt moderation that does not prevent the reader from admiring the charismatic detective, or rejecting the job so well done by his prime screen impersonator, William Powell.

The Latin mottos of the institutions where Wright/Van Dine was educated are *Veri iustique scientia vindex* ("Knowledge is the guardian of truth and justice.")—St. Vincent College, and *Veritas* ("Truth")—Harvard University.

3. Erle Stanley GARDNER (1889–1970)

Born on July 17, 1889, in Malden, Massachusetts, Erle Stanley Gardner was educated at Palo Alto High School and spent one month at the Valparaiso University School of Law. He studied law on his own and passed the (California) state Bar exam in 1911. A successful lawyer for many years, he published his first short story in 1923 and soon became an enormously prolific author of mystery novels, divided into several series. The most extensive and popular is the "investigating attorney Perry Mason" series including *The Case of the Velvet Claws* (1933), *The Case of the Lucky Legs* (1934), *The Case of the Howling Dog* (1934), *The Case of the Curious Bride* (1934), *The Case of the Stuttering Bishop* (1936), *The Case of the Haunted Husband* (1941) and *The Case of the Golddigger's Purse* (1945). The "Cool and Lam" series also consists of many novels, such as *The Knife Slipped* (1939), *Double for Quits* (1941), *Some Women Won't Wait* (1953) and *Cut Thin to Win* (1965). The "D.A. Doug Selby" series includes such titles as *The D.A. Calls It Murder* (1937), *The D.A. Draws a Circle* (1939), *The D.A. Cooks a Goose* (1942) and *The D.A. Breaks an Egg* (1949). He also wrote two novels of the "Terry Clane" series, two of the "Gramps Wiggins" series, plus some other fiction and nonfiction books. Among Gardner's numerous distinctions are a Grand Master Award and an Edgar Award—both from the Mystery Writers of America. At the time of his death (he died on March 11, 1970, in Temecula, California), Gardner was the bestselling American author of the 20th century.

The popularity of Gardner's novels has been manifested in countless big-screen and TV adaptations. Several films, all based on the Perry Mason novels and most starring Warren William in the part of the attorney, were made in the 1930s. The most memorable ones are Alan Crosland's *The Case of the Howling Dog* (1934, co-starring Mary Astor), Michael Curtiz's *The Case of the Curious Bride* (1935, co-starring Margaret Lindsay), Archie Mayo's *The Case of the Lucky Legs* (1935, co-starring Genevieve Tobin) and William Clemens's *The Case of the Velvet Claws* (1936, co-starring Claire Dodd)—all with William as Mason. The actor was replaced in that role by Ricardo Cortez in *The Case of the Black Cat* (1936, co-starring June Travis) and by Donald Woods in William Clemens's *The Case of the Stuttering Bishop* (1937, co-starring Ann Dvorak). In terms of TV, the most long-lasting series was *Perry Mason* with Raymond Burr as Mason and Barbara Hale as his secretary, Della Street; as many as 271 episodes of the series were made in the years 1957-1966.

Latin references have been found in three novels by Gardner and in one of his short stories. The first novel of interest here is *The Case of the Stuttering*

Bishop ([1936] 1988) with a couple of Latin expressions, both used several times. Here are a few of the examples of the legal term *Res Gestae* as used in court by attorney Perry Mason and Judge Knox several times:

> "That's all she told me. I took the letter out. A young man opened the door when I rang the bell at Brownley's house. I gave him the letter. He said he'd take to Mr. Brownley. I asked him what his name was ..."

> "Just a moment," Mason snapped. "I object to any conversation between these two people on the ground that it is merely hearsay and not part of the **Res Gestae**.

> "Sustained," Judge Knox ruled. [pp. 139-140]

> "I won't admit any statement as to what was in the letter nor whom it was from," Judge Knox ruled, "but I will admit, as part of the **Res Gestae**, any statements that might have been made by Mr. Bownley as to what he intended to do or where he intended to go."

> ...

> "I will reserve a ruling," Judge Knox said, "but I'll leave it in if the subsequent testimony shows it to be what I consider part of the **Res Gestae**."

> "It's too remote to be part of the **Res Gestae**," Mason objected. [p. 141]

The argumentation about the issue keeps going on between Mason and the judge, and, in fact, the phrase **Res Gestae** ('things done/exploits,' or, better 'facts admissible as evidence in court,' or better still, 'events/circumstances/ remarks that relate to a particular case') is used in the same context three more times on p. 141 and, once again, on p. 157. However, despite the legal application of the phrase in modern times, the original and complete version of the phrase, *Res Gestae Divi Augusti* ('The Deeds of the Divine Augustus'), was a monumental inscription composed by Augustus Caesar (formerly Octavianus; 63 B.C.–14 A.D.), Julius Caesar's great-nephew and adoptive son and a member of the Second Triumvirate before he became the first Roman emperor. The text of the inscription was left by Augustus in his will and subsequently carved on many buildings.

The other legal term in Latin introduced to the reader by Gardner in this book is *corpus delicti* ('the dead body of the victim'), and here are a couple of samples of the context, both being a part of an extensive scene where Mason himself explains the meaning of the phrase and its ramifications to Della Street, his secretary, and Paul Drake, the head of the Drake Detective Agency:

> "The term, ***corpus delicti***, means the body of the Offense. In order to show it, in a charge of homicide, the Prosecution must show death as the *result*, and the criminal agency of the defendant as the *means*. Now the Prosecution's going to run up against one big hurdle on the ***corpus delicti*** business. They can't show death, and if they're not careful, I can trap them into being crucified by their own proof." [p. 151]
>
> "Could you keep Sacks from testifying if you tripped them up on this ***corpus delicti*** business?" Drake asked.
>
> "That's exactly the point," Mason told him. "That's why I'm making this defense. I can beat the case on the ***corpus delicti***, I'll get Julia Branner off temporarily." [pp. 152-153]

The reason why it is possible for Mason to take advantage of the *corpus delicti* idea is the fact that the body of the murder victim, Mr. Brownley, has never been found. The issue reemerges a few pages later, and the phrase is used again, as many as five times, on pp. 154, 157 (three times here) and 159.

Two other well-known Latin phrases commonly used in law appear in Gardner's mystery *The Case of the Golddigger's Purse* ([1945] 1962). One of them is *post mortem* (literally 'after death'), referring to an examination of a dead body to determine the cause of death; the other one is *habeas corpus* (literally: 'that you have the body'), referring to a recourse allowing to report an unlawful detention. Both expressions are used by Perry Mason in a conversation with Paul Drake, the already mentioned private detective and aide-de-camp to Mason (Sally Madison is the titular "golddigger," also Mason's client as a murder suspect):

> Mason nodded, "I've had it coming to me once or twice," he admitted, "but what makes me sore is to think that they'd really hang it on me in a case where we were absolutely innocent and only trying to help a young fellow who had T.B. get enough money to take treatments that would cure him. Hang it, Paul, I'm really in a mess this time, and they've got Della roped into it. That's what comes of trusting a golddigger. Oh well, there's no use conducting **post-mortems**. By the time the police let me get in touch with Sally Madison she'll have been bled white. I'm getting out a writ of ***habeas corpus*** and that of course will force their hand. They'll have to put a charge against her. But by the time they do that, they'll have really put her through a clothes

ringer. Keep working Paul, and if you get anything new, let Della Street know. [p. 119]

The latter expression is also used some pages later, during a telephone conversation between Della Street and her boss:

"Okay, Chief, anything else?"

"That's all. What's new?"

She said, "I'm glad you phoned. I filed the application for a writ of **habeas corpus** and Judge Downey issued a writ returnable next Tuesday. They've now booked Sally Madison on a charge of first-degree murder."

"I suppose they booked her as soon as they learned of the writ," Mason said.

"I guess so."

Mason said, "All right, I'm going up to the jail and demand an audience with her.

"As her attorney?"

"Sure." [p. 136]

Gardner has published a number of short fiction works, but the only short story featuring Perry Mason is "The Case of the Irate Witness," originally published in a 1953 issue of *Collier's* and widely reprinted ever since, in *Sleuths of the Century* (2000) among others. A relatively rare legal Latin term, a subpoena *duces tecum* ('you will bring with you'), is used by the attorney to demand that a key witness appears at the trial with certain objects. Here is the interesting scene:

"Are you ready?" the judge asked.

Mason turned. "I am quite ready, Your Honor. I have one witness whom I wish to put on the stand. I wish a subpoena **duces tecum** issued for that witness. I want him to bring certain documents that are in his possession."

"Who is the witness, and what are the documents?" the judge asked.

Mason walked quickly over to Paul Drake. "What's the name of that character who has the garbage-collecting business," he said softly, "the one who has the first nickel he's ever made?"

"George Addey."

The lawyer turned to the judge. "The witness that I want is George Addey, and the documents that I want him to bring to court with him are all the twenty-dollar bills that he has received during the past sixty days." [p. 189]

In *The Case of the Daring Decoy* ([1957] 1993), one more Perry Mason novel, Gardner furnishes his prose with two Latin phrases, both legal terms, the first one of which, *res gestae* (spelled in lower case this time), was already introduced in his mystery *The Case of the Stuttering Bishop*. The context, again, is a scene in court where Mason questions the admissibility of certain facts, regarding a murder victim, offered by witness Robert King, a clerk at the Redfern Hotel, but the phrase is used by two other men, the prosecutor and the judge:

'You had seen that young woman during her lifetime?'

'I had.'

'Where and when?'

'She had entered the hotel and stated that she wanted a suite somewhere on the sixth or seventh floor, preferably the seventh. She stated that—'

'Never mind what she stated,' Mason said. 'I object on the ground that it's incompetent, irrelevant and immaterial.'

'This is very definitely part of the **res gestae**,' Marvin Elliott said. It accounts for certain facts which otherwise would be confusing.'

'I think I will sustain the objection to the conversation,' Judge DeWitt said. 'You may ask what she did as part of the **res gestae**.' [p. 211]

The other phrase, *rigor mortis* (literally 'stiffness of death,' or, better, 'postmortem rigidity'), is used multiple times in the same trial; the examples (all quoted except for one more on p. 215 and one on p. 222) are part of a scene which depict the questioning of Dr. Klenton C. Malone, an autopsy surgeon:

> 'Why didn't you perform the autopsy that night?'
>
> 'There was not that much urgency about it. The district attorney wanted to have certain information by nine o'clock in the morning. I started the autopsy so I could give him the information he wanted.'
>
> '*Rigor mortis* had developed when the body was discovered?'
>
> 'I understand it had.'
>
> 'When does **rigor** develop?'
>
> 'That is variable, depending upon several factors.'
>
> ...
>
> 'Did you consider *rigor mortis* in connexion with determining the time of death?'
>
> 'I did not. I determined the time of death from the contents of the stomach and intestines.'
>
> 'Did you know when the last meal was ingested?'
>
> 'I was told that time could be fixed with great certainty. I know that death occurred approximately two hours after the last meal had been ingested.' [p. 214]
>
> 'You didn't consider *rigor mortis* as an element in fixing the time of death?
>
> 'I did not. There were indications that *rigor mortis* had set in almost immediately.'
>
> ...
>
> '*Rigor mortis* begins at the chin and throat muscles and slowly spreads downward until the entire body is involved. Then **rigor** begins to leave the body in the same order in which it was formed.' [p. 215]

3. Erle Stanley GARDNER (1889–1970)

One of the most popular and most prolific American mystery writers, Erle Stanley Gardner (referenced in numerous books by his peers, especially Paul Levine) embellished his highly entertaining books with an impressive variety of Latin phrases from the legal field, which, as a whole, provide one more unambiguous argument negating the wrongful and, unfortunately, quite prevalent belief that Latin is a dead language. Even though he did not study for more than a month at Valparaiso University, it is still a good idea to quote its Latin motto: *In luce tua videmus lucem* ("In Thy light we see light.").

4. Brett HALLIDAY (1904–1977)

David Dresser, better known as Brett Halliday (one of his several pen names), was born in Chicago, Illinois, on July 31, 1904, but grew up in Texas. After an adventurous youth consisting of a stint in the U.S. 5th Cavalry Regiment and several odd jobs in the Southwest, he graduated from Tri-State College of Engineering in Angola, Indiana. An engineer and surveyor in Texas for several years, he started writing in the late 1920s, publishing his first novel, *Divided on Death*, in 1939. He wrote mysteries, westerns and romances, but is probably best remembered as the author of a series of novels featuring private detective Michael Shayne. His last novel was *Win Some, Lose Some* (1976). He died on February 4, 1977, in Santa Barbara, California.

While there are about a dozen movies based on the characters he created, the ones adapted from his novels include Eugene Forde's *Michael Shayne: Private Detective* (1940; starring Lloyd Nolan and Marjorie Weaver)—from the novel *The Private Practice of Michael Shayne* (1940); Sam Newfield's *Murder Is My Business* (1946; featuring Hugh Beaumont, Cheryl Walker, Lyle Talbot and George Meeker)—based on the novel *The Uncomplaining Corpse* (1940); and Newfield's *Three on a Ticket* (1947; starring, again, Hugh Beaumont and Cheryl Walker, as well as Paul Bryar)—from the novel *The Corpse Came Calling* (1942).

Halliday's novel *This Is It, Michael Shayne* ([1950], 1968) is set, like most of the Shayne stories, in Miami, Florida. The first out of the two murder victims is uncompromising reporter Sara Morton, who dies because Shayne did not respond to her messages soon enough. The Latin reference appears in a scene where narrator/protagonist Shayne discusses Morton's case (involving her coworker Carl Garvin) with his good friend Tim Rourke, who, just like Morton, is a tough reporter.

> Rourke's slaty eyes showed surprise. "Sure, I run into him now and then." He grinned and added, "Morton and Garvin got along just like that," holding up both index fingers and moving them apart the full length of his arms.

> "Why?"

> "She worried him. Garvin's not a newspaperman. Just a glorified office boy for her syndicate. He's probably a tenth cousin to a vice-president. He sits on his lazy butt and draws a fair salary for clipping an occasional story and rewriting it over the wire. I think he took a

journalistic course in some swanky eastern college, and do those guys ever think they know their stuff," he added with heavy sarcasm.

"What control did he have over Morton? Shayne asked. "What she did in Miami and what she wrote?"

"Damn little. He was afraid she'd upset the ***status quo*** ['the existing state of affairs'] by sending out stuff so hot the syndicate would begin to wonder why he'd been sitting on it."

Several Latin references have been found in *Murder Takes No Holiday* (1960), Halliday's novel set partially in Miami and mostly on an island, a notorious smugglers' haven, where the detective is supposed to rest after recovering from an almost deadly car accident. Tim Rourke, just like Shayne's loyal secretary, Lucy Hamilton, are again among the minor characters. The first Latin reference is a part of Shayne's interrogation by the island's local police:

"In the morning we will have it out with the inspector, and you can give us all the corresponding details which you have apparently been skipping over."

"The morning—" Shayne began hotly.

"Will be too late," the sergeant said. "I believe you told us that already. But we have nobody's word for it but yours, do we? And your ***bona fides*** [one's 'honesty and sincerity of intention'] are hardly of the best." [p. 108]

The next reference appears in the continuation of the scene where Shayne's interlocutor is still Sergeant Brannon:

I know all about your kind. But you may come to regret that it ever entered your mind to play ducks and drakes with our backward little provincial constabulary. What you need is time for reflection, and I'm the man who can give it to you."

Shayne, too, was beginning to get angry. "Did you ever hear of a writ of **habeas corpus** [literally 'that you have the body,' a recourse allowing to report an unlawful detention]?"

"Often. You Americans stole it from us, you know. But I don't think it will apply in your case." [pp. 111-112]

4. Brett HALLIDAY (1904–1977)

The clause quoted in the last paragraph, very well-known in legal circles, is also interesting from the grammatical point of view. Its verb, *habeas* (from the second-conjugation *habeo habēre* – 'to have/hold'), is in the Present Active Subjunctive, second person singular form, and its direct object, *corpus* (the accusative singular of the third-declension noun *corpus corporis* – 'body'), has the ending *-us* (rather than *–em* added to the base *corpor-*) only because its gender is neuter.

A Latin word frequently used in English is a part of a narrative text, without italics (confirming its generally-acceptable application), of a paragraph where Shayne, having searched the hotel room of Vivienne Larousse, a woman offering him some help, examines a number of random objects, including a letter that might contain some revealing information:

> It was on a letterhead of the American consul, addressed to Mlle. Vivienne Larousse at a St. Albans hotel. In stiff official language it listed the conditions under which French citizens could be assigned a **quota** ['portion/part'] number for permanent admission to the United States. Larousse's chances, the consul seemed to feel, were not good. [p. 133].

The same word is used by Shayne at the end of the book in a more philosophical context, when he confronts the dying murderer and smuggler, Martha (Baines) Slater:

> Two interns jumped out of the ambulance with a stretcher. Shayne remained at the girl's side.
>
> "You had your full **quota** of luck with Slater," he said. "He knew you shot him, but he wanted you to take the plane and get away with the diamonds, because he thought it was his fault." [p. 189]

Brett Halliday's position in literature is not exactly on a par with such masters of the detective genre as Dashiell Hammett, Raymond Chandler, James M. Cain or Erle Stanley Gardner, but his mysteries have been popular for an extensive period of time. Even though his Latin references, consisting mainly of legal terms and some general expressions, are relatively scarce and hardly original or insightful, they illustrate how Latin is used in everyday language; hence, his prose does count in the overall picture of the role of the ancient language in modern fiction and, indirectly, in modern intellectual life.

5. Ellery QUEEN (Manfred B. Lee, 1905–1971; Frederic Dannay, 1905–1982)

Originally created as the protagonist of *The Roman Hat Mystery* (1929) for a mystery novel competition, Ellery Queen became the pseudonym of cousins Manfred Bennington Lee (real name: Emanuel Benjamin Lopofsky) and Frederic Dannay (born Daniel Nathan), who, as a team, wrote a substantial number of crime and detective novels (mostly with Queen as the hero) as well as compiled and commentated on the material submitted to *Ellery Queen's Mystery Magazine* (founded in 1941). They also edited a number of anthologies and collections by other writers, including such big names as Dashiell Hammett and John Dickson Carr. The most successful series of books by the team, all featuring Ellery Queen and/or Inspector Richard Queen (the detective's father), include *The Dutch Shoe Mystery* (1931), *The Green Coffin Mystery* (1932), *The Siamese Twin Mystery* (1933), *The Chinese Orange Mystery* (1934), *The Spanish Cape Mystery* (1935), *The Door Between* (1937), *The Devil to Pay* (1938), *The Dragon's Teeth* (1939), *Calamity Town* (1942), *The Murderer Is a Fox* (1945), *The Origin of Evil* (1951), *The Scarlet Letters* (1953) and *The Finishing Stroke* (1958). The Ellery Queen novels, subsequently written by other authors, kept appearing until the early 1970s. The awards won by the original team include the Special Edgar Award for ten years' service through *Ellery Queen's Mystery Magazine* (1950), the Grand Master Edgar Award (1961) and the Special Award on the 40th anniversary of the publication of *The Roman Hat Mystery* (1969)—all from the Mystery Writers of America, the organization that established the Ellery Queen Award in 1983 "to honor writing teams and outstanding people in the mystery-publishing industry." The two cousins, who together held the position of the President of the Mystery Writers of America in 1946, died about a decade apart: Lee on April 3, 1971, in Roxbury, Connecticut; Dannay on September 3, 1982, in New York.

Between the big screen and television, there were a number of actors portraying Ellery Queen. Those that impersonated the protagonist fairly successfully (all in theatrical movies) include Donald Cook—in Lewis D. Collins's *The Spanish Cape Mystery* (1935; co-starring Helen Twelvetrees and Berton Churchill); Eddie Quillan—in Ralph Staub's *The Mandarin Mystery* (1936; featuring Charlotte Henry and Rita La Roy), from *The Chinese Orange Mystery*; Ralph Bellamy—in four films including Kurt Neumann's *Ellery Queen, Master Detective* (1940, from *The Door Between*) and two pictures directed by James P. Hogan, *Ellery Queen and the Perfect Crime* (1941, based on *The Devil* to Pay) and *Ellery Queen and the Murder Ring* (1941, loosely based on *The Dutch Shoe Mystery*)—all three co-starring Margaret Lindsay and Charley Grapewin; William Gargan—in three films including James P. Hogan's *A Close Call for Ellery Queen* (1942; also co-starring Margaret Lindsay and Charley Grapewin), from *The Dragon's Teeth*. The actors that played Queen on television include Richard Hart, Lee Bowman, Hugh Marlowe, George Nader, Peter Lawford, Jim Hutton and others.

Several Latin references have been found in *The Dutch Shoe Mystery* ([1931] 1968), a book in which the famous detective is investigating the murder of Abigail Doorn, a rich patient of the Dutch Memorial Hospital, in a diabetic coma, strangled just before she is supposed to undergo a serious operation. The first Latin phrase (very well-known and common also in English; hence, there is no need to translate it) appears at the very beginning of the book, in fact, in the first line of Chapter One, in a sentence about Ellery Queen's father:

> Inspector Richard Queen's **alter ego** [literally: 'the other I,' better: 'a second self'], which was in startling contrast with his ordinary spry and practical old manner, often prompted him to utter didactic remarks on the general subject of criminology. [p. 17]

The term *alter ego* was originally coined by Cicero (see the entry on Wolfe), who used it to illustrate the existence of 'a second self', a 'trusted friend.' It became widely recognized in the eighteenth century when Franz Anton Mesmer (1734–1815), a German doctor interested in astronomy, developed hypnosis as a means to separate the *alter ego*.

The second phrase, also quite well-known in English, is a part of the answer Dr. John Minchen, a friend of Ellery Queen's, gives to the detective's question regarding the use of anesthesia in surgical operations:

> "Fair question," admitted Minchen. "And it's true that in most cases—virtually all cases—anesthesia is used. But diabetics are funny people. You know—or rather I suppose you don't know—that any surgical operation is dangerous to a chronic diabetic. Even minor surgery may be fatal. Had a case just the other day—patient came into the dispensary with a festered toe—some poor devil. The doctor in charge—well, it's just one of those unforeseeable accidents of dispensary routine. The toe was cleaned, the patient went home. Next morning he was found dead. **Post mortem** examination showed the man to be full of sugar. Probably never knew it himself. [p. 24]

5. Ellery QUEEN

The phrase *post mortem* (literally meaning 'after-death') is normally, just like in the above quotation, used as a modifier; thus, it is appropriate in that case to hyphenate the English translation. Sometimes, however, it stands for a shortened version of the complete phrase 'after-death examination,' and then the hyphen is a matter of choice or opinion. The Latin version of the phrase, by the way, is also used on p. 93, in Ellery Queen's response to Dr. Moritz Kneisel's explanation of his rather indifferent attitude toward death, noticed and inquired about by the detective. Here is the whole paragraph (containing another Latin expression) where the scientist, regarded as a "genius," discloses his rather rare philosophy:

> Kneisel's soft eyes became suffused with a queer surprise. "My dear sir!" he protested. "Death is hardly a cause for emotion in the scientist. I am interested in the fatality, naturally, but not to the point of sentimentality. After all—" He shrugged, and a whimsical smile appeared on his lips. "We're above the bourgeois attitude toward death, aren't we? '***Requiescat in pace***' ["Rest in peace."], and all that sort of thing. I should much rather quote the Spaniard's cynical epigram—'She is good and honored who is dead and buried.'" [p. 93]

The expression *Requiescat in pace* (R.I.P), referring to the wish that the soul of the dead person remains untormented after death, began to appear on tombstones in the eighth century, especially by graves of Roman Catholics.

The next Latin reference takes place toward the end of the book, when Ellery Queen has already a pretty good idea who committed to crime and is sharing his update with those involved in the investigation:

> From the adhesive on the lace I conjured a professionally minded person connected with the Dutch Memorial Hospital; from the tongues I conjured a woman.

> "It was the first indication that the impersonator was not only posing as another individual but also as an individual of the opposite sex. ***Id est*** ['that is'], a woman made up as a man!" [p. 202]

What is interesting about the Latin phrase in the above quotation is that it is very well-known in English, but rather in the abbreviated form, *i.e.*, and in writing rather than in speech. Using it in the original Latin unabbreviated form in a conversation testifies to the authors' competence in the ancient language, or, at least, to their extensive exposure to it.

There are some other Latin references in the book that are worth presenting without their contexts since all or most of them appear in many other entries of this publication. Here is the list, along with the English translations and page numbers:

Rigor mortis (literally 'stiffness of death,' better: 'postmortem rigidity,' p. 20);

Quod erat demonstrandum ('That which was to be shown/demonstrated/proven,' p. 204);

vincit omnia veritas ("Truth conquers everything," p. 198).

An abundance of Latin references have also been encountered in the authors' *Calamity Town* ([1942] 2003), a novel set in Wrightsville, a small New England town where the detective moves incognito for, at first, a short period of time and then decides to stay longer in order to solve the murder mystery. Suspicious circumstances suggesting that Jim Haight is planning to murder his wife, Nora, followed by an unexpected murder of Jim's sister, Rosemary (in reality, his first wife), a guest in the house of Queen's landlords (Nora's parents), make the detective more than indirectly involved in the case. The first reference appears in a narrative part opening Chapter 6 and listing the preparations for Jim and Nora's wedding by Nora's mother, Hermione (Pat is Nora's younger sister, in cahoots with Ellery):

While Nora and Pat were in New York shopping for Nora's trousseau, Hermione held technical discussions with old Mr. Thomas, sexton of the First Methodist Church; horticultural conferences with Andy Birobatyan, the one-eyed Armenian florist in High Village; histrionic conversations with the Reverend Dr. Doolittle *in re* ['with regard to'] rehearsals and choirboy arrangements; talks with Mrs. Jones the caretaker, with Mr. Graycee of the travel agency, and with John F. at the bank on intrafamiliar banking business. [p. 45]

A famous Latin sentence is quoted by Pat when caught by Ellery snooping in Nora's room and, subsequently, admitting her knowledge of his real identity:

Ellery's jaw waggled. "You little demon," he said admiringly. "You've known me all along."

"Of course," retorted Pat. "I heard you lecture once on *The Place of the Detective Story in Contemporary Civilization*. Very pompous it was, too."

"Wellesley?"

"Sarah Lawrence. I thought at the time you were very handsome. *Sic transit gloria.* Don't look so concerned. I shan't give your precious incognito away." [p. 60]

The Latin expression quoted above is a shortened version of the sentence *Sic transit Gloria mundi* ("Thus passes the Glory of the world.") used at the papal coronation ceremonies between the fifteenth and nineteenth centuries.

One more Latin quotation appears at the end of the book, in the penultimate chapter. Queen returns to Wrightsville and meets with Pat and Carter Bradford (County Prosecutor and Pat's ex-fiancé still in love with her) to expose the murderer. Their conversation, taking place in *Roadside Tavern*, is being eavesdropped on by the local drunkard, Andy Anderson, whose non-sequitur recitation of poetry is unexpectedly followed by the following monologue:

"*O vita, misero longa! Felici brevis!* ["O life, long for/to the wretched man, brief for/to the happy man."]" croaked Mr. Anderson. "Friends, heed the wisdom of the ancients ... I suppose you are wondering how I, poor wretch, am well-provided with lucre this heaven-sent day. Well, I am a remittance man, as they say, and my ship touched port today. *Felici brevis!* ['Brief for the happy man.']" And he started to fumble for Patty's glass. [p. 344]

The Latin quotation, a wise saying from the proverb collection by Latin writer Publilius Syrus (a Syrian brought to Rome as a slave in the first century B.C.), is grammatically interesting because it demonstrates different endings of different-declension adjectives within the same case. Thus, *longa* is a first-declension adjective (to be exact, the feminine version of the first/second adjective *longus longa longum* – 'long'), and *brevis* is a two-termination third-declension adjective (from *brevis brevis breve* – 'short/brief'), also feminine and also in the nominative singular case as both of them have to match the number, gender and case of the subject *vita* – 'life.' The other pair of adjectives, *misero* ('poor/wretched/miserable') and *felici* ('happy') are both in the dative case, the different endings resulting, again, from different declensions they belong to, the former being an example of the first/second declension (*miser misera miserum*), the latter of the third declension (one termination *felix felix felix*, or, as it is usually listed in a dictionary, *felix felicis* – 'fruitful/lucky/happy' – with just one, common for all genders, form followed by the genitive-case form/ending); both serving and matching (in number, gender and case) the implied masculine, singular indirect object, such as 'one/man/person/human being.'

Again, the presented excerpts illustrate only some of the numerous references found in the book. Thus, here is the list of the remaining ones:

Doryphora decemlineata (name of a beetle that is a serious pest of potatoes, p. 156);

Summa cum laude ('with highest praise,' p. 195);

Ave, Caesar! ("Hail, Caesar!" p. 207);

Homo ('human being,' p. 338).

A reverse case of a Latin reference, an English translation of a well-known Latin proverb, is rather rare in literature; therefore, it is worth mentioning here even more. It comes from the mouth of Lola, Nora's older sister, as an epithet about newspaperwoman Roberta Roberts:

"Apparently it's enough for Roberta Roberts, too," mumbled Ellery.

"Miss **Love-Conquers-All**?" Lola shrugged. "If you ask me, that dame's on Jim's side so she can get in where the other reporters can't." [p. 169]

The famous aphorism, very well known in its Latin version, *Omnia vincit amor*, originates from Book X of *Ecloquoes* by Vergil (see the entry on Lewis). Interestingly, it is used here as an epithet.

Just a few Latin references have been found in *The Origin of Evil* ([1951] 1972), Queen's novel about a series of unusual anonymous gifts (including a dead dog in a casket and poisoned tuna- fish salad) received by wholesale jewelers Leander Hill and Roger Priam and the latter partner's heart attack leading to his death. The only reference that is worth quoting within its context is the one that appears in a conversation between Queen and Laurel Hill, the woman who asks him to investigate the mystery, regarding a missing pillbox and alluding to Queen's unpleasant experience:

"Could it have been your pillbox?"

"I suppose it could, but—"

"And you never found the one you lost?"

She looked at him worried. "Do you suppose it was?"

"I'm not supposing much of anything yet, Laurel. Just trying to get things orderly. Or just trying to get things." Ellery opened the door and looked out cautiously. "Be sure to tell your muscular admirer that I'm returning you to him *virgo intacto*. I'm sort of sentimental about my clavicles." He smiled and squeezed her fingers. [pp. 82-83]

The Latin phrase quoted by Queen has a grammatical or spelling error, as the ending of the past perfect participle, *intacto* (from the third-conjugation verb *tango tangĕre tetigi tactum*, preceded by the negative prefix *–in*), cannot be '-o' in any case. While *virgo* (a third-declension feminine noun *virgo virginis*) is used in the nominative singular form, the modifier, in order to match it in number, gender and case, needs to be *intacta*. Thus, the whole phrase, after the correction, means literally 'untouched maiden/virgin,' or simply 'a woman who has never had sexual intercourse.'

The other two Latin references discovered in the novel are scientific names; here they are:

Quercus agrifolia ('California live oak,' p. 47);

Hyla regilla ('Pacific tree toad,' p. 93).

The novel *The Fourth Side of the Triangle* (1965), though credited to Ellery Queen, was ghost-written by Avram Davidson (1923-1993). However, just like the original books by the famous team, it does have a few Latin references. Two of them deserve to be presented along with their contexts. The first one is a part of a narrative passage where writer Dane McKell's dilemmas regarding his relationship with Sheila Grey (soon to be murdered) are unveiled to the reader:

Whether he adored her because of what she was or in spite of it did not matter. Her reason for being was threatened, and who else was there to remove the threat?

Now a rather leering interloper crept into his thoughts.

What to do next ... break up the affair, certainly, but how? He asked the question, not rhetorically—he had no doubt that it could be done—but in order to organize his *modus operandi* ['a particular way/method of doing something'] ... That was when the intruder crept in. [p. 27]

The second Latin phrase appears in passage narrating a court scene, at a point when Dane's father, Ashton (also romantically acquainted with, by now, the murder victim), takes the witness stand (O'Brien is the defense attorney):

When Ashton resumed the witness box, being admonished that he was still under oath, O'Brien said, "Mr. McKell, I am going to ask you a painful question. What was your underlying reason for disguising yourself each Wednesday as a nonexistent Dr. Stone—even going so far as to conceal the disguise from your own chauffeur?"

"I didn't want my family or anyone to know about my visits to Miss Grey." The courtroom rustled. "In this," added the elder McKell bitterly, "I seem to have failed with a bang."

It was an unfortunate metaphor. Someone in the courtroom tittered, and at least one newspaper reporter dodged out to pone his paper the "expert psychiatric opinion" that the **lapsus linguae** ['a slip of the tongue'] might well have been a Freudian slip by which the accused confessed his guilt. [p. 93]

The other two Latin references encountered in the book are by far less impressive; they are single Latin words, a preposition (governing the accusative case) and a masculine noun (of the second declension, in the nominative singular form):

cum ('with,' p. 119);

modus ('measure/rule/way/mode/manner,' p. 152).

The mysteries by Ellery Queen, just like those by S. S. Van Dine and John Dickson Carr (all inspired by Sir Conan Doyle and Agatha Christie), are prime examples of what is considered to be the Golden Age of detective fiction, where more important than action are the carefully plotted clues and solutions. The protagonist is a somewhat snobbish, but definitely well-educated individual (Harvard)—such a profile additionally illustrated by the multitude of those Latin references that are interjected by Queen himself—and detection is more of a hobby for him than a profession. He solves the complicated cases either by himself or with the help of his policeman father, revealing, in the process, such traits as patience, careful analysis of all available clues and thorough deduction based on a variety of observations, including the psychological profiles of all the suspects. The multiple Latin references that embellish the authors' novels—ranging from legal terms to everyday expressions to ancient proverbs—provide an apt illustration and strong evidence of the vitality and perpetual assets of the ancient language.

Lee's alma mater was New York University, from which he graduated cum laude in 1925 with a degree in English. Its Latin motto, carried by its impressive seal, is *Perstare et Praestare* ("To persevere and to excel."), consisting of two present active infinitives from the first conjugation verb *sto stare* ('to stand'), each modifying its meaning by use of a different prefix. The impressive and long list of other famous alumni of NYU includes Andrew D. Hamilton, Rudy Giuliani, Martin Scorsese, Woody Allan, Meg Ryan, Billy Crystal and Anne Hathaway.

6. John Dickson CARR (1906–1977)

Born on November 30, 1906, in Uniontown, Pennsylvania, John Dickson Carr, a son of a congressman, graduated from Haverford College in 1929 and, between the early 1930s and 1948, lived in England. A prolific writer since 1930, Carr wrote novels, plays, short stories and nonfiction (including a biography of Sir Arthur Conan Doyle, 1950). His novels, rightly regarded as the "Golden Age" mysteries, are divided, depending—in most cases—on the protagonist's name, into the following series: "Henri Bencolin"—e.g., *It Walks by Night* (193) and *Castle Skull* (1931); "Dr. Gideon Fell" (English)—*The Blind Barber* (1934), *The Hollow Man* (1935, US title: *The Three Coffins*), *To Wake the Dead* (1938), *The Crooked Hinge* (1938), *The Case of the Constant Suicides* (1941), *Below Suspicion* (1949) and *Dark of the Moon* (1967); "Sir Henry Merivale" (English)—*The Plague Court Murders* (1934), *And So to Murder* (1940), *The Skeleton in the Clock* (1948) and *The Cavalier's Cup* (1953); in addition to his "Colonel March" short stories and about a dozen historical mysteries, including *Captain Cut-Throat* (1955), *The Ghost's High Noon* (1970) and *Deadly Hall* (1971). A winner of two Special Edgar Awards from the Mystery Writers of America, as well as their Grand Master Award (1963), Carr, a member of the exclusive British Detection Club, died on February 28, 1977, in Greenville, South Carolina.

While Carr's stories were the basis for many TV series, the few major feature films inspired by his works include Francis Searle's *The Man in Black* (1934; featuring Betty Ann Davies, Sheila Burrell and Sidney James)—from Carr's radio series *Appointment with Fear*; Fletcher Markle's *The Man with a Cloak* (1951; starring Joseph Cotten, Barbara Stanwyck and Louis Calhern)—from his story; and Julien Duvivier's *The Burning Court* (1962; featuring Nadja Tiller, Jean-Claude Brialy and Perrette Pradier)—from his novel of the same name.

Latin references have been found in four of Carr's mysteries, all featuring Dr. Fell. *The Blind Barber* ([1934] 1988), set mostly on board the ocean liner *Queen Victoria* on her way from New York City to Southampton, is a story about the theft of some reels of film, significant because of a serious diplomatic scandal being one of its possible ramifications. The characters include mystery writer Henry Morgan, who relates the story to Dr. Fell (after disembarking), his friends Peggy Glenn and Captain Thomasse Valvick, Curtis Warren, who made the film of his Uncle Warpus's political speech, Captain Whistler (in charge of the ship), Dr. Kyle (the ship doctor) and the titular "blind barber," who is supposedly a criminal and, thus, the most obvious suspect.

The first Latin word appears in a paragraph in which Warren, worried about the remaining reels of film being unguarded, runs to his cabin despite the captain's attempts to stop him:

> Captain Whistler, ***imprimis*** ['in the first place'], objected to being addressed as "barnacle," and described horrible surgical tortures he would like to perform. [p. 44]

The other Latin references are related to the fact that Warren, considered insane by the captain, is held captive in a padded cell on Deck D, and his fellow passengers, sorry for him, decide to smuggle some gifts to console him. The first quotation addresses the philosophical irony of his predicament, the second one gives details about the second gift.

> ***Sic volvere parcae!*** ["Thus span the Parcas!"] To solace him in captivity they could not share, Peggy Glenn presented him with a bottle of whisky (full size) and Henry Morgan with one of his old detective-novels. [p. 102]

> As a gentleman burglar, Lord Gerald was hot stuff. His thrilling escapes from captivity under heavy guard made Mr. Harry Houdini look like a bungler who had got out of clink only with a writ of ***habeas corpus*** [literally 'that you have the body,' a recourse allowing to report an unlawful detention]. [p. 104]

While the second Latin expression is very well known among lawyers and law enforcers, much more interesting, from both cultural and grammatical standpoint, is the first reference, a sentence extracted from Vergil's *Aeneid*, Book I, line 22, which can be better translated as "So the fates decree." For the 'Parcas' (the word usually capitalized) are personifications of 'Fates'—three sisters, Clotho (Spinner), Lachesis (Measurer) and Atropos (Inevitable) who, through dividing among themselves the acts of spinning the thread of life, measuring the thread and cutting it at a strictly defined moment, together decide about one's fate. The quoted line appears almost at the beginning of the epic, when the author/narrator, after his impressive invocation, gives the reader a general introduction to the story itself. The middle part of the sentence, *volvere*, is supposed to be the Perfect Active Tense, third person plural form of the third-conjugation verb *volvo volvĕre volvi volutum* ('to roll/spin/undergo'); it is used here instead of *volverunt* (the correct form in this context), and is thus an example (quite common in Vergil's verse) of a poetic device known as 'syncope.'

A rather fascinating Latin reference was also found in *To Wake the Dead* ([1938] 1988). The main characters of the novel, in addition to Dr. Gideon Fell, are wealthy young man Christopher Kent, his close friend Dan Reaper and Superintendent Hadley who, along with Fell, investigates the murder of a couple of victims related to Christopher, Josephine (whose body is discovered by Christopher) and her husband, Rodney Kent, murdered two weeks earlier.

The same exactly Latin sentence is quoted twice, both times in relation to an object found at the murder scene, a room at the Royal Scarlet Hotel in Piccadilly, London. The person that shows the detectives the bracelet and makes the discovery possible is the hotel manager, Mr. Kenneth Hardwick.

> Square, black, polished and dully gleaming, it had engraved on in two lines in Roman script just large enough to read. **Claudite jam rivos, pueri**, said the inscription, **sat prata biberunt** ["Now stop the currents, young men, the meadows have drunk enough."]. Behind Hadley's shoulder Dr. Fell was making vast and seething noises of excitement. [p. 208]

> "You can see for yourself that there's not a scrap of writing, or place for writing, or any secret hanky-panky, except that **Latin** inscription. Do you mean there's a secret hidden in that, like an acrostic or some such thing? **Claudite jam rivos, pueri, sat prata biberunt**. This is more in your line, Fell." [p. 253]

The quoted line comes from Vergil's *Eclogues*, Book III, line 111 (more on Vergil in the entry on Lewis), and is a good example of metaphor or allegory (extended metaphor) since the implied meaning of the sentence is something like "Stop the music, young men, we have enjoyed it sufficiently." Grammatically, three words are of interest: *Claudite* is the Present Active Imperative plural form of the third-conjugation verb *claudo claudĕre* ('to shut/close'); *pueri* is the vocative plural (same as nominative plural or, for that matter, genitive singular) form of the second-declension masculine noun *puer pueri* ('boy'); and *biberunt* is the Perfect Active Indicative, third person plural form of the third-conjugation verb *bibo bibĕre*.

Carr's novel *The Crooked Hinge* ([1938] 1988) is considered (according to mystery writer Edward D. Hoch) to be "one of the most impossible" crime mysteries of all time, and it does include some supernatural elements. Set in a village near Kent, it is focused on solving an inquest which of the two men that claim to be Sir John Farnleigh is the real one. The first paragraph including a Latin phrase is a part of a scene in which the first Farnleigh, while discussing the case with two men on his side, Nathaniel Burrows and Brian

Page, addresses the credibility of Kennet Murray, young Johnny's tutor, who at that point remains neutral:

> "I think we have discussed that before. It was the first thing that occurred to me, of course; and, considering the steps we have taken, you yourself have been satisfied of Mr. Murray's **bona fides** [being 'genuine/real']. Have you not?" [p. 361]

The second Latin reference appears much later in the book, when Dr. Fell and Scotland Yard Inspector Elliot investigate the mysterious murder of the first Farnleigh. The Latin sentence (whose translation is provided by the author himself) is closely related to a book that ties Farnleigh's murder with that of Victoria Day, a spinster who was strangled in her cottage the previous summer. Present at the scene is also Kennet Murray, now testifying in favor of the second claimant, who temporarily uses the name 'Patrick Gore.' Gore is the one that answers Fell's questions.

> "Yes. That book-plate has not been used in the family since the eighteenth century."
>
> Dr. Fell's finger traced out the motto. "'**Sanguis eius super nos et super filios nostros**,' Thos. Farnleigh, 1675. 'His blood be upon us and upon our children.'" [p. 431]

Unlike in the previous three novels, where the Latin references are more or less tied with the stories, in *The Case of the Constant Suicides* ([1941] 1988), the quotation appears at the very last line of the book when Dr. Fell has already solved all the murder cases, and a minor punchline is offered by the author. Here is the final paragraph of the mystery:

> Laden with the luggage, the porter trudged dispiritedly along the platform after them. **Floreat scientia!** ["Let knowledge flourish!"]. The wheel had swung round again. [p. 660]

The closing quotation happens to be a part of the crest of the Massey University of New Zealand. While *scientia* is obviously the (first-declension feminine) Latin noun (in the nominative case) which the English word 'science' is derived from, the second word, *floreat*, is the Present Active Subjunctive form (used as 'jussive') of the second-conjugation verb *floreo florēre* ('to bloom/flower/flourish').

In addition to winning some of their prestigious awards, John Dickson Carr was, in 1949, the President of the Mystery Writers of America. While his foremost creation, Dr. Gideon Fell, is regarded by British novelist Kinsley Amis as one of the three greatest successors to Sherlock Holmes (G. K. Chesterton's Father Brown and Rex Stout's Nero Wolfe being the other two), the author's other series are equally captivating, and his work as a whole certainly belongs to the detective fiction highlights of the first half of the twentieth century. Furthermore, his fresh and imaginative Latin references, only occasionally justified by the legal application, constitute an additional asset to the readers, especially the ones alluding to the classics. The Latin motto of his alma mater, Haverford College, is *Non doctior, sed meliore doctrina imbutus* ("Not more learned, but steeped in a higher learning"). It is grammatically interesting because of three of its words: *doctior* is the comparative form of the perfect passive participle *doctus docta doctum* ('learned/skilled'); *imbutus* is the perfect passive participle (in the masculine gender, thus justifying the choice of the pronoun 'he' in the first clause) of the third-conjugation verb *imbuo imběre imbui imbutum* ('to steep/saturate'), meaning 'steeped/ saturated'; and *meliore* is the comparative form of the adjective *bonus bona bonum*, matching, in gender (feminine) and case (ablative), the noun *doctrina* ('teaching/instruction'), thus together meaning 'better/higher learning.' The ablative case, furthermore, is the case with the largest number of possible applications, including, as in this particular example, 'location' or 'the place where,' which explains why it is possible and correct to use the preposition 'in' in the English translation, sometimes missing or implied in Latin in such circumstances.

7. Ross MACDONALD (1915–1983)

Ross Macdonald (real name: Kenneth Millar) was born on December 13, 1915, in Los Gatos, California, to Canadian parents who moved back to Canada when he was a child. After his parents' separation, he was raised by his mother in Vancouver, British Columbia. He graduated from Kitchener Collegiate Institute in Ontario, the University of Western Ontario and the University of Michigan (with a Phi Beta Kappa key and a Ph.D. in English literature). He and his wife, college friend Margaret Sturm (better known as mystery writer Margaret Millar), moved to the United States in 1938 and settled in Santa Barbara, California, during World War II, when Kenneth served in the Navy. He started his writing career (as Kenneth Millar) with a Chet Gordon novel, *The Dark Tunnel* (1944), which was followed by another novel featuring the same character, *Trouble Follows Me* (1946). His other novels published under his real name include *Blue City* (1947) and *The Three Roads* (1948). He is best known for his eighteen Lew Archer mysteries (all written as Ross Macdonald)—including *The Moving Target* (1949), *The Drowning Pool* (1950), *The Ivory Grin* (1952), *Find a Victim* (1954), *The Barbarous Coast* (1956), *The Galton Case* (1959), *The Zebra-Striped Hearse* (1962), *The Chill* (1964), *The Far Side of the Dollar* (1965, Crime Writers' Association's Gold Dagger Award), *Black Money* (1966) and *The Underground Man* (1971)—and many short stories featuring the same private investigator. Both Millars served as Presidents of the Mystery Writers of America: Margaret in 1957, Kenneth in 1965. A winner of the Grand Master Award by the Mystery Writers of America, Macdonald died on July 11, 1983, in Santa Barbara.

The first two of the Lew Archer mysteries were turned into successful movies, both starring Paul Newman: *The Moving Target* as *Harper* (1966; co-starring Lauren Bacall, Julie Harris, Arthur Hill, Janet Leigh and Robert Wagner), directed by Jack Smight; and *The Drowning Pool* under the same title (1975; co-starring Joanne Woodward, Anthony Franciosa, Murray Hamilton and Gail Strickland), directed by Stuart Rosenberg; the name of the protagonist in both is changed to Lew Harper (which explains the title of the first film). The other notable screen adaptations of Macdonald's works include Paul Wendkos's *The Underground Man* (1974; featuring Peter Graves, Sharon Farrell, Celeste Holm, Jim Hutton and Vera Miles) and Michael Miller's *Criminal Behavior* (1992; starring Farrah Fawcett, A Martinez and Dakin Matthews), based on *The Ferguson Affair* (1960)—both TV productions.

Four Latin references have been found in *The Three Roads* ([1948] 1991), Macdonald's early novel set in California, mostly in Hollywood. While on the surface it is a love story—the protagonists being successful screenwriter Paula West and amnesiac war veteran Lt. Bret Taylor—in reality, it is a mystery regarding Taylor's murdered wife.

The first two Latin references appear at the beginning of the story, when Paula talks with Commander Wright, the doctor running the hospital where Taylor is a patient. In the first excerpt, Wright explains Taylor's mental state to Paula (who hopes to win Bret back after his wife's death); in the second one, he talks about Taylor's deceased wife, Lorraine:

> "I have no deep respect for words. They're my business after all. But 'insanity' sounds so hopeless."
>
> It isn't necessarily hopeless. But I didn't mean to imply that Taylor is insane. Insanity is a legal concept, and from the legal point of view he's **compos mentis** ['sane,' or 'having full control of one's mind']. He goes through intelligence tests in a breeze. His orientation is still uncertain, but he could probably leave here tomorrow and get along for the rest of his life as well as most." [p. 10]

> "She was pretty enough—I've got to acknowledge that—but she used too much make-up, she didn't know how to dress, she didn't know how to wear her hair. Those are trivial things, but they can mean a good deal to a jilted woman. She wasn't even a good housekeeper. There were used glasses and full ashtrays on the tables and chairs. I shouldn't be catty like this, should I? **Nil nisi bonum**. [p. 15]

The second Latin expression is a shortened version of the proverb of *De mortuis nihil nisi bonum*, meaning 'About the dead, nothing but good things.' (This Latin proverb, spelled out exactly the same way as in the quoted excerpt, also appears, on page 215, in Macdonald's novel *The Zebra-Striped Hearse* ([1962] 1993). It needs to be acknowledged that this famous aphorism was translated to Latin from Greek.

In the next quoted excerpt, containing a very well-known Latin phrase, the narrator reveals Bret's thoughts about his past:

> The landmarks of his external life—his boxing championship in college, his graduation **summa cum laude** ['with highest praise'], his Washington appointment, the publication of his book on the Age of Reason—these things lost all their significance when he looked at them from below, from the vantage point of darkness. [p. 45]

7. Ross MACDONALD (1915–1983)

The last Latin phrase appears in a scene where Bret, trying to solve the mystery of his wife's murder, follows Paula to a motel and is stopped by the man running it:

> "I can't stand here," Bret said. "She may come out any minute."
>
> "So what! I thought you wanted to see her."
>
> "Not her. The man."
>
> "Come in here." He led Bret through a door marked "Office" and closed the Venetian blind over the front window. "What's the deal, Lieutenant? You trying to catch them ***in flagrante delicto*** ['in the act of wrongdoing'], like they say?"
>
> "No, nothing like that. Who's registered in 106?"
>
> "That's the kind of information I only give to the cops—" [p. 182]

Macdonald's mystery *The Galton Case* ([1959] 1970) has two Latin references. The protagonist of the novel is private detective Lew Archer, who is hired by his acquaintance lawyer Sable to find Anthony Galton, the only son of rich Maria Galton, who, after twenty years, has not given up hope to see her son despite the criminal circumstances of his disappearance.

The first Latin phrase is a part of a scene following a seemingly unrelated crime, the murder of Peter Culligan, a young man working for and living with the Sables:

> Sable must have read the look in my face. "This is an unsettling thing to me, too. It can't conceivably relate to Alice and me. And yet it does, very deeply. Peter was a member of the household. I believe he was quite devoted to us, and he died in our front yard. That really brings it home."
>
> "What?"
>
> "***Timor mortis***," he said. "The fear of death." [p. 37]

While the Latin phrase is used here literally, it should be noted that it originated in a responsory of the Catholic Office of the Dead, in the third Nocturn of a canonical hour of Christian liturgy (Matins or Mattins) or the vigil.

While checking the story of a John Brown, a boy who claims to be Anthony Galton's son, Archer goes to the sheriff's substation where a note from Deputy Mungan, with the second Latin reference, is handed to him by another deputy:

> He took a long envelope out of a drawer and handed it across the counter. It contained a hurried note written on yellow scratch-pad paper:

> *R.C phoned me some dope on Fred Nelson. Record goes back to S.F. docks in twenties. Assault with intent, nolle-prossed. Lempi gang enforcer 1928 on. Arrested suspicion murder 1930, **habeas-corpused**. Convicted grand theft 1932. Sentenced "Q." Attempted escape 1933, extended sentence. Escaped December 1936, never apprehended.*

> Mungan. [p. 105]

The bold-printed phrase, based on the Latin expression *habeas corpus* (literally meaning 'that you have the body,' a recourse allowing to report an unlawful detention) is used here (something rather unusual) with an English '-ed' ending to turn the form into a past participle, which implies that the suspect had to be released due to the lack of evidence of his crime.

Another novel by Macdonald, *Black Money* ([1966] 1970), featuring Lew Archer once again, offers a couple of Latin references as well. The detective is hired to collect information about Francis Martel, a presumed French political refugee, the man his client's fiancée, Ginny, decided to marry instead. The first Latin reference is a part of an excerpt which depicts the conversation between Archer and Martel:

> "But you're not the only person involved, now that you've married a local girl.

> He saw my point. "Very well. I will tell you why I am here, in return for a **quid pro quo** ['one thing for another']. Tell me who is the man who tried to take my picture."

> "His name is Harry Hendricks. He's a used-car salesman from the San Fernando Valley."

> Martel's eyes were puzzled. "I never heard of him. Why did he try to photograph me?"

> "Apparently someone paid him. He didn't say who." [p. 464]

The other reference found in the novel is tied to the manuscript of a book by Ginny's secret lover Tappinger ("Taps"), which Archer finds in Martel's study, where the detective is brought by Ginny's mother, Mrs. Fablon, who is concerned about Martel's threat to kill Ginny, Taps and himself:

> The most recent version, which Tappinger had been working on when I first came here Monday, was lying on top of the desk.
>
> "Stephen Crane," it began, "lived like a god in the adamantine city of his mind. Where did he find the prototype of that city? In Athens the marmoreal exemplar of the West, or in the supernal blueprint which Augustine bequeathed to us in the **Civitas Dei**? Or was it in Paris the City of Arts? [p. 620]

The book mentioned in the excerpt, usually translated as *The City of God*, was written by Augustine of Hippo. Originally published in 426 A.D. under the title *De civitate Dei contra paganos* (*About the City of God against the Pagans*), it is considered to be one of the author's most significant works, all dealing with Christian philosophy and theology.

Writing in the tradition of detective fiction by Dashiell Hammett and Raymond Chandler (the resemblance going far beyond the Californian setting), Ross Macdonald is unquestionably one of the top mystery writers of the mid-twentieth century. The Latin references encountered in his prose, a combination of general, legal and religious expressions, constitute one more example of how the ancient language invades, in the positive sense of the word, modern fiction and, indirectly, modern discourse not only among academic people.

The mottos of the educational institutions attended by Kenneth Millar are *Veritas Vincat* ("May truth prevail")—Kitchener Collegiate Institute in Ontario, *Veritas et Utilitas* ("Truth and Usefulness")—the University of Western Ontario, and *Artes, Scientia, Veritas* ("Arts, Knowledge, Truth)— the University of Michigan. While, interestingly, all the three mottos have one word in common, 'truth' (one of many assets of the author's novels), the first one incorporates a verb in the Present Active Subjunctive, third person singular form, *vincat*, and the last one constitutes an example of a poetic device known as 'asyndeton' (multiple commas and no conjunction).

8. William X. KIENZLE (1928–2001)

Born on September 11, 1928, in Detroit, Michigan, and educated at Sacred Heart Major Seminary in Detroit, William Xavier Kienzle was a priest for many years before he became an enormously successful mystery writer. He is the author of twenty-four novels, all featuring Father Robert Koesler, including, *The Rosary Murders* (1978), *Death Wears a Red Hat* (1980), *Mind Over Murder* (1981), *Shadow of Death* (1983), *Sudden Death* (1985), *Marked for Murder* (1988), *Body Count* (1992), *No Greater Love* (1999) and *The Gathering* (2002). A winner of the National Book Award for Mystery, he died on December 28, 2001, in West Bloomfield, Michigan.

Unfortunately, there is only one movie based on Kienzle's amazing works; it is the screen version of his very first novel, *The Rosary Murders*. It was directed by Fred Walton, who wrote the screenplay with Elmore Leonard, another great mystery writer. The cast of the film includes Donald Sutherland (as Koesler), Charles Durning, Belinda Bauer, Josef Sommer and James Murtaugh.

The targets in *The Rosary Murders* ([1978] 1989), a novel set (like all of the author's books) in Detroit, are priests and nuns, and the serial killer operates during Lent. The first murder takes place on Ash Wednesday, and, by the time there are eight victims (four priests and four nuns), the police anticipate the ninth and tenth strikes (the overall number corresponding to the number of the commandments) to occur on Good Friday. Both the pattern of the murders and the probable names of the last two victims are figured out by Father Robert Koesler, who cooperates with Lt. Koznicki, the policeman in charge of the case. Koesler is also the only person to find out—through the murderer's confession— the motivation behind the crimes; however, because of the seal of the confessional, he would not be able to share the information with anyone.

Out of the numerous Latin references encountered in the book, the first one worth quoting in its context appears early in the story, when Koesler is invited to dinner by Pompilio, another priest:

> "***Disputatur apud peritos.***" Pompilio didn't know much **Latin**, but when tripped over an appropriate phrase like "The experts are in dispute," he liked to throw it in for everyone's amazement. [p. 3]

The literal translation of the Latin quotation is 'It is being disputed/discussed among the experts,' which implies that the first-conjugation verb *disputo disputare* ('to debate/discuss' or 'to argue/dispute') is used in the Present

Passive Indicative Tense. The passive ending '-tur' implies a third person singular subject; the choice of 'it' in the English translation is justified by the fact that the predicate is meant to be impersonal.

A nice reference, combining, or rather separating, two elements of the same proverb to accomplish a humorous effect, is made by the narrator in a paragraph concerning Father Fred Palmer (strongly inclined to overeat and avoid exercising), who ends up dying with a black rosary tied around his left-hand fingers (just like in all the cases of the murder victims), but his death happens to be of natural causes. The scene takes place at the health club, where the priest's program is supposed to include weights, board, pool, sauna and whirlpool.

> Palmer affectionately waved at the young man and worked himself and his gear through the door. I wonder, the priest thought, if it's possible to have a **mens sana** ['sane mind'] without the **corpore sano** ['healthy body']. It seemed workable to him. [p. 92]

When faced with the dilemma whether he can break the seal of the confessional in order to help the police catch the murderer, Koesler looks up historical documents:

> He found it. Noldin's **Summa Theologiae Moralis, De Sacramentis** [*Summary of Moral Theology*, Volume III: *On Sacraments*]. He leafed through until he found "**De poenitentia**"—on penance—and located "**de obligatione sigilli**—on the obligation of the seal. [p. 176]

One more humorous Latin reference was found toward the end of the book, in a scene where priests Farmer, Pompilio and Koesler discuss the motive of the crimes:

> "Did you notice that the police were unable to come up with a motive for the killing?" Pompilio asked.
>
> "Yeah," Farmer commented, "that's almost as bad as one of your whodunits without an ending."
>
> "Or," said Koesler, "***amplexus reservatus.***"
>
> Both Farmer and Pompilio looked up from their papers inquiringly.
>
> "Withdrawal from sexual intercourse without ejaculation," explained Koesler.

Farmer and Pompilio returned to their newspapers, each distracted by the new thought. [p. 292]

The remaining Latin words or phrases found in the book, in addition to one referring to the language itself (p. 165), are listed below, without their contexts, along with their English translations and page numbers:

sine qua non ('a thing/person absolutely necessary,' used in the dedication);

consensus ('consensus,' 'general agreement,' p. 4);

ad hoc (literally 'for this,' or, 'when necessary or needed,' p. 40);

pro tem (a shortened form of *pro tempore* – 'for the time being,' p. 112);

"tutior pars" ('the safer path,' p. 177);

M.O. (an abbreviation of *modus operandi* – 'a particular way/method of doing something,' pp. 233, 253, 260);

deus ex machina ('a god from a machine,' i.e., 'an unexpected/miraculous power,' p. 242);

pro forma ('as a matter of form or politeness,' p. 245);

Bona ('goods,' p. 246).

While Kienzle's first novel, *The Rosary Murders*, is a meticulously conceived and executed murder mystery, the author's twenty-first book, *No Greater Love* ([1999] 2000), is a powerful morality tale told in flashbacks with murder constituting its multidimensional climax. Father Robert Koesler is still one of the main characters, an observer and a catalyst of the main theme, Deacon Al Cody's dilemma resulting from his father's pressure to stick to his vocation against all odds.

The book abounds in Latin references; however, most of them are words or phrases interjected here and there. Among the exceptions are three which, even though not directly related to the main plot, deserve to be presented in their rather unusual contexts. The first two are parts of a long scene depicting the dream of Patty Donnelly, who (in that dream) first is ordained a priest and then elected the first female Pope, and her first decision as a Pontiff is moving the seat of all Catholicism from the Vatican to Maui, Hawaii.

> All the while, white smoke billowed from the special vent on the roof of the chapel. Hundreds of thousands of people crowded into St. Peter's Square.
>
> The new Pope—Popess?—stayed just out of view behind one corner of the balcony.
>
> A Cardinal came out on the balcony and read from an impressive scroll: '***Annuntio vobis gaudiam magnum. Habemus Papam!*** ["I announce you a great joy. We have a Pope!"]
>
> The crowd went wild. Then it quieted to hear the most important part of that "great joy"—the name of the new Pope.
>
> "**Patriciam** …" The crowd became hushed. Was that Cardinal looped? He couldn't be serious. It sounded for all the world as if he'd said **Patriciam**. Feminine for Patrick! Patricia? Impossible. [p. 162]
>
> She realized this would be a jolt to the lifestyle of Italy, and particularly to Rome. But the people must remember—and here she was grateful that she had paid attention in Ecclesiology class—that, ***Ubi Petrus, ibi Ecclesia*** (Where Peter—in this case, Petra—is, there is the Church). [p. 165]

The third of those references is a part of the passage where the narrator reveals Andrea Zawalich's thoughts and concerns regarding her close friend Patty Donnelly's obsession:

> Andrea Zawalich propped the book against a statue of the Blessed Mother on her desk. At the base of the statue were the words ***Sedes Sapientiae***—Seat of Wisdom.
>
> She had been trying to study, but she was preoccupied.
>
> She kept thinking of her friend, perhaps her best friend, Patty Donnelly. As far as Andrea could see, Patty was on a treadmill to oblivion. [p. 169]

Below is the list of the remaining Latin references discovered in *No Greater Love*. It does not include the cases where the Latin language itself is mentioned—on pp. 17, 73, 131, 163—either by the writer/narrator or one of the characters.

sacerdos ('priest,' p. 45);

vera doctrina ('the True Doctrine,' p. 67, 73);

magisterium (here: 'the Pope,' p. 74);

a fortiori ('not entirely refuted,' p. 79);

status quo ('the existing state of affairs,' p. 94);

Nolo ('I do not wish/I refuse,' p. 162);

volo ('I wish/I want,' p. 162);

Sanctae Romanae Ecclesiae ('of Holy Roman Church,' p. 162);

Cardinalem ('cardinal,' in the accusative singular case, p. 162);

Episcopum ('bishop,' in the accusative singular case, p. 162);

lapsus linguae ('slip of a tongue,' 238);

causa finita ('the discussion is over,' p. 240).

From a grammatical standpoint, two items on the list are of interest. Both *volo* and *nolo* are examples of the first principal part, the former of the irregular verb *volo velle volui* ('to wish/want' or 'to be willing') and the latter, being the former's negative counterpart, of the irregular verb *nolo nolle nolui* ('to be unwilling/wish not to/refuse'). Furthermore, the first of the two verbs should not be confused with the first-conjugation verb *volo volare volavi volatum* ('to fly'), which is easy to do as their first principal parts are identical, both having present stems with a short vowel –'*vŏl-*.'

William X. Kienzle is unquestionably a unique name among mystery writers or writers in general. Not only did he leave priesthood (the reason for which he reveals briefly in an interview printed at the end of the paperback edition of *No Greater Love*), but, in the second stage of his life, he got married, and his wife, Javan Herman Andrews Kienzle (to whom *No Greater Love* is dedicated), is the one that ended up publishing, after his death, his biography, *Judged by Love*. Though, as a mystery writer, he needed to deal with killings, many of his novels are much more than mysteries: filled with insightful ideas, they can definitely compete with, and even surpass in quality, a lot of mainstream fiction works. Needless to say, the numerous Latin references encountered in the two novels presented above, as well as many others waiting to be discovered in his other books (e.g., in the posthumously published *The Gathering*, 2002, where Latin lexicon pops up on whichever page you happen to open to), constitute a rare treasure and offer a strong argument against ignoring or underrating the significance of the ancient language as a part of modern discourse and literature.

9. Tom KAKONIS (1930–2018)

Born on November 13, 1930, in Long Beach, California, to a Greek father and an American mother, Tom E. Kakonis was educated at the University of Minnesota (B.A.), South Dakota University (M.S.) and the University of Iowa (Ph.D.). During his interesting and adventurous life, he found pleasure in a variety of jobs, and before he became a novelist, he was a lifeguard, an army officer, a technical writer and a college professor. His first novel, *Michigan Roll*, was published in 1988 and was followed by *Criss Cross* (1990), *Double Down* (1991), *Shadow Counter* (1993), *Blind Spot* (1997), *Flawless* (2014) and *Treasure Coast* (2014). Kakonis is also the author of the nonfiction book *Statement and Craft: Means and Ends in Writing* (1971). He died in Grand Rapids, Michigan, on August 31, 2018.

Kakonis's very first book, *Michigan Roll* (1988), contains an impressive number of Latin references. The protagonist of this crime novel, Timothy Waverly, is a well-educated, 36-year-old ex-convict, getting his life on track after eight years' imprisonment for killing his wife's divorce lawyer. He takes a brief vacation from his professional gambling (he is a first-class card player) in Florida and goes to Traverse City, Michigan, hoping to see his now ten-year-old son. Instead, he helps a lady in distress, Holly ("Midnight") Clemmons, and unintentionally gets involved in a deadly confrontation with the Chicago mafia, originally provoked by the greed of Holly's half-brother, Clay, who is now in hiding.

The first Latin expression is a part of a paragraph describing two dangerous men, Gilbert Hawkins, alias Gleep, and Christian Skaggs, alias Shadow, sent by the mafia to retrieve the missing merchandise (drugs) and punish the insolent "thieves." They are the same two mobsters that would (some time later) bother Midnight Clemmons and require Waverly to step in:

> Shadow wore rust-colored slacks and a pale-blue sport shirt with flame patterns rising through it. His partner, an inordinately large man, was dressed all in black, a hulking **memento mori** ["remember you must die"], come to call. [p. 23]

The grammatical significance of the highlighted quotation consists in two rare forms: the future imperative, second person singular form (present does not exist) of the verb *memini meminisse* ('to remember') and the present infinitive form of the deponent verb *morior mori* ('to die'). Furthermore, the former verb is truly unique, as its two principal parts look like the Perfect Active Indicative forms (first person singular and infinitive, respectively), but they have the sense of and are translated as the Present Active Indicative Tense.

The same two characters are the pretext for the second Latin phrase. It appears in a scene where the two mobsters warn garage owner Dale Moon what will happen to him if he does not do what they "request":

> As they pulled away from the station, Gleep said to his partner, "You sure got some way with the words." Genuine admiration.
>
> But Shadow was not to be cheered. This **coitus interruptus** of the spirit drained all the natural zest he took in his work right out of him. [p. 95]

The literal translation of the Latin phrase is 'interrupted intercourse,' which can be further explained as 'sexual intercourse in which the penis is intentionally withdrawn before ejaculation.' The expression, naturally, is used by the author in a metaphorical way.

A rather unusual linguistic reference becomes a part of Waverly's sarcastic reaction to the tortures he receives from Shadow:

> He straddled Waverly and placed his thumbs inside the corners of his mouth, fitting them carefully, clear of the teeth. And then he began to tug laterally.
>
> As the pain widened across his head, Waverly smothered a rising shriek by forming the words **Risus Sardonicus**, seeing them, focusing on them, and picturing the distended smile being shaped on him now, smile of death, smile that says Look, the joke's on you, monstrous joke and somehow you missed it, biggest laugh of them all. [p. 151]

While the literal translation of the phrase is 'sardonic smile,' the medical definition is 'fixed contraction of the facial muscles resulting in a peculiar distorted grin.' What is interesting about the phrase is that it is a combination of a Latin (fourth declension, masculine) noun, *risus risūs* ('laughter/smile/grin/ridicule') derived from the second-conjugation verb *rideo ridēre risi risum* ('to laugh/smile'), and an adjective that is originally Greek.

The next Latin reference, a somewhat modified version of or a possible pun on the internationally well-known phrase *magna cum laude*, appears in a flashback paragraph, relating prison life (Chop or Chopper is the nickname of Waverly's buddy and survival master, Wesley):

After Waverly was graduated from the Forensic Center, **magna cum sane** ['with great sanity'], and returned to Jackson for the remainder of his sentence, Chop sought him out and advised him: "Nobody can give you your nuts and nobody can take them away." [p. 215]

There are also some references to the Latin language itself, all rather self-explanatory and all resulting from the fact that Waverly and Chop had a special deal in prison, the former teaching the latter ancient languages and English literature, and the latter teaching the former how to survive. In the first passage, Waverly, once in Michigan, plans to visit his old prison buddy and looks for an appropriate gift for Chop:

> Still, he felt a twinge of guilt, so when he came on a large bookstore, new to him, he pulled over. Chop had long since mastered **Latin** and was well into Greek, so Sanskrit had to be next. Half for a joke he'd buy him a Sanskrit grammar if he could find it. [p. 32]

The ancient language is also mentioned in a passage where Waverly tells Midnight, after they get to be intimate, about his prison experience (pp. 131-132), and, once again, in a scene where Waverly does finally visit Chop in prison, and they have a warm but rather disappointing (to Waverly) chat:

> "It's me, Waverly. You remember."
>
> "Waverly?"
>
> "Anglo-Saxon Waverly. **Latin** Waverly. Remember?"
>
> A thin wolfish smile cracked the sunken face. "Course I remember. You think they got to me yet?" [p. 265]

The remaining, relatively minor, Latin references (two of them being a normal part of the English language, hence, not italicized) encountered in *Michigan Roll* do not require to be presented in their contexts. Here is the list:

> **dictum** (a perfect passive participle from the third-conjugation verb *dico dicĕre dixi dictum*, used as a substantive, literally meaning 'something said,' in fact being a synonym of such nouns as 'saying, maxim, axiom, proverb, epigram, etc.' pp. 50, 74);
>
> ***Religio Medici*** (*The Religion of a Doctor*, a book by Sir Thomas Browne, 1643, p. 1240;

quota ('a fixed minimum or a particular number required,' p. 255).

Several Latin phrases and quotations have been found in Kakonis's psychological mystery *Flawless* (2014), the author's last book. Its main character is Michael Woodrow, a young financial consultant who also happens to be a serial killer of promiscuous women during his business trips to different parts of the country. His father, Norman, is a well-educated ex-convict who served his time for killing his own wife (when Michael was a child) and who now, living with his son, gradually begins to suspect Michael of the atrocious acts he reads about in the newspaper. One day, he is also visited by Victor Flam, a private "researcher"/investigator ("top tracker on Florida Gold Coast") on the trail of the serial killer. The first Latin expression appears in a passage relating a conversation between Michael and his father (and also, once again, on page 316):

> His infelicitous choice of words effectively arrested that line of conversation. Michael steered it down another avenue. "What about that book you're working on? Any progress?"
>
> "A little. It goes slowly."
>
> "It's a biography, is it?"
>
> "Yes, a biography," Norman said. Because he didn't want to follow that topic, he added quickly, in **non sequitur** (a clause referring to something that does not logically follow the previous topic or statement), "The new neighbor is a pleasant-seeming young lady."
>
> "Really."
>
> Norman described his afternoon encounter with the pleasant-seeming woman.
>
> Michael chuckled, a little patronizingly and without much mirth. "For you to spend an hour with someone, she must be pleasant."
>
> "It wasn't a full hour." [p. 51]

The next reference, a well-known quotation, is mentioned in a scene where Norman talks to the pleasant-looking neighbor, Lizabeth Seaver, who, in the meantime, has met Michael and fallen in love with him, apparently with reciprocation. The topic of their conversation is a recent incident in which Norman defended Lizabeth from her aggressive ex-husband:

"It was heroic, Norman."

He shrugged. "You supply the sand, I'll do the kicking."

"It was all so fast," she said, the sally unacknowledged, "so ... sudden."

"Good thing too. Another thirty seconds and you'd have been summoning the EMS unit. For me, that is."

"How did you do it, anyway?" she asked, voice small but charged with wonder, genuine curiosity. "You don't strike me as the brawler type."

"***Mens sana in corpore sano.*** ["A sound mind in a healthy body."]"

"What?"

"Sound mind in a sound body. Semi-sound, both places."

"Be serious, Norman."

"I am. It's all a matter of the head you're in."

"Where'd you learn that? Those Japanese warriors you were telling me about?"

"There, and elsewhere."

"Where, elsewhere?"

"Elsewhere." [p. 203]

The third Latin phrase happens to emerge in less dramatic but rather complicated circumstances during one of the meetings (this one related to the Hobbes College project) that Michael Woodrow participates in as a consultant. The other names that are mentioned in the quoted passage are members of the board:

> Dr. Hilda sitting off to one side, pursed-lipped, glaring, poised and waiting, taut as a coiled cat about to spring. Dr. H. on her feet in impassioned rebuttal, well-rehearsed, well-delivered, and freighted with well-timed bursts of ridicule ("Crisis? What crisis? I submit to you that a businessperson's grasp of the issues and problems of higher education is likely to be clouded by a, shall we say, bottom-line mentality.") Himself seething under the sneered and wholly gratuitous **ad hominum** assaults; the spineless board, flying in the face of irrefutable evidence, electing to take the Stoltz plan "under advisement" and to render its considered judgment later (for it was, after all, homecoming weekend, and the insistent thump of a marching band could be heard in the distance, a steady pounding in his ears). [p. 269]

The Latin phrase is clearly misspelled here as the form '*hominum*' (genitive plural) should not be preceded by the preposition '*ad*' (governing the accusative case). Thus, the correct form, with the noun in the accusative singular, should be '*ad hominem*' (literally meaning 'against the man/person'), which is a phrase usually used to modify an argument or statement directed against a particular person rather than against the position or view expressed/taken by that person.

The next passage including a Latin reference is a part of Norman's biographical book, or rather diary, from the entry dated August 24, 1958, a Sunday morning in Long Beach:

> I'm slouched on a bench at the shore end of the pier. Exactly why I'm here I don't fully understand. A belated pilgrimage? Whimsical search? Perhaps a resolution, of sorts. Impossible to say.
>
> Lived only twenty miles up the road, yet in all the years I've been out here never once undertook the journey. Have, in fact, scrupulously avoided this place (though I've found my way to Newport and Laguna and even to San Diego often enough, prowling for new scams, new marks).
>
> But the true ***axis mundi*** (literally: 'axis of the Earth' or 'celestial/cosmic axis,' often referring to the 'Sacred Sites Where Heaven Meets Earth') of my existence is Santa Monica, that oddly displaced community boxed between monster city and sea, insulated, in those days, as a midwestern hamlet. [p. 298]

The final quotation from *Flawless* does not include a Latin word or phrase, but rather an unusual English derivative from the Latin noun '*spelunca*' ('cave'), a word definitely not used in the spoken language too often. It is used by the narrator in a passage describing and analyzing (from Michael's point of view) the awkward situation between Norman, Lizabeth and Michael:

> Norman had kept a curious distance, almost as though he were deliberately avoiding them. Once, at Lizabeth's insistence, he came by for dinner, but he seemed to have an uncomfortable sense of his own tinny presence, didn't linger long.
>
> Fine by him. For over the course of those days and under her gentle ministrations, the contagion of her artless joy, some of the unearthed horror at what he'd done, who he'd been, some of it, a share at least, dissolved and scattered like ashes driven by a healing wind. He likened himself to a **spelunker** ['caveman'] lost in the depth of a black and terrifying cave, miraculously come across a narrow passage, tiny portal, and emerging, bruised and shaken, eyes stung by the light, but rescued at last. [p. 328]

Frequently compared to Elmore Leonard, Tom Kakonis is going to be remembered as the author of a handful of remarkable thrillers with realistic backgrounds, charismatic characters and unique plot resolutions. However, he was not only a first-rate novelist, but also a true scholar and probably a genuine fan of the classical culture, frequently reaching for Latin words and embellishing his prose with relatively rare expressions and quotations. As a college student, he came across the following Latin mottos: *Commune vinculum omnibus artibus* ("A common bond for all arts")—at the University of Minnesota, and *Veritas* ("Truth")—at South Dakota University.

10. Joe GORES (1931–2011)

Born in Rochester, Minnesota, on December 25, 1931, Joseph Nicholas Gores studied English Literature at both Notre Dame University and Stanford University (M.A. in 1961). He was a private investigator for twelve years before he began writing mysteries set in the San Francisco Bay Area. In addition to his short story collection and six novels involving Detective Agency Dan Kearney and Associates, e.g., *Dead Skip* (1972) and *32 Cadillacs* (1992, an Edgar Award nominee), and two Dashiell Hammett-related novels—*Hammett* (1975, Japan's Falcon Award) and *Spade & Archer* (2009)—Gores wrote eight other novels, notably *A Time of Predators* (1969, an Edgar Award winner) and *Come Morning* (1986, an Edgar Award nominee). Gore is only one of two authors to win the Edgar Award in three separate categories: Best First Novel, Best Short Story and Best Episode in a TV series. He died on January 10, 2011, in Greenbrae, California.

While Gore wrote scripts for episodes of several crime TV series in the late 1970s and 1980s—such as *Kojak, Mrs. Columbo, Magnum, P.I.* and *B. L. Stryker*—the only big-screen adaptation of his work is Wim Wenders's *Hammett* (1982; featuring Frederic Forrest in the titular part, Peter Boyle, Marilu Henner, Roy Kinnear and Elisha Cook, Jr.).

Latin references have been discovered in two of Gores's works, *Hammett* ([1975] 1976) and *Spade & Archer*. The former is an audacious undertaking in which the author makes Dashiell Hammett the protagonist, here in the role of a retired Pinkerton detective and aspiring writer, reluctantly, at the age of thirty-four, involved in a complex and dangerous case of major crime, prostitution and political corruption. The first Latin phrase appears in a scene where Hammett, in the midst of his investigation, walks into a bar, known as Dom's Dump, at two o'clock in the morning and is about to start a chat with the bartender:

"That way for the bar, sir."

"Thank you, my good man."

Hammett spoke with the considered enunciation of one whose condition makes of the term "drunkenness" a ***non sequitur*** [a clause referring to something that does not logically follow the previous topic or statement]. His eyes had a slightly glassy, slightly hooded look, like the eyes of a resting hawk. He laid his stick on the bar and placed his freshly blocked and newly banded Wilton beside it." [pp. 149-150]

The expression '*non sequitur*' (literally meaning 'it does not follow,') is a clause rather than a phrase because it does include a verb, '*sequitur*' (from '*sequor sequi*'), which, being a deponent verb, despite having a passive ending '*-tur*,' is really translated in the active voice. However, the third person singular ending allows us to conclude that the implied subject is most likely 'it.'

The second passage worth quoting because of a Latin reference is related to a murder scene. The victims are Heloise Kuhn and her son, Andy, two small-time criminals who have been holding by force Crystal Tam, a Chinese prostitute (one of the main characters of the book, a villain, in fact), and, as a result, got themselves killed. Jimmy Gibson is a witness of the murder circumstances; Hammett, the local sheriff, his deputy and Doc Straub arrive there first:

> "Who found the bodies?" asked Hammett, apparently idly.
>
> "Jimmy Gibson from the farm a mile down the road. Heard a shotgun here twice, figgered it was Andy shootin' crows so he come down to see could he tag along. That Andy'd shoot anything that moved. Only just as Jimmy come out of the trees up the ravine, a big man he didn't know come running out of the barn. He jumps in a big black car and goes tearin' out of here. So Jimmy naturally looked in and saw—"
>
> "Didn't get a plate on the car, I guess."
>
> "Big and black. That's it. If he had to guess, he'd say a Reo."
>
> Doc Straub came out of the barn wiping his hands on his handkerchief. "You figgered they was gonna raise up from the dead or something, Jeremy, you run me out here to see 'em ***in situ*** ['in position/in the original place']?"
>
> "Just going by the book, Chet," said the sheriff in a soothing voice. "What can you tell me about the deaths?" [pp. 191-192]

The final Latin reference happens to be in the self-explanatory opening paragraph of the author's Acknowledgments. I do not see any reason why it should not be shared with the reader. It goes like this:

> On a book such as this, a great many people must be conned by the writer's enthusiasm into doing much of his work for him. If I have forgotten anyone, please—***mea culpa*** ['my fault]. [p. 261]

10. Joe GORES (1931–2011)

Quite a few Latin references have been found in *Spade & Archer* (2009), a book which, as its subtitle suggests, is a prequel to Dashiell Hammett's legendary novel *The Maltese Falcon* (1929). A number of characters from the classic novel also appear here: Sam Spade, his partner Miles Archer and his wife, Iva, Sam's secretary, Effie Perrine, two cops (Dundy and Tom) and even the assistant DA Bryan. The context of the first quotation is private investigator Spade confronting a man who was reported as missing (Robert Flitcraft) and eventually turned up under a different name (Charles Pierce):

> "I was sent here to find and identify the man our informant thought was Flitcraft. I've done that. Charles Pierce is Robert Flitcraft. No definite instructions beyond that, but there's the bigamy question. Wife here, wife in Tacoma. Kids from both marriages . . ." For the first time Spade addressed Pierce directly as Flitcraft. "Of course since you left your first wife extremely well fixed you could claim you thought that after all this time she would have divorced you ***in absentia***—[literally: 'in/during absence,' better: 'while not present' (at the event being referred to)]." [p. 10]

As the story develops, some eighty pages later, cops Dundy and Tom Polhaus bring Spade to a crime scene (four murdered men, all criminals) and the three detectives discuss the possible scenarios:

> Spade said to the sheriff, "How long have they been dead?"
>
> "Coroner says different times most like. I wanted you to see 'em here **in situ** [a phrase already translated in this entry], like the feller says, fore he moved 'em." [p. 94]

Another eighty pages later, Spade, using the false name 'Eric Gough,' tries to obtain information about Penny Chiotras, an old friend of Effie's and now also his client, from her employer, in fact, as it turns out, former employer, Desmond Cole, junior partner of the firm 'Hartford & Cole: Stocks and Bonds.' For Sam finds out that Penny is not employed there anymore, which means that she lied to him. He mentions Collin Eberhard (which is missing in the cited excerpt), the major victim of the second part of the book, whose murder, by the police believed to be a suicide, is the cause of Penny's dangerous predicament:

> "Penny started out as a secretary right enough, but she soon became a **de facto** ['in fact/in effect/in reality'] broker, near as damn to swearing. We were urging her to get her own license when she had to leave." [p. 170]

The same Latin phrase as above also appears in a scene where Sam confronts Penny about her lies (pp. 186-187). Because it is used in exactly the same lexical context, it would be redundant to quote the whole passage.

However, a couple of pages later, when Sam is still talking with Penny, he uses another Latin phrase in place of the previous one:

> Animation lit her face. "I told Effie I was working—"
>
> "Yeah. But not where. And not where you were living. You had a head for the business, so pretty soon you were handling bits and pieces of some of Hartford and Cole's accounts like a **bona fide** ['genuine/real'] broker. 'Near as damn to swearing' is the way Cole put it to me. One of the accounts was Eberhard's." [p. 188]

The final Latin reference in the book happens to be a phrase in Sam's thoughts during his exchange with Archer after their secretary leaves the room:

> Spade spoke with what seemed like admiration. "Does that mean you know who's doing it? ... Are they in it for the money? Or for something else?"
>
> "Of course for the money. This ain't nickel-and-dime stuff, Sam. This is big-time, organized thievery."
>
> Spade said thoughtfully, "Maybe someone in the labor movement wants to disrupt the **status quo** ['the existing state of affairs'], like the Wobblies kept trying to do up in Seattle after the union movement got squashed by all those ex-servicemen coming home needing jobs." [p. 237]

The 1986 President of the Mystery Writers of America, Joe Gores, was a distinguished writer of the crime and detection genre, a generally-respected continuator of the Dashiell Hammett tradition. Considering his impressive contribution to the Latin-quotation database, it should not be surprising to see an abundance of Latin words in the information regarding the places of his education. For, while the outer ring of the logo of the University of Notre Dame has a Latin inscription "*Sigillum Universitatis Dominae Nostrae a Lacu*" ("The seal of the University of Notre Dame of the Lake"), the college's motto is "*Vita, Dulcedo, Spes*" ("Life, Sweetness, Hope"), three attributes referring to the Blessed Virgin Mary. Furthermore, the motto of Stanford University is *Semper virens* ("Ever flourishing").

11. Joseph WAMBAUGH (1937–)

Joseph Aloysius Wambaugh, Jr. was born on January 22, 1937, in East Pittsburgh, Pennsylvania, to an Irish-German family (his father was a police officer). He was educated at Chaffey College (A.A.) and California State University, Los Angeles (B.A. and M.A.). Before he became a full-time writer, he served in the United States Marine Corps and was a policeman in southern California, which experience inspired his first novel, *The New Centurions* (1971), and most of his later novels and nonfiction books. His novels include *The Blue Knight* (1972), *The Choirboys* (1975), *The Black Marble* (1978), *The Glitter Dome* (1981), *The Delta Star* (1983), *The Secrets of Harry Bright* (1985), *Fugitive Nights: Danger in the Desert* (1992), *Finnegan's Week* (1993), *Hollywood Station* (2006) and *Hollywood Hills* (2010). His best nonfiction books are *The Onion Field* (1981), *Lines and Shadows* (1984), *Echoes in the Darkness* (1987) and *The Blooding: The True Story of the Narborough Village Murders* (1989). His notable awards include the Special Edgar Award (1974, for *The Onion Field*), Edgar Award for Best Motion Picture Screenplay (1981, for *Black Marble*), Edgar Award for Best Fact Crime (for *Fire Lover*, 2003) and Edgar Grand Master Award (2004).

Several of Wambaugh's works have been turned into Hollywood movies. They include three theatrical productions that the author liked—Richard Fleischer's *The New Centurions* (1972; starring George C. Scott, Stacy Keach, Jane Alexander and Scott Wilson), Harold Becker's *The Onion Field* (1978; featuring John Savage, James Woods, Franklyn Seales and Ted Danson) and Becker's *The Black Marble* (1980; starring Robert Foxworth, Paula Prentiss and Harry Dean Stanton); and one—Robert Aldrich's *The Choirboys* (1977; featuring Charles Durning, Lou Gossett, Jr., Perry King and Clyde Kusatsu)—that the author strongly disapproved of and, as a result, forced the studio to delete his name from the credits. The television adaptations include Robert Butler's *The Blue Knight* (1973; starring William Holden, Lee Remick, Joe Santos and Sam Elliott), Stuart Margolin's *The Glitter Dome* (1984; featuring James Garner, Margot Kidder and John Lithgow) and Gary Nelson's *Fugitive Nights: Danger in the Desert* (1993; starring Sam Elliott, Teri Garr and Thomas Haden Church). Wambugh contributed screenplays to most of the above-mentioned films, as well as to numerous episodes of several TV series, and, also, he appeared himself as an actor in two episodes—as Truxton in an episode of *Police Story* (1973-1987; featuring Scott Brady, Mel Scott, Don Meredith, Joe Santos and many others) and as Desk Sergeant in an episode of

The Blue Knight (1975-1976; starring George Kennedy, John Steadman and Barbara Rhoades).

The major theme of Wambaugh's novel *The Secrets of Harry Bright* ([1985] 1986), set (like most of the author's work) in southern California, is the investigation of millionaire Victor Watson's son's murder case, assigned to two LAPD officers, Sidney Blackpool and Otto Stringer. The only Latin reference appears in a passage where the two cops try to obtain some more information about the circumstances of the murder (Jack Watson was found inside a Rolls-Royce in the California desert with a bullet in his head) in a phone conversation with Lieutenant Sanders of the Palm Beach Police Department:

> "Too bad there wasn't a gun found at the scene," Sidney Blackpool said. "You coulda maybe figured it to be a suicide where the car rolled off the hill after the kid shot himself."
>
> "No gun," the lieutenant said. "And a very bad angle for a right-handed suicide."
>
> "About how many people live in those canyons?"
>
> "No people. About sixty dirtbag methamphetamine dealers. No **Homo sapiens** [literally: 'wise man,' better: 'human being,' a member of the species] allowed in Solitaire Canyon. They cook up speed in those shacks, but it's almost impossible to get probable cause to bust them." [p. 108]

One of the author's later novels, *Hollywood Station* (2006), is a multi-episode chronicle of the Hollywood Division cops' everyday work on the streets of the city. The colorful characters include the Oracle (a sergeant), Fausto Gamboa, Budgie Polk, Mag Takara, Nathan Weiss (a.k.a. Hollywood Nate, due to his acting aspirations) and Wesley Drubb. There are several Latin references in the book. The first one appears in a self-explanatory passage revealing the plans of two criminals, Cosmo Betrossian and his girlfriend Ilya:

> Cosmo and Ilya had never committed an armed robbery prior to the jewelry store job. The hand grenade idea came from something he had heard from one of the addicts who had read about it in a San Diego newspaper. The reason the addict had mentioned it to Cosmo at all was that the robbers who did it were Armenians who were supposed to be connected with Russian Mafia. Cosmo had to laugh. He had stolen their idea and their **modus operandi** ['a particular way/method of doing something'], and it had been easy. And it had all come to him because he was an Armenian émigré. [p. 113]

The second phrase—just like the first one, quite common in everyday English—is applied by the narrator in the scene where two policewomen from the Vice Squad, Budgie and Mag, are acting as decoys:

> The vice cops had said that they expected long tall Budgie to get some suspicious questions about being a police decoy, but Mag was so small, so exotic, and so sexy that she should reassure anybody. And indeed, the businessman was not interested in her **bona fides** ['being real/genuine'].
>
> He said, "You look like a very clean girl. Are you?" [p. 159]

The next and final two (identical) references, both being a single Latin word used in connection with an English word (paraphrasing the Marine Corps motto), appear, first several pages later (after Mag gets beaten up), in a dialogue between some other policemen discussing the misfortunate incident, and then again, toward the end of the book, when the Oracle's ashes are being scattered by his colleagues from the famous "HOLLYWOOD" sign:

> But all Fausto said to him before he and Benny Brewster left the scene was "This is a crummy job, Merv."
>
> The Oracle opened a packet of antacid tablets, and said, "Old dogs like you and me, Fausto? It's all we got. **Semper** ['always'] cop." [p. 171]
>
> The ladder was in place beside scaffolding, and when he had climbed halfway up, Budgie yelled, "That's high enough, Fausto!"
>
> But he kept going, puffing and panting, pausing twice until he was all the way to the top. And when he was there, he carefully opened the lid from the urn and turned it upside down, saying, "**Semper** cop, Merv. See you soon."
>
> And the Oracle's ashes blew away into the warm summer night, against the backdrop of HOLLYWOOD, four stories high, under magical white light supplied by an obliging Hollywood moon. [p. 338]

Praised for his authenticity and highly realistic approach to police work, Joseph Wambaugh is also a competent and prolific writer with an impressive number of superior books to his credit. While his realistic prose has been inspiring many writers and filmmakers, his Latin references, simple but aptly applied, constitute a modest illustration of the inclusion of Latin phrases in modern English, both written and spoken.

The Latin motto of Wambaugh's alma mater, California State University, Los Angeles, is *Vox, Veritas, Vita* ("Voice, Truth, Life"), which is also a nice example of alliteration.

12. Robert K. TANENBAUM (1942–)

Born in Brooklyn, New York, in 1942, Robert K. Tanenbaum is a successful lawyer, a prolific novelist and a well-known politician (he served two terms as Mayor of Beverly Hills and was a City Council Member from 1986 to 1994). He was educated at the University of California, Berkeley, on a basketball scholarship, earning his Juris Doctor from Boat Hall School of Law. In addition to three non-fiction books, Tanenbaum wrote nearly three dozen crime novels, including *Material Witness* (1993), *Corruption of Blood* (1995), *Falsely Accused* (1996), *Irresistible Impulse* (1997), *True Justice* (2000), *Absolute Rage* (2002), *Fury* (2005), *Escape* (2008), *Betrayed* (2010), *Outrage* (2011), *Fatal Conceit* (2014) and *Without Fear of Favor* (2017). The only screen adaptation of Tanenbaum's work is Mel Damski's TV production *Badge of the Assassin* (1985; starring James Woods, Yaphet Kotto and Alex Rocco), based on his non-fiction book of the same name (1979). Tanenbaum was its co-executive producer.

Just a few Latin references have been found in Tanenbaum's *Corruption of Blood* ([1995] 1996), a thriller about the reopening of the JFK assassination investigation. The most insightful of them appears in a passage where Marlene Ciampi, Manhattan Assistant District Attorney Roger "Butch" Karp's wife, talks on the phone with lawyer Harley Blaine about his client, Richard Ewing Dobbs:

"The point being," Marlene put in, "that if you thought Mr. Gaiilov was a double, then you'd expect him to try to cover for Dobbs, the master spy, but if you thought he was on the level, then Dobbs had to be innocent."

The man chuckled, a dry rustling sound. "Yep, you got it. I reckon you can figure out the rest. I called a meeting in Judge Palmer's chambers with the U.S. Attorney, Paul Garrigan, and I told him that I intended to call Armand Gaiilov as a witness. Well, when that got back to the CIA it let the skunk loose in amongst the choir. There was a great gnashing of teeth, I expect, and it must've brought the internal battle to a head. The last they wanted was a fella who they didn't know whether he was a spy or not getting hauled up in open court under oath to testify about Dick Dobbs. So they said they wouldn't do it, couldn't do it, for national security reasons, and I said in that case, I'd settle for a *subpoena **duces tecum*** ['a writ ordering a person to attend a court and bring something']—the transcripts of all their debriefs of Gaiilov. Well, of course, they said I couldn't have that either. [p. 224]

The other Latin references in the book are in fact abbreviations of the word *versus* ('against') in such phrases as *People v. Melville* (p. 113) and *U.S. v. Dobbs* (p. 220), plus one botanic name, *Brunfelsia floribunda*, which denotes a brush from Brazil.

Tanenbaum's novel *Escape* (2008) has two parallel themes: a filicide committed by Jessica Campbell, a highly educated woman and politician's wife, and a plot to destroy the United States designed by an American organization in collaboration with international Islamic terrorists. While the main protagonist, District Attorney Roger "Butch" Karp, is the prosecutor in Jessica Campbell's trial, he and his daughter, Lucy (alias Marie Smith), are also engaged in the multi-level and complex investigation aimed to prevent the plot from being successful. Moreover, Karp's wife, Marlene, and their thirteen-year-old twin sons, Isaac and Giancarlo, as well as Marlene's father, Mariano Ciampi, would accidentally end up being at the crime scene and, thus, participate, in their own ways, in the fight against terrorism.

The novel is rich in legal terms. One that is apparently adopted by the English language as it is spelled by Tanenbaum without italics is *caveat*, which, in addition to meaning 'warning' or 'caution,' can be defined as 'a notice that certain actions are not allowed to be taken without letting the person who gave the notice know about it ahead of time.' The term is used by the author/narrator in a passage regarding the connection between some mosques and terrorism:

> Even in the mosques whose imams preached assimilation into the main-stream community and whose congregation publicly denounced the violence of Islamic extremists, there had been no great effort to cooperate with law-enforcement agencies in identifying possible terrorists in their midst. And the denunciations always seemed to come with some **caveat** that the United States was a target because of its support for Israel. Some of the 9/11 hijackers had worshiped at such mosques and even let their extremist views be known to various members of the congregation.

The most interesting of the Latin references found in the book, being at the same time the only complete sentence among them, is the one that appears in the crucial conversation between Assistant District Attorney Vinson Talcott "V. T." Newbury, who has staged some dramatic and painful circumstances to justify his fake resignation from Karp's office in order to penetrate a terroristic group, and his uncle, Dean Newbury, deeply involved in international terrorism, also guilty of fratricide (he has poisoned V. T.'s father for his selfish and illegal reasons). Quoted below is an excerpt in which V. T. pretends to be interested in his uncle's illegal organization and everything that stands behind it:

12. Robert K. TANENBAUM (1942–)

> When V. T. held up his hand for the drink, his uncle noted the ring on his finger. "Looks good on you," he said, holding up an exact copy of his own hand. "The triskele. Three golden spiral legs joined in the middle against a field of black. Symbol of the Isle of Man." He held the ring out as if to study it from a distance. "It's really a stylized version of three human legs joined in the middle and running, an ancient symbol that shows up in ancient art from Celtic ruins to Spain and Sicily. '*Quocunque jeceris stabit.*'"
>
> "Wherever you will throw it, it stands," V. T. translated, raising his glass to his nose to inhale the aroma of leather and spices.
>
> "Ah yes, you were the **Latin** scholar in boarding school," Dean Newbury recalled. "It's appropriate, too, as the motto of our families for more than two hundred years." [p. 238]

While the translation of the quotation offered by the author is basically correct, the two verbs used in the two clauses of the sentence are worth commenting on. The first form, *jeceris* (from the third-conjugation verb *iacio iacěre ieci iactum* – 'to throw'), is in the Future Perfect Tense, whereas in English, in such a context, it is usually expressed by a present tense due to the conditional connotation. Furthermore, the second form, *stabit* (from the first-conjugation verb *sto stare steti statum* – 'to stand'), is in the Future Tense, which tense can also be kept in the English translation due to the fact that it appears in a result clause, even though Tanenbaum's translation chooses to put it in the Present Simple Tense.

Another legal term, *sua sponte* (meaning 'of one's own will' or 'of one's own accord'), appears later in the book during the trial, in Judge Dermondy's response to defense attorney Linda Lewis's exclaim "Mistrial!"

> Dermondy raised his hand to silence her. "Miss Lewis, your initial comment about relevance was ill-advised. If the witness Swanburg's testimony was not relevant I would have so ruled ***sua sponte***. [pp. 364-365]

The expression *postpartum* or *post-partum*, modifying the mother's condition after birth (unlike *postnatal*, which refers to the infant's condition), is a compound composed of the Latin preposition 'post' (meaning 'after') and the accusative singular form of the fourth-declension masculine noun *partus partūs* (meaning 'birth' or 'delivery'). Since Jessica Campbell's lawyer bases her defense on the defendant's mental state before, during and after committing the crime of killing her three children, the statements of two psychiatrists, Dr. Harry Winkler and Dr. Louise "Niki" Nickles, regarding

Jessica's mental health are frequently quoted both in and out of court. Thus, the word *postpartum* is used in combination with 'depression' on pp. 73, 75, 77, 95, 133, 175, 205, 206, 303, 308, 309, 400, 405-409, 437, 439, 479, 480, 496; with 'psychosis' on pp. 83, 437, 496; and with 'schizophrenia' on p. 437.

The remaining Latin references discovered in *Escape*, mostly legal, all quite well known and presented also in other entries of this book, are listed below along with the page numbers where they appear in Tanenbaum's novel:

bona fide ('in good faith,' pp. 9, 432)

Semper Fi ('Always faithful,' pp. 48, 432)

pro bono ('free of charge,' pp. 66, 187, 253)

persona non grata ('an unwelcome person,' pp. 86, 165)

prima facie ('based on the first impression,' pp. 399, 400)

Robert K. Tanenbaum, in addition to being a famous public figure in the areas of politics and the law, is one of the most accomplished writers of legal thrillers. The numerous Latin references encountered in his prose, especially in his complex novel *Escape*, offer a strong contribution to the statement that even now, in the first couple of decades of the twenty-first century, Latin is far from being a dead language. The Latin motto of his alma mater, the University of California, Berkeley, is *Fiat Lux* ("Let there be light").

13. Sara PARETSKY (1947–)

Born in Ames, Iowa, on June 8, 1947, Sara Paretsky studied political sciences at the University of Kansas, graduating *summa cum laude* in 1967 with a B.A. diploma, and got her M.B.A. diploma and Ph.D. in history from the University of Chicago in 1977. She started writing in the mid-1970s and published her first (out of over twenty) crime novel in 1982. Her most important distinctions include the Cartier Diamond Dagger Award for lifetime achievement by the Crime Writers' Association (2002) and the Grand Master Award by the Mystery Writers of America (2011). Not counting David E. Peckinpah's television production *When Danger Follows You Home* (1997; with JoBeth Williams), for which she co-wrote the screen story, the only movie inspired by Paretsky's prose is Jeff Kafew's *V.I. Warshawski* (1991; starring Kathleen Turner, in the titular role, Jay O. Sanders and Charles Durning), which was based on a few of her novels featuring the fascinating private investigator. While it is rather hard to name the most remarkable of her works, the ones listed below, in which examples of Latin references have been found, definitely belong to Paretsky's foremost accomplishments.

Paretsky's fourth novel, *Bitter Medicine* ([1987] 1988), is, as usual, set in Chicago and, as usual, follows the investigations of private eye V.I. Warshawski. A Latin reference appears in a scene where the female detective talks on the phone with Murray Ryerson, head of the crime desk at the *Herald-Star* (a crime reporter Warshawski has known and been collaborating with, in one way or another, since Paretsky's first book):

> "You know more than you're telling, sweet pea. Yarborough has the IckPiff files—didn't take much of a newspaperman to get that out of a secretary who isn't used to the press. But I want to know what's going on. His reaction was just all out of proportion. Besides, he accused you of swiping them to begin with. You want to comment before I transmit my story?"
>
> I thought for a second. "Ms. Warshawski, the eminent private investigator, was reached in her office late in the day. On hearing of the allegations from Crawford, Meade, she replied in classical **Latin**, '*Ubi argumentum?*' ["Where is the proof?" or "What is the matter?"] and suggested that her learned colleague blow it out of his ears."

"Vic, come on. What gives with IckPiff? Why is a two-hundred-dollar-an-hour man like Dick Yarborough representing a lowlife like Dieter Monkfish?"

"The Constitution guarantees a right to counsel," I began sonorously.

Murray cut me off. "Don't dribble legal shit at me, Warshawski. I want to talk to you. I'll meet you at the Golden Glow in half an hour." [p. 174]

In Paretsky's fifth novel, *Blood Shot* ([1988] 1989), the narrator/protagonist, detective Warshawski, reluctantly revisits her old south Chicago neighborhood in order to help a childhood friend, which eventually leads to her uncovering of a big-time chemical corruption. A famous Latin quotation is rather unexpectedly included in a narrative paragraph revealing the detective's thoughts and feelings:

I hunted around for the phone book. It had somehow gotten buried under a stack of music on the piano. Naturally enough, Humboldt's number wasn't listed. Frederick Manheim, Attorney, had an office at Ninety-fifth and Halsted and a home in neighboring Beverly. Lawyers with large incomes or criminal practices don't give their home numbers. Nor do they usually hide out on the southwest side, away from the courts and the major action.

I was restless enough to want to move now, call Manheim, get the story from him, and gallop down to Oak Street to confront Humboldt. "*Festina lente*" ["Rush slowly"], I muttered to myself. Get the facts, then shoot. It would be better to wait until morning and make the trek down south to see the guy in person. [p. 126]

One of the most complex and engaging works by Paretsky is *Tunnel Vision* (1994, her eighth novel), where V.I. Warshawski once again, against all odds, tackles an extremely difficult and dangerous case and unveils a big-scale corruption involving seemingly respectful businessmen and local politicians. The first Latin phrase appears in a paragraph relating the dialogue between Victoria, the narrator/protagonist, Phoebe, her idealistic long-time friend, and Camilla, one of Vic's boyfriend's four sisters (African-American policeman, Sergeant Conrad Rawlings, is the boyfriend):

Phoebe screwed her face up in a tight ball, not wanting to bend but knowing compromise was inevitable. "Give me fifteen, Vic, and we'll see."

"In writing, Phoebe, and it's a deal."

"Camilla's a witness here."

I shook my head. "Nonprofits eat you alive, and **pro bono** ['out of good will/free of charge'] work is the biggest devourer of all. In writing or not at all. I won't do like your legal staff—charge you a full hour for ten minutes' work. It'll be fifteen real-time hours." [p. 25]

The phrase *pro bono* is used three more times in the book: in a passage where Vic approaches Donald Blakely, the president of Gateway Bank, hoping to get an introduction to someone at Century Bank (p. 45); during Vic's conversation with Fabian Messenger, a corrupt lawyer and an abusive husband and wife (p. 61); and in her exchange with MacKenzie "Ken" Graham, a computer-savvy college kid (suspended for hacking), who eventually turns out extremely helpful to Vic (p. 181). Except for the excerpt from p. 61, where it is Ken who uses the phrase, the user of the Latin term is consistently Vic. The reason why this particular Lain expression appears four times in the book is not only to illustrate the author's familiarity with Latin legal terminology, but also, or primarily, to reveal the protagonist's major characteristics. For Warshawski, a daughter of Italian and Polish immigrants (her father was a Chicago policeman), has shown repeatedly that, in addition to being a tough and determined investigator, she is a dedicated liberal and idealist, a defender of the poor, the homeless and the abused ones against their exploitation by the rich, by the corrupt and by the abusive. Consequently, she often offers her services practically free of charge; as a result, she constantly finds herself in financial difficulties.

The next excerpt is a part of a scene focused on the problems of Tamar Hawking, a woman who, having been abused by her husband, lives in tunnels with her children but eventually appears in Vic's office asking for help:

A few minutes later Whiting phoned back: there was already a **bona fide** ['genuine/real'] missing persons search for Hawkings on file. Leon Hawkings, of an address on West Ninety-fifth Street, had notified them six months ago that his wife had disappeared, taking their three children with her. So if anyone on the beat found her, they would call her old man first. [p. 35]

The penultimate Latin quotation appears in a series of dramatic occurrences. After being assaulted and spending some time in a hospital, Vic stays overnight at the home of her old friends, Max and Lotty Loewenthal, then, when still trying to solve the problem of Deidre Messenger's murder, she and Max are arrested by the INS agents (and almost deported to Romania as illegal aliens) but are eventually freed when Vic's lawyer, Freeman Carter, arrives at the scene and steps in:

> When I told him he was not supportive. "You're not getting much sympathy from me on that one. In the first place, finding Deidre's murderer is a job for your friend Conrad, and in the second, why should any business open its books to you? Just because you want to know something they don't want to tell you does not constitute **prima facie** ['based on first impression/sufficient to establish a fact unless disproved'] grounds of wrongdoing." [p. 267]

The title of Chapter 41 is **The Quid Pro Quo** ('One thing for another,' p. 273), and the phrase appears again a few pages later in a narrative paragraph, where Warshawski arrives at an important conclusion regarding the connection between Phoebe and Alec Gantner, a senator's son involved in an illegal business with Jasper Heccomb, the Head of Home Free, and Donald Blakely, a money-hungry banker:

> I searched the paper feverishly but could find no other mention of the company. I shoved the paper aside and stared sightlessly out the window. So that was Phoebe's **quid pro quo**. Draw Lamia women away from their project and Alec Gantner will get the FDA to approve preliminary trials. But why had she done it? [p. 275]

Originally referring to either intentional or unintentional substitution of one medicine for another (which may have caused serious consequences for the patient), the phrase quoted in the last excerpt has eventually developed its more general meaning, referring to any sort of substitution or exchange.

In her short story "Grace Notes" (1995), a part of the magnificent compilation *Sleuths of the Century* (2000), Paretsky's private eye, V.I. Warshawski, is confronted with her distant cousin (on her mother's side), Tony, who unexpectedly arrives in Chicago (from Italy), motivated by his selfish and dishonest search for a hidden treasure among the forgotten family belongings. A minor Latin reference, inserted between two English words, appears in the protagonist/narrator's description of the woman working for the corrupt lawyer hired by Tony:

> Ranier's assistant-**cum**-receptionist was buried in Danielle Steel. When I handed her my card, she marked her page without haste and took the card into an inner office. After a ten-minute wait to let me understand his importance, Ranier came out to greet me in person. [p. 546]

13. Sara PARETSKY (1947–)

Vic Warshawski goes back to south Chicago once again in *Fire Sale* (her novel number thirteen, [2005] 2006). This time the detective volunteers to coach the girls' basketball team of her alma mater and once again gets involved in scandalous and dangerous corruption. The Latin references appear toward the end of the book and are associated with the unusual linguistic inclinations of Coach Mary Ann McFarlane, a warm and caring character, here offering help to Vic and shelter to two of the kids, Josey and Billy:

> "I wanted to call you, Coach Warshawski," Josie said, "but Billy was afraid you might still be working for Mr. William. So we came here, because Coach McFarlane was the person who helped Julia when she got pregnant."
>
> I shadow-punched Mary Ann. "What was that you said to me this afternoon—about not knowing the Dorrado girls very well?"
>
> She gave her grim smile. "I wanted them to go to you, Victoria, but I'd promised I'd keep their secret safe until they were ready to tell it. Trouble is, I thought Billy was hiding while he sorted out the ethics of his family's business—I didn't know 'til I heard him just now that they'd witnessed Bron's death. If I'd known that, please believe I'd have called you ***quam primum famam audieram*** ["as soon as I had heard the news"]."
>
> Mary Ann breaks into **Latin** when she's agitated—it calms her down, but makes it hard for people like doctors and nurses to know what she's saying. I don't follow her easily myself, and, right now, I was too overwhelmed by Billy's narrative to make the effort. [p. 482]

The last Latin quotation is alluring because of a poetic device, 'syncope' ('a purposeful omission of sounds or letters within a word'), being a part of it: the correct spelling of the very last word, *audieram*, is *audiveram* (Pluperfect Active Indicative), the correct perfect stem used in this context, *audiv-*, derived from the third principal part of the fourth-conjugation verb *audio audire audivi auditum* ('to hear' or 'to listen to').

A few pages later, when Victoria announces her intention to take the kids (who seem to be in danger because they "know too much") to her own place and expresses her concerns about Mary Ann's safety, the philosophically-inclined lady comes up with a response that includes, not unexpectedly, a reference to Latin:

"When I do come back, I'm going to take you home with me. I don't like leaving you here with Coach McFarlane—you're too exposed, and it puts her in danger."

"Oh, Victoria, my life is too close to the end to worry about danger," Mary Ann protested. "I like having young people in the place. It keeps me from brooding over my body. They're looking after Scurry, and I'm teaching them **Latin**—we're having a grand old time. [p. 485]

The 2015 President of the Mystery Writers of America, Sara Paretsky, is a prolific crime fiction writer and a creator of one of the most charismatic female detectives. Both in the way she chose to live her own life and in the manner she limns Victoria Warshawski and some other characters of her prose, Paretsky seems to have been genuinely inspired by the Latin mottos of her almae matres—*Videbo visionem hanc manam quare non comburatur rubus* ("I will see this great vision in which the bush does not burn")—of The University of Kansas; and *Crescat scientia; vita excolatur* ("Let knowledge grow from more to more; and so be human life enriched.")—of The University of Chicago. Both impressive from the standpoint of their deep meaning, they are also interesting because of their grammatical content. Together, in addition to a verb in the Future Active Indicative—*videbo* (from *video vidēre* – 'to see'), they include two verbs in the passive voice—*comburatur* (from *comburo comburĕre*, 'to burn') and *excolatur* (from *excolo excolare*, 'to polish/to burn'); and two verbs—*crescat* (from *cresco crescĕre*, 'to spring forth/to arise') and *comburatur* (from the verb already mentioned)—in the Present Subjunctive (jussive) form (third person singular), whose application here is to express a general wish.

14. Paul LEVINE (1948–)

Paul Levine was born on January 9, 1948, in Picture Rocks (near Williamsport), Pennsylvania. He was educated at the Pennsylvania State University and the University of Miami (J.D., 1973). Levine practiced law for many years and taught at the University of Miami before he turned to writing. He is famous for his superior legal thrillers featuring (most of the time) either Jacob (Jake) Lassiter, an ex-Penn State linebacker and lawyer—e.g., *To Speak for the Dead* (1990), *Mortal Sin* (1994), *Fool Me Twice* (1996)—or another couple of lawyers, Steve Solomon and Victoria Lord, e.g., *Solomon Vs. Lord* (2005), *The Deep Blue Alibi* (2006) and *Trial & Error* (2007). Occasionally, as in the case of *Bum Deal* (2018), all of the three lawyers appear in the same novel as both friends and legal opponents. The protagonist of his novel *9 Scorpions* (1998) is Lisa Fremont, an ex-stripper who, after getting a law degree from Stanford University, works as a Supreme Court law clerk. One of Levine's several distinctions is the John D. MacDonald Award for Excellence in Florida Fiction. (Levine dedicated his novel *Mortal Sin* "To the memory of John D. MacDonald, whose tough love for an embattled Florida inspires us still.")

Levine has contributed his teleplays to a number of episodes of several TV series (usually credited as Paul J. Levine)—notably *First Monday* and *JAG*—but the only screen adaptation of his published prose is Peter Markle's TV movie *Jake Lassiter: Justice on the Bayou* (1995; with Gerald McRaney as the titular protagonist), based on *To Speak for the Dead*. The setting of the story was moved from Miami to New Orleans, which explains the subtitle of the movie.

An abundance of Latin references have been found in three of Levine's novels—*Mortal Sin, Fool Me Twice* and *Bum Deal*. Set in the Florida Everglades, *Mortal Sin* (1994) has Jake Lassiter (also the narrator of the book) struggle almost as much with his infatuation with an unusual woman, now known as Gina Florio, as with the dangers created by the crime and corruption represented by Gina's current husband, Nicky Florio, whom, at the beginning of the novel, he happens to defend in court. Scattered on the pages of the book are over thirty Latin phrases, out of which number, for practical reasons, only eight have been selected for the presentation in their context. Most of the Latin sayings come from the mouth of Doc Charlie Riggs, Jake's close friend.

When Jake weighs his chances to win the case against Nicky, who is accused of causing the death of local politician Peter Upton, and thinking about the possible motive, he suddenly remembers the words that Charlie used to say:

> *When there's no explanation for the death, always ask,* **cui bono**, *who stands to gain.* [p. 22]

The phrase is composed of two words in the dative case, an interrogative pronoun *cui* (from 'qui, quae, quod') and a neuter noun *bono* (from 'bonum'); thus, the closest literal translation, rather awkward and not completely correct, is something like "for whose goodness").

The next couple of quotations are related to Lassiter's injury in a football game and a photograph of that particular moment, blown up and framed, given to him by Riggs on the day he retired from the game. Here is the exchange explaining the reasoning behind the gesture:

> "You want me to remember the pain so I don't miss the game so much."
>
> "No, you'll do that without any prompting. As Cicero said, ***Cui placet obliviscitur, cui olet meminit***. We forget our pleasures, we remember our sufferings."
>
> ...
>
> "I want you to examine the consequences of your actions before you act. ***Respice finem*** ["consider the end"]. You have a tendency to ..."
>
> "Break the china."
>
> "Precisely. And usually your own." [pp. 26-27]

What needs to be clarified about the first reference (see the entry on Wolfe for more information on Cicero) is that the two clauses constituting the sentence have been switched around in the translation offered by Riggs (Levine). The second reference has been notably used by Russian writer Leo Tolstoy (1828–1910) in his novella "The Death of Ivan Ilyich" (1886): the expression, in its Latin version, is stitched by the titular protagonist onto his luggage to keep reminding him about mortality. This particular reference may imply that Riggs, in addition to being a Latin aficionado, is also a very well-read person.

While the two friends discuss the case in detail, there are circumstances triggering two more Latin quotations:

> Charlie shook his head. "Whatever happened to the concept '***de mortuis nihil nisi bonum***' [literally: "nothing about a dead person unless it is good"]?

"Damned if I know."

"Speak kindly of the dead," Charlie answered. [p. 40]

And how about this little ditty, 'Seek the truth,' or however the hell you say it."

"***Quaere verum***," he instructed me. "And you're the lad who told me that isn't the lawyer's job." [p. 41; the same Latin phrase also appears on p. 208]

Another line worth quoting here (a sentence including two present participles playing the role of nouns, both in the nominative plural form) is Charlie's remark regarding love, which is expressed in a scene where both Jake and he catch Gina in an amorous situation with Rick Gondolier, a guy handling her husband's gambling business:

"Jake, you're not involved with that woman again, are you?"

That woman sounded like a communicable disease. I didn't answer him.

Charlie sighed. "***Amantes sunt amentes***. Lovers are such lunatics." [p. 66]

While *Quaere verum* is a quotation obtained from Horace's *Epistles*, *Amantes sunt amentes* is an aphorism cited in William Shakespeare's comedy *A Midsummer Night's Dream*.

In the next scene, where Vergil's *Aeneid* gets to be quoted, Jake and Charlie are joined by Granny Lassiter, to whom the two gentlemen pay a visit and by whom they are treated to her own brew and kibitz. The topic of their conversation is love again, or, rather, Jake's unwelcome relationship with Gina:

Charlie patted his lips with a dish towel Granny used for a napkin. "As Virgil asked, '***Quis fallere possit amantem?***' Who can deceive a lover?"

"Easy," I answered. "The lover's lover."

"Ah, the cynic in you speaks."

"The voice of experience," I said.

"Just so you haven't taken up with that cheerleader again," Granny said, sipping at her drink. "Son, that girl was nothing but trouble." [p. 110]

The famous sentence quoted above comes from the *Aeneid* by Vergil (see the entry on Lewis), Book IV, line 296, where it is used as a rhetorical question in the form of aposiopesis (a device consisting in a sudden breaking off in speech) in order to comment on Dido's premonition, her ability to subconsciously sense Aeneas's deceit as he is secretly making preparations to leave her.

Two pages later, Charlie quotes another great poet, Publius Ovidius Naso, commonly known as Ovid (see the entry on Adams), but the words (from *Metamorphoses*) constitute the Latin equivalent of an arrogant or narcissistic statement by Jake's opponent, Nicky, who made the comment about his own grandeur and immunity. Jake quotes Nicky: "The gods make their own rules." And Charlie offers the translation: "***Sunt superis sua iura.***" [p. 112]

There are a lot of other significant Latin quotations in *Mortal Sin*. To save space, I am listing them outside of their context, with their English translations and the page numbers:

Vincit veritas ("Truth wins out." p. 29);

bona fide ('genuine/real, p. 33);

alma mater ('nourishing mother,' p. 62);

Non semper ea sunt quae videntur ("Things are seldom what they seem." pp. 63, 300);

ergo ('therefore,'p. 92);

locus delicti ('crime scene,' pp. 101, 177);

alibi ('elsewhere,' p. 108);

non sequitur ('it does not follow,' p. 127);

in flagrante delicto ('in the act of wrongdoing,' p. 154);

corpus delicti ('the dead body of the victim,' p. 177);

post facto ('after the fact,' p. 177);

dramatis personae ('list of characters,' p. 177);

Deo volente ('God willing,' p. 177);

doctus cum libro ('book smart,' p. 178);

quid pro quo ('one thing for another,' p. 194);

Sapiens nihil affirmat quod non probat ("A wise man states as true nothing he cannot prove." p. 265);

Quod avertat Deus! ('What God keeps off!' p. 300);

de minimis ('too trivial/minor,' p. 300).

At least two of the items on the list deserve some additional information regarding their genesis. The axiom *Non semper ea sunt quae videntur* is attributed to Phaedrus (full name: Gaius Julius Phaedrus; c. 15 B.C.–c. 50 A.D.), a Roman fabulist born in Macedonia, who used it in Book IV, fable 2, line 5.1; and the maxim *Sapiens nihil affirmat quod non probat* appeared in the paper Guglielmo Carchedi (born in 1938), Professor at Amsterdam University and an author of several works on economics, wrote in his response to Italian professor Ernesto Screpanti's critique of his Karl Marx's transformation procedure.

Some of the other quotations deserve special attention due to the grammatical forms they consist of. While the first quotation on the list is a good example of a Latin sentence where the subject follows the verb/predicate rather than the other way around (quite a common practice), there are a couple of more items there worth addressing. For the list includes an example of the ablative of means – *bona fide* (literally meaning 'in good faith,' with the preposition implied), a sample of the 'deponent verb' in the Present Indicative Tense, third person singular – *sequitur* (from *sequor sequi* – 'to follow') and two interesting cases of the present participle, both in the ablative singular case – *volente* (from the irregular verb *volo velle* – 'to wish/want') and *flagrante* (from the first-conjugation verb *flagro flagrare* – 'to blaze/burn/glow/flame').

Also brimming with Latin references is *Fool Me Twice* (1996), another legal thriller by Levine featuring Jake Lassiter in the role of narrator/protagonist. While Granny Lassiter and Doc Charlie Riggs are two more characters that tie this novel with *Mortal Sin*, another interesting detail that the two books have in common is Jake's affair with a married woman or, rather, sleeping with his ex-girlfriend (here it is Josephina Jovita "Jo Jo" Baroso) who is now married, which fact, again, becomes the reason for all his serious problems. Another significant character is Kip or Kippers (real name: Sylvester Houston Conklin), Jake's half-nephew, a movie buff, currently taken care of by Jake.

The first two Latin quotations appear in a scene where Charlie (a retired coroner) is eager to tell Jake and Granny one of his stories (this one about two rival biologists and poisonous nasal spray used by one of them as a result of his professional jealousy), and the other two are rather reluctant to listen to it. However, finally, Riggs gets his chance and, in fact, starts with quoting Horace and concludes with a phrase regarding God:

"C'mon, Charlie, I was only kidding. What's your story?"

"Charlie shot me a look over his shoulder. "The moral might have been summed up by Horace when he wrote '*Ira furor brevis est.*'"

Horace had such a way with words," I agreed.

"'Anger is brief madness,'" Charlie translated. [p. 36]

"Did it kill the rival?"

"***Dei gratia***, by the grace of God, no. The chemical in the nasal spray changed the properties of the beta-propiolactone. Stung like the devil but didn't cause permanent damage." [p. 37]

The first of the two references comes from *The Odes* of Horace (see the entry on Wolfe), and its complete version, *Ira furor brevis est, animum rege: qui nisi paret imperat*, means "Anger is a brief madness: control your temper, which commands unless it obeys." The second one is an expression that sometimes accompanies royal titles.

When Jake finds a dead body of a man (Kyle Hornback) in his room, he is interrogated by the police, and, at the end of the scene, Charlie arrives and utters two sentences using Latin, one an exclamation and one a question:

"***Deus miseratur!***" Charlie Riggs proclaimed. "Now where's the ***corpus delicti?***" [p. 70]

While the latter phrase is well known and has been already translated in this entry, the former Latin quotation, most likely misspelled because what is meant here is probably the subjunctive form of the second conjugation verb (in its deponent version) *misereor misereri*, correctly spelled *misereatur*, which, together with *Deus*, means "May God be merciful" or, simply, "God be merciful" (Psalm 67 from the biblical Book of Psalms).

14. Paul LEVINE (1948–)

The next Latin quotation appears in a court scene as it is thrown in by Judge T. Bone Coleridge at the trial of Kip. The boy is accused of vandalism (illegal painting) that was triggered by the unannounced cancellation of the show of *Casablanca* after he took a bus to Miami just to see the film.

> "... and while I may not read everything in the law books," he continued, gesturing to a shelf of pristine copies of the *Southern Reporter*, "Ah believe there are only three possible pleas—guilty, not guilty, and **nolo con-ten-dere** ["I do not wish to contest") ..." [p. 74]

Since the literal translation of the clause *nolo contendere* may not be clear, it is appropriate to add that the legal interpretation of the clause is a plea by which the defendant accepts conviction without, however, admitting his guilt.

During the recess, Jake calls Riggs to find out about the autopsy report on Kyle Hornback and gets a response partially in Latin:

> "Charlie, please!"
>
> "All right, all right. **Vincit qui patitur.** He who is patient prevails. Hornback's blood was loaded with barbiturates." [p. 75]

The reference happens to be the motto of Berea College, which was taken from the family seal of Reverend John A. R. Rogers, whose ancestor, John Rogers, was the first Christian martyr to be burned alive during the persecutions of the sixteenth century. A translation somewhat better than the one provided by Riggs is "He who suffers conquers," as *patitur* is the Present Tense, third person singular of the deponent verb (passive in form, active in meaning) *patior pati passus sum* ('to suffer/undergo' or 'experience'). The adjective 'patient,' used in Charlie's translation, is, however, an apt English derivative from the present participle form of the verb (*patiens patientis*), because one of its meanings can be 'capable of enduring.'

Two more quotations are related to the same trial. The first passage reveals Jake's thoughts about the defender; the second one is used by Jake in his narrative part relating his exchange with the judge:

> Besides, Kornblum had done the job. I wouldn't have to pay him for his services, but I would defend him **gratis** ['free of charge'] on his pending DUI charge.
>
> ...

"Not exactly, Your Honor. The deprivation of the movie unleashed his anger at earlier abandonments."

"Well, we can't have him painting up the town every time they change the double feature at the mall, can we?"

It is difficult to respond to a complete ***non sequitur*** [translated earlier], so I didn't try. [p. 80]

Among the other Latin references found in *Fool Me Twice*, at least two are worth quoting without their context, even though they have been already presented in the discussion of *Mortal Sin*: **Non semper ea sunt quae videntur** ("Things are seldom what they seem," p. 39) and **Cui bono** ("Who stands to gain?" p. 64, 237).

Levine's novel *Bum Deal* (2018) is also rich in Latin quotations. While Jake is still the main character/narrator, two other lawyers, Steve Solomon and Victoria Lord, also play important roles in the unusual case of alleged uxoricide, where the defendant happens to be Victoria's former boyfriend. Jake stays on friendly terms with Steve and Victoria and is even invited to their upcoming wedding despite the fact that he and the engaged couple end up being opponents in the case.

The first Latin word is used by Judge Melvia Duckworth in a conversation with Jake about the case:

> "One **caveat** ['warning'], soldier. Should you want out, you gotta ask before an indictment is handed up. If you're walking point, I won't have you throwing down your rifle and jumping into the bushes just as you're about to engage the enemy." [p. 40]

While the usual translation of *caveat* is 'warning,' the literal translation of the second-conjugation verb *caveo cavēre* ('to take care that …'), here in the third person singular active subjunctive form, is 'let him/her take care/make sure that' or, somewhat better, 'let him/her beware.'

The next quotation depicts Jake's opinion about Phil Flury, a lawyer from the DA's office that Jake does not like. The sentence follows Jake's (accepted) apology for poking the other man in the chest:

> He'd never done any manual labor, and I doubted he could bench-press a single volume of **Corpus Juris Secundum** [*Second Body of the Law*], the ancient legal encyclopedia. [p. 47]

14. Paul LEVINE (1948–)

The defendant, Clark Calvert, is a well-educated and tremendously intelligent man, but also an arrogant narcissist (not guilty, after all), which shows while he is being interrogated by Jake:

> "You could have said 'sensual needs.' Or 'sexual needs.' But you used the word *carnal*. You're a physician, and you drop **Latin** words like a butterfingered receiver with the football. My old pal Doc Charlie Riggs taught me a little of that ancient language. *Carnal* come from the **Latin** word meaning 'flesh' or 'meat,' and it's related to the word *carnage*, which relates to murder and slaughter. So maybe your subconscious chose that word, and you were really saying that Sofia filled your murderous needs."

> He barked a little laugh. "Bravo, Counselor! You've combined your rudimentary knowledge of **Latin** with your slipshod knowledge of Freud. And eureka! You've caught me. I confess. ***Nolo contendere!*** [a clause translated and explained earlier in this entry]" [p. 90]

In the next passage, Calvert, when asked about his relationship with his wife, Sofia (apparently missing; by the police suspected to be murdered), keeps revealing his unusual traits:

> "That might have scared away most men."

> "Do you think I fit into that category? 'Most men.' Or would you find me more **sui generis** ['one of a kind' or 'unique']?" [p. 97]

The next scene is an unexpected appearance of Señor Pepe Suarez, an arrogant millionaire having State Attorney Raymond Pincher in his pocket, at Jake's office:

> "Your friends served me with this shit," he said, meaning Solomon and Lord.

> I examined the document. A subpoena **duces tecum** [literally: 'you will bring with you'] requiring Suarez to appear at trial and bring documents related to a trust he had formed for Sofia. [p. 212]

When Jake is sharing his thought regarding his tactics at the trial with the reader, he uses another Latin phrase:

I needed to plant in the jurors' minds the idea that Calvert was getting a lap dance while his wife's limbs were going into **rigor mortis** ['stiffness of death'] in the trunk of the Ferrari. [p. 215]

A couple of other phrases are used during a meeting before the trial in the judge's chamber with the following participants: Judge Gridley, defenders Victoria Lord and Steve Solomon and prosecutor Jake Lassiter.

"The defense has filed three motions **in limine** [literally: 'at the threshold,' meaning: 'at the beginning']," Judge Gridley said. "First one seeks to preclude Dr. Harold Freudenstein from testifying to certain matters on grounds of doctor-patient privilege." [p. 234]

The other Latin expressions from *Bum Deal* worth quoting here but not necessarily in their context include *flexor digitorum longus* (p. 178), the name of a muscle in a foot; *Et tu, Brute?* (p. 269), a quotation from Shakespeare's *Julius Caesar* which here illustrates Jake's reaction to one of the court testimonies; and 'a **prima facie** case' (p. 284), literally: 'a case based on first impression,' better: 'the establishment of a legally required rebuttable presumption.'

The extent of Paul Levine's incorporation of Latin expressions in his fiction is overwhelming. If all of them were discussed in this publication, there would be no need to reach for any other books by any other authors; they would simply be sufficient to fill out the volume. There are two rather obvious reasons for this kind of Latin "feast" in Levine's prose. One is the genre of his novels, legal thriller; the other one is his educational background, which, in fact, leads to two more Latin expressions. For, while the motto of the Pennsylvania State University is expressed in English only, "Making Life Better," Levine's postgraduate alma mater, the University of Miami, offers two things in Latin: its motto, *Magna est veritas* ("Great is the truth"), and the degree that Levine earned there, *Juris Doctor* ('the doctor of law'), the highest law degree in the United States.

15. Elizabeth GEORGE (1949–)

Born on February 26, 1949, in Warren, Ohio, Susan Elizabeth George was educated at the University of California, Riverside. She is a novelist specializing, just like Martha Grimes, in mysteries set in the United Kingdom, and her recurrent protagonist is Scotland Yard Inspector Thomas Lynley. Her first novel, *A Great Deliverance*, was published in 1988 and was followed by nearly twenty more books of the Lynley series—including *Payment in Blood* (1989), *Well-Schooled in Murder* (1990), *For the Sake of Elena* (1992), *Playing for the Ashes* (1993), *Deception of His Mind* (1997), *In Pursuit of the Proper Sinner* (1999), *A Traitor to Memory* (2001), *A Place of Hiding* (2003), *With No One as Witness* (2005), *What Came Before He Shot Her* (2006), *Careless in Red* (2008), *This Body of Death* (2010), *Just One Evil Act* (2013) and *The Punishment She Deserves* (2018)—and several other novels, such as *The Evidence Exposed* (2001), *I, Richard* (2002) and *The Edge of Nowhere* (2012). She is a winner of the Agatha Award (1988) and the Anthony Award (1989)—both for Best First Novel; Grand Prix de Littérature Policière in the International Category (for the same book, 1990) and Audie Award for Mystery (*The Punishment She Deserves*, 2019). The first eleven Lynley books were adapted by the BBC into a series entitled *The Inspector Lynley Mysteries* (2001-2008), with Nathaniel Parker and Sharon Small portraying the detective and his assistant, Barbara Havers, respectively.

Latin references have been discovered in two of George's novels, *Well-Schooled in Murder* ([1990] 1991) and *A Traitor to Memory*. The former follows Inspector Lynley and Sergeant Barbara Havers as they investigate the murder of Matthew (Mattie) Whateley, a thirteen-year-old student of Bredgar Chambers, a fictional, relatively prestigious private school in West Sussex. The boy's naked body, revealing evidence of tortures, was found near a cemetery during a weekend which he was supposed to spend with a classmate's family.

The first two references, both rather minor and both appearing early in the story, are **postmortem** ('after-death,' p. 58), an expression found in the narrator's paragraph explaining the feelings of Mattie's parents, Kevin and Patsy, and ***pater*** ('father,' p. 69), a word uttered by Havers, sarcastically expressing her feelings about the curriculum and snobbery of the institution, when she finds out about the prospects of seeing the school.

The word 'prospectus,' referring in the book to a printed document that advertises the school, directly derived, or "borrowed," from the fourth-declension masculine Latin noun *prospectus prospectūs* ('outlook/view/prospect'), is used by the narrator in two different places. It appears for the first time in a short and general, but rather informative, passage presented below. The context of its second appearance (on pp. 117-118), which is not presented here, is the description of the dorm room of Brian Byrne, the student who is responsible for all the evil and whose estranged father, Giles, is the most influential member of the Board of Governors (he was also the one who sponsored Mattie).

> The school's **prospectus** might well give lip service to an egalitarian approach to education. The reality was much different. [p. 89]

The next two references, both offering complete Latin sentences, are tied to the character of Chas Quilter, the senior prefect of the school indirectly but deeply involved in Matt's death. The first of the two references appears for the first time on p. 218 (in an exchange between Colonel Bonnamy and his daughter, Jean, whose hospitable house was frequently visited by Matt). Lockwood, mentioned in the first of the two excerpts, is the name of the Headmaster.

> When asked to do so, Chas took a seat at the table himself, a chair next to Lockwood. It was as if by choice of seating, battle lines had been drawn, with the Headmaster and his senior prefect on one side of the conflict, and Lynley and Havers on the other. Loyalty to school, Lynley thought and readied himself to see whether Chas would also show loyalty to the school's motto. ***Honor sit et baculum et ferula*** ["Let honor be both staff and rod"]. The next few minutes would tell the tale. [pp. 289-290]

> He remembered a **Latin** phrase that had been one of many he had been forced to memorise as a fourth form student. ***Nam tua res agitur, paries cum proximus ardet.***

> Alone, he whispered the translation into the listening room. "'For it is your business, when the wall door catches fire.'" [pp. 291-292]

The second of the two references, which can be somewhat better translated as "You should be concerned when your neighbor's wall is on fire," comes from Horace (see the entry on Wolfe).

The last reference is also related, though indirectly, to Chas and his multiple sins and problems. It appears in a conversation between Lynley and Simon St. James, Lynley's classmate at Eton and now a famous forensics expert, following their discovery of Chas's dead body with a rope around his neck.

15. Elizabeth GEORGE (1949–)

Coincidentally, it was St. James's wife, Deborah, who found Matt's body (in the same location) at the beginning of the book.

> When they were in the car heading back to West Sussex, St. James broke into Lynley's thoughts. "What is it, Tommy? You're not thinking it's not a suicide, are you?"
>
> "No. Chas Quilter took his own life. As far as he could see, it was either kill himself or tell the truth. There was nothing else for it. Death seemed the better alternative to him." Lightly, Lynley struck the steering wheel with his fist. "It says it right on the wall of that miserable chapel. I read it. Damn it all, I *read* it, St. James."
>
> "What?"
>
> "***Per mortes eorum vivimus.*** Through their deaths we live. The school's blasted memorial to its old boys who died in war. And he bought into it, damn him." [p. 376]

One more Latin reference that has been found in the book (on p. 203), **Quid pro quo**, but ignored until this point, also appears in the next novel by George, and it is about to be discussed in its context there.

While most of the Latin quotations in *Well-Schooled in Murder* refer in one way or another to Bredgar Chambers, the school that the murder victim attended, it is surprising and rather disappointing that the protagonist, Detective Inspector Thomas Lynley, who himself is an alumnus of Eton College, an independent boarding school famous especially for its classical studies program, does not contribute any material in support of the thesis of this project.

Two Latin references, both popular phrases used in several languages, have been encountered in *A Traitor to Memory* ([2001] 2009), another mystery by George. Inspector Lynley and his partners, Barbara Havers and Winston Nkata, investigate the murder of Eugenie Davies, an elderly woman who gets run over on a quiet street in London. As it turns out, the case seems to be related to a crime that took place over twenty years ago and was conducted by a policeman who is now Superintendent Malcolm Webberly.

The first Latin reference was found in the passage relating a telephone conversation between Richard Davies, Eugenie's husband, and their son, Gideon. Gideon is the narrator of the chapter, and psychologist Dr. Rose is one of the people they refer to in their long exchange.

"What happened?" I asked.

"I won't discuss this."

"It's why Mother left us, isn't it?"

"I've told you—"

"Nothing. You've told me *nothing*. If you're so intent on helping me, why won't you help me with this?"

"Because *this* has sod all to do with your problem. But digging it all up, dissecting every nuance, and dwelling on them ***ad infinitum*** ['forever/endlessly'] are brilliant ways to side-step the real issues, Gideon."

"I'm going at this the only way I can."

"Bollocks. You're following her dance steps like a nancy boy."

"That's bloody unfair."

"Unfair is being asked to stand one side and watch your son throw his life away. Unfair is having lived solely for that son's benefit for a quarter of a century so that he can become the musician he wishes to be, only to have him fall to pieces the first time he has a setback." [p. 201]

Later in the book, Richard and Gideon, both being accomplished musicians, become the inevitable topic of a conversation between Lynley and Havers as the two law enforcers speculate about a possible motive of the murder. The second reference comes up in a paragraph presenting Havers's opinion on the matter:

"So what if we've had been looking at it wrong?" Havers asked.

"In what way?"

"I accept that Richard Davies wants Gideon to play again. If he had an issue with his playing—like jealousy or something, like his kid being more of a success than he is and how can he handle that—then he probably would have done something a long time ago to stop him. But from what we know, the kid's been playing since he was just out of nappies. So what if Eugenie was going to meet Gideon in order to *stop* him ever playing again?"

"Why would she do that?"

"What about **quid pro quo** ['one thing for another'] to Richard? If their marriage ended because of something he'd done—" [p. 617]

A holder of an honorary doctorate in humane letters from California State University, Fullerton (2004), and an honorary Master's degree in Fine Arts from the Northwestern Institute of Literary Arts (2010), Elizabeth George is unquestionably one of the foremost crime fiction writers of her generation. Her novels are much more than pure mysteries as, in addition to spinning an intricate puzzle, they offer a rich social background for all of the events, as well as complex, imaginative and psychologically plausible relationships between the characters, both primary and secondary. Her genuine talent and evident erudition are further enhanced by her inclination to embellish her prose with carefully selected Latin references, including both popular expressions and rare quotations. The Latin motto of her alma mater, the University of California, Riverside, is *Fiat Lux* ("Let there be Light"), and that of California State University, Fullerton, from which she received her honorary doctorate, is *Vox, Veritas, Vita* ("Voice, Truth, Life"), the former offering an example of a semi-deponent verb, *fio fieri factus sum* ('to become/be made'), in the Present Subjunctive Tense, and the latter being a nice example of alliteration.

16. Scott TUROW (1949–)

Scott Frederick Turow was born on April 12, 1949, in Chicago, Illinois. After graduating from Amherst College in 1970, he studied writing for two years at Stanford University and then attended Harvard Law School. He has been an assistant U.S. attorney in Chicago and a partner in the law firm of Sonnenschein, Nath & Rosenthal. His first novel, *Presumed Innocent* (1987), was a major bestseller, and was followed by such successful works of fiction as *The Burden of Proof* (1990), *Pleading Guilty* (1993), *The Laws of Our Fathers* (1996), *Personal Injuries* (1999), *Reversible Errors* (2002), *Ordinary Heroes* (2005), *Identical* (2013), *Testimony* (2017) and *The Last Trial* (2020). His major nonfiction books are *One L* (1977) and *Ultimate Punishment: A Lawyer's Reflections on Dealing with the Death Penalty* (2003).

While several novels by Turow have been turned into either a TV series or a TV movie—e.g., *The Burden of Proof* (1992; starring Hector Elizondo, Brian Dennehy and Mel Harris) and *Pleading Guilty* (2010; featuring Mädchen Amick, Jason Isaacs and Isabelle Fuhrman), the only feature film based on his work is Alan J. Pakula's *Presumed Innocent* (1990; starring Harrison Ford, Brian Dennehy, Raul Julia and Bonnie Bedelia).

The protagonist of Turow's second novel, *The Burden of Proof* (1990), is Alejandro "Sandy" Stern, a defense lawyer who, while dealing with the trauma caused by his wife's suicide, is looking for distraction through representing in court his brother-in-law, Dixon Hartnell, an immensely rich businessman investigated by a federal grand jury. One of the two Latin references found in this book appears first in a conversation between Sandy and Dixon:

"We must answer certain questions at the threshold, Dixon. What are they investigating? Who is it they seek to prosecute? Is it, in particular, you?"

"Do you think this thing's about me?"

"Probably," said Stern evenly.

Dixon did not flinch, but he took his cigar from his mouth and very carefully removed the ash. He finally made a sound, quiet and ruminative.

"This is a **subpoena *duces tecum*** ['a writ ordering a person to appear in court with relevant documents'], Dixon—a request for records.

Ordinarily, the government would not send two agents to serve it. The prosecutors were attempting to deliver a message. [pp. 37-38]

The same legal term is used once again, much further in the book but in reference to the same documents, by Sonny Klonsky, another lawyer, in an exchange with Sandy:

"I think this is fair, Sandy," said Sonny. "I really do. The fact that you have the safe just isn't privileged. All we want is the safe and to know that we have everything that was in it. We'd be entitled to get the thing if he'd left it at MD, where it belonged. We can't allow someone to avoid a **subpoena** *duces tecum* by conveying what we want to his lawyer." [pp. 398-399]

The second Latin reference, being another legal phrase, comes up in a suspenseful scene after the documents are obtained by Sandy with the help of a crook named Remo. They remove the documents from the safe in the house owned by Dixon and Sandy's sister and, when still there, they sense that someone is approaching:

"Hide," said Stern.

"Hide?" asked Remo. "What for?" An eyebrow lowered. "You mean this ain't really your sister's?"

"Of course it is. But I prefer not to be apprehended in this silly exercise."

"I been caught," said Remo. "Lots. I don't never hide. Guys get shot like that. Just siddown. Be quiet."

...

Remo was right, Stern thought. His own reactions were juvenile. Particularly if it was the houseman or the driver, there would be real danger in some effort to avoid him. But Stern's skin still crawled. Dixon would never let him live this down. He would ridicule, threaten—whatever advantage he could wring from having caught Stern *in flagrante* burglary ['in the act of wrongdoing'] would be utilized repeatedly. Stern crept into the carpeted corridor, stepping forward with breathtaking precision, like a pantomime character. [p. 415]

16. Scott TUROW (1949–)

Turow's legal thriller *The Laws of Our Fathers* (1996) is tied with *The Burden of Proof* by means of the character of Sonia "Sonny" Klonsky, who, in addition to taking over the narration of the book, presides over the trial of Nile Eddgar (a probation officer), accused of murdering his mother. The only Latin reference discovered in the book appears in a court scene where Judge Klonsky is addressing Homicide supervisor Tommy Molto. The Latin sentence is translated by the writer/narrator:

> "Judge, the defense had this information," says Tommy. "They had the statements of the witnesses. Our theory is obvious."
>
> The book on Tommy is that he cannot stand down when he should not bother firing, and I lose my patience with him now.
>
> "Look, Mr. Molto, are you suggesting that the defendant would find it helpful to try to pick a jury on the same day the state's theory of the case is detailed on the front page of the *Tribune*?" Molto is mocked by another rollicking burst of spectator laughter, ringing loudest from the press section. "***Res ipsa loquitur***, Mr. Motto. Remember that phrase from law school? The thing speaks for itself. Doesn't it? Again, I'm sure it wasn't you. But you should remind everyone on your side what their obligations are and let them know that if there's a repetition, there will be a hearing." [p. 52]

It is worth pointing out that the legal doctrine quoted in the last excerpt dates back to 1863, when it was applied by the court to an English tort case, Byrne versus Boadle, ruling that it was not necessary for the plaintiff to come up with direct evidence of the defendant's crime (who breached his duty while being responsible for the barrel).

Set, just like Turow's most books, in the fictional Midwestern Kindle County, Illinois, *Personal Injuries* (1999) is an enormously complex novel expertly tackling the problem of legal corruption. It is narrated by attorney George Mason, but the two protagonists (who, unexpectedly, end up having a romantic relationship) are Robbie Feavor, a lawyer whose successes have been accomplished by bribery, and FBI agent Evon Miller, who is assigned to supervise him in the details of a big sting he is forced to participate in order for his crimes to be forgiven. Out of many other characters that crowd the story, two—Judge Magda Medzyk, a woman personally engaged in the case, and Alf Klecker, an electronics expert—are also mentioned in the following excerpt, where the only Latin reference has been found.

Robbie was in and out of Medzyk's chambers in ten minutes. He said he'd spent most of the time waiting for her to get off the bench. Magda had made her law clerk stand in the room as a witness, which had proved a mistake, because she had been unable to keep herself from crying near the end.

"She's pretty Catholic," said Robbie to Evon on the way out. "She turned herself in to the Supreme Court Judicial Disciplinary Committee." He had suggested nails through the palms might have saved her time, which was when she's asked him to leave.

They emerged from the courthouse with Klecker a few steps ahead. Evon was supposed to cover Robbie from the rear, but he was still smarting from the visit. What he felt worst about, he said, was that Magda had seemed resigned to the world of locked closets and prim restraints where she's been cloistered when they'd first taken up. "She's at less than zero now" was how he put it. Whatever he'd given her had been jettisoned as she'd yielded again to the *in terrorem* ['into/about fear'] lectures she'd practiced on herself over a lifetime, [pp. 360-361]

Inducted as a Laureate of The Lincoln Academy of Illinois, Turow was recognized with the Order of Lincoln by the Governor of Illinois in 2000; he also received the Robert F. Kennedy Center for Justice and Human Rights 2003 Book Award. These distinctions prove that Scott Turow is not only an excellent lawyer and a first-rate novelist, but also a sensitive person deeply involved in the matters of mankind. The Latin references encountered in his prose, furthermore, offer a nice set of examples of how Latin phraseology is still dominating the modern English language, at least in the field of law and law enforcement.

The Latin mottos of the educational institutions attended by Turow are *Terras Irradient* ("Let them enlighten the lands")—Amherst College, *Semper virens* ("Ever flourishing")— Stanford University, and *Veritas* ("Truth")—Harvard.

17. Joseph FINDER (1958–)

Born on October 6, 1958, in Chicago, Illinois, Joseph Finder spent several years of his childhood in Asia. He was educated at Yale University, graduating *summa cum laude* and Phi Beta Kappa, and Harvard, where he received his master's degree. He started his writing career in 1990. He is best known for his Nick Heller series, consisting of five novels including *Vanished* (2010) and *Guilty Minds* (2016). His other major works, all in the thriller genre, include *The Moscow Club* (1991), *Extraordinary Powers* (1994), *High Crimes* (1998), *Paranoia* (2004), *Killer Instinct* (2006), *Suspicion* (2014) and *The Fixer* (2015).

Out of Finder's overall number of novels (seventeen), three have been filmed so far, all under the same title—two as theatrical productions: *High Crimes* (2002), directed by Carl Franklin and starring Jim Caviezel, Morgan Freeman and Ashley Judd; and *Paranoia* (2013), directed by Robert Luketic and featuring Liam Hemsworth, Gary Oldman, Harrison Ford and Amber Heard; and one as a TV movie: *Suspicion* (2018), directed by Brad Anderson and starring Jeri Ryan and Sofia Bryant.

There are several Latin quotations in *Guilty Minds* (2016), Finder's excellent thriller set in Washington, D.C., dealing with corruption, slander and manipulation among politicians and retired law enforcement officers. The main character (and the narrator), Nick Heller, is a private investigator from Boston brought to the capital city to clear the name of the chief of justice of the Supreme Court, Jeremiah Claflin. He looks for help wherever he can find it. One of the men he has a meeting with is Senator Patrick Brennan, a man he has previously worked for. It is the senator who reveals his weakness for Latin and provides most of the following quotations:

> He glugged a couple of fingers of bourbon into two glasses and handed one to me. Then he clinked his glass against mine. "In the words of Horace, **fecundi calices quem non fecere disertum?**" He paused, and then translated. "Whom have flowing cups not made eloquent?" [p. 71]

> He put his palms like a priest conferring a benediction. "**Sigillum confessionis**," he said. "The seal of the confessional." [p. 72]

> "Jerry Claflin is a deeply honorable man," Brennan went on. "Perhaps a bit of a stickler, to my taste. But a brilliant jurist. You know, I'm sure, about his contribution to **mens rea** law."

"***Mens rea*?** I forgot ..."

"Criminal intent. Literally, 'guilty mind.'"

"Right."

"It matters whether the defendant intended to commit the crime. What the defendant meant to do. Anyway, Jerry will always be celebrated for clarifying the vexed 'conditional intent' problem of ***mens rea***."

...

"But this story is just scurrilous, and it will damage him. As Virgil tells us in *The Aeneid*, ***fama, malum qua non aliud velocius ullum***. There is no evil swifter than a rumor."

...

"So who benefits from the destruction of Jeremiah Claflin's career?"

"Ah. That old shopworn phrase ***cui bono***—who benefits?" [p. 75-76]

An impressive combination of legal, religious and literary quotations, the above excerpts include even lines by ancient Roman poets Horace (see the entry on Wolfe) and Vergil (see the entry on Lewis). The *Aeneid* reference comes from Book IV, line 174, where *Fama* is capitalized as it refers to *Dame Gossip* or *Rumor*, a personified phenomenon (with physical appearance described in detail) who in that particular passage swiftly carries the news about Dido and Aeneas's love affair all the way to African chieftain Iarbas, Dido's rejected suitor now determined to start a war against Carthage.

The next passage refers to another man approached by Nick for help, Frank Montello, his information broker. However, this time the Latin phrase is a part of the protagonist/narrator's description of the other man's modus operandi:

> Montello picked up his phone after six long rings. His voice was faint and muffled, as it always seemed to be, as if you'd just interrupted him doing something far more important than talking to you. He operated in the gray zone between law enforcement and private investigation, a place I tried not to go except ***in extremis*** ['in extreme circumstances']. [p. 107]

The last Latin quotation found in the book is the narrator's reiteration of Senator Brennan's remark concerning Jeremiah Claflin:

Claflin, Senator Brennan had said, was known for clarifying the concept of **mens rea**. Which struck me as ironic, since in Washington, pretty much everyone had a guilty mind. [p. 380]

The significance of the last passage lies in the ambiguity of the phrase *mens rea*, which also corresponds to the meaning of the book's title and, not surprisingly, to its message. Thus, we can say that the Latin language plays an important, not to say crucial, role in this remarkable novel, definitely far beyond being a stylistic embellishment.

Another interesting thing about this particular book by Finder is that in its Polish translation (2019), entitled *Z premedydacją* (meaning: literally, *With Premeditation*, or, better, *Premeditated*), Przemysław Hejmej uses two additional Latin phrases, *ad hoc* (p. 71) and *de facto* (p. 235), the exact context of which does not need to be presented here, providing, nevertheless, further examples of how Latin remains prevalent in modern fiction.

Latin references have been found in two other novels by Finder: **Mens Sana in Corpore Sano** ("A sound mind in a healthy body." p. 201) in *Vanished* (2009) and **Habemus papam** ("We have a pope." p. 270), the announcement traditionally given in the papal conclave upon the election of a new pope, in *Buried Secrets* (2011).

The motto of Finder's undergraduate alma mater, Yale, is *Lux et Veritas* ("Light and Truth"), and that of his graduate school, Harvard, is *Veritas* ("Truth"). While the concept of truth seems to be important to both of his universities, Finder himself is an outstanding author, truly talented and truly original, and, what is relevant for this book, he has not forgotten what he had learned in one of his most significant liberal arts courses, Latin. His references/quotations, found in several of his works, are exemplary and enormously enlightening.

18. Greg ILES (1960–)

Born on April 8, 1960, in Stuttgart, Germany, where his father was in charge of the U.S. Embassy Medical Clinic, Greg Iles was educated at the University of Mississippi, from which he graduated in 1983. He is a popular novelist living in Mississippi, where most of the stories of his books take place. His major novels include *Spandau Phoenix* (1993), *Black Cross* (1995), *Mortal Fear* (1997), *The Quiet Game* (1999), *24 Hours* (2000), *Dead Sleep* (2001), *Sleep No More* (2002), *The Footprints of God* (2003), *Turning Angel* (2005), *True Evil* (2006), *Third Degree* (2007), *Natchez Burning* (2014) and *Cemetery Road* (2019). In addition to writing, Iles loves music and is an accomplished guitarist performing with famous bands.

Iles's second novel, *Black Cross* (1995), is a World War II thriller, in which an American pacifist, Dr. Mark McConnell, and a fanatical Jewish killer, Jonas Stern, selected and prepared for the mission by Brigadier Smith and with blessings from Winston Churchill himself, are sent to Germany to stop the Nazis from using a new deadly weapon called Sarin. The book's only Latin reference appears in one of the crucial, and rather self-explanatory, passages of the story:

Stern actually snapped to attention.

Churchill beamed. "This is my sort of fellow, Duff. You've chosen well, I think.

"He'll do," Smith said grudgingly. "But I'm afraid we really must go. The schedule, you know."

"H-Hour," Churchill said with relish. "And right into Germany! What I wouldn't give to go with you." He stood up and vigorously shook both McConnell's and Stern's hands.

McConnell thought of something else he wanted to ask, but by then the brigadier had whisked them out of the room and along the dim corridor.

The driver of the Humber met them at the outside door.

"Follow him," Smith said. "I'll join you in a moment."

As they passed outside, McConnell looked back. They were exiting from a different door, and above it he knew he saw the words: **Pro Patria Omnia**. Now he realized what Duff Smith had said to his pilot over Loch Lochy. He had not said to head for "checkers" but *Chequers*, which was the country residence of the British prime minister. As he followed Stern back to the Lysander, McConnell wondered if Adolf Hitler knew what words were engraved above the door of that house, and what they meant.

All for the Fatherland. [p. 285]

The narrator/protagonist of Iles's novel *The Quiet Game* ([1999] 2005) is Penn Cage, a prosecuting attorney who, after his wife Sarah's death, decides to leave Houston, Texas, and return, with his four-year-old daughter Annie, to his childhood Natchez, Mississippi, where he hopes to find peace and an atmosphere conducive to his new career as a novelist. But, when still on the plane to get there, he is approached by another passenger, a woman named Kate, who, in addition to claiming to be his fan (she is having a copy of his novel in her hand), opens an old wound of his, trying to interview him about the criminal he made convicted to death years ago.

The only Latin reference found in the book appears in the first of a few paragraphs in which Cage responds to some of Kate's questions and gives her the details of the traumatic incident:

> "Arthur Lee Hanratty vowed to kill me after his arrest. He said it a dozen times on television. I took his threats the way I took them all, **cum grano salis** ['with a grain of salt']. But Hanratty meant it. Four years later, the night the Supreme Court affirmed his death sentence, my wife and I were lying in bed watching the late news. She was dozing. I was going over my opening statement for another murder trial. My boss had put a deputy outside because of the Supreme Court ruling, but I didn't think there was any danger. When I heard the first noise, I thought it was nothing. The house settling. Then I heard something else. I asked Sarah if she'd heard it. She hadn't. She told me to turn out the light and go to sleep. And I almost did."

...

> "I saw his teeth in the dark, and I knew he was smiling. I pointed my pistol at his head. He started backing through the door, using Annie as a shield. Holding her at center mass. In the dark, with shaking hands, every rational thought told me not to fire. But I had to."

...

"He was halfway through the door when I pulled the trigger. The bullet knocked him onto the patio. When I got outside, Annie was lying on the cement, covered in blood. I snatched her up even before I looked at the guy, held her up in the moonlight and ripped off her pajamas, looking for a bullet wound. She didn't make a sound. Then she screamed like a banshee. An anger scream, you know? Not pain. I knew then that she was probably okay. Hanratty ... the bullet had hit him in the eye. He was dying. And I didn't do a goddam thing to help him." [pp. 14-15]

One of the possible origins of the quoted phrase is *Naturalis Historia* by Pliny the Elder (full name Gaius Plinius Secundus; c. 23–79 A.D.), a Roman natural philosopher and a naval and army commander, in reference to the discovery of a recipe for an antidote to a poison. His exact words were *addito salis grano* ('having added a grain of salt').

Another mystery and thriller by Iles, *Sleep No More* (2002), develops its suspenseful plot from the complications in the lives of businessman John Waters and his family, triggered by a reappearance of the man's lover's soul from twenty years ago in another female's body. The first of the two Latin references that have been encountered in the book is a part of an interior description:

Entering his own space was a relief after Cole's chaotic office. When they remodeled the two-story warehouse, Waters had taken the office with the most frontage on the bluff. Now he had two massive windows that gave an unsurpassed view of the Mississippi River, and unlike Cole, he had planned his **sanctum sanctorum** ['the holy of holies,' thus, in some situations: 'a very private or secret place'] around it. He'd even added an outdoor balcony, fighting the Historical Preservation Commission all the way. [p. 136]

The second reference comes up in a passage that is much more closely related to the main theme of the novel, explaining some of the aspects of the plot:

Waters stared at the handcuffs, a shining little metaphor for his situation. He recalled Eve cuffing him to the bed at the Eola. Thinking of that made him think of Mallory, not as she was now, but when they were together. In those days, Mallory had bound him with scarves, not handcuffs. He saw himself tied to the headboard of her parents' bed, wondering if Ben Candler and his wife would come home unexpectedly and discover their princess **in flagrante delicto** ['in the act of wrongdoing']. When he thought of Ben Candler, he felt something shift deep in his mind, and he saw what Mallory had described earlier: the local politician who liked to take secret snapshots of little girls. In the dark glow of that image was born his next move in the emotional chess match he would have to play for possession of his life and family. [p. 319]

In *Turning Angel* (2005), Iles returns to his recurrent protagonist, Penn Cage, who, in this book, tries to help his friend Drew Elliott be cleared of the murder charge after a naked body of Kate Townsend—a female student of St. Stephen's Prep, the school the two men are board members of—is found by the Mississippi River. The only two Latin references have been found in the middle of the book, in two paragraphs relating narrator Cage's thoughts and feelings during his visit to the cemetery (Ellen is the name of Drew's wife):

"Appearance **versus** ['against/in contrast to'] reality," I say softly. That sounds like the title of an essay I was forced to write in high school English class.

As I stare over the gravestones at the angel's androgynous features, several faces seem to project themselves onto the white stone, slowly morphing from one into another like the faces in the classic Sinéad O'Connor video. Mia first. The angel most resembles her, with its oval face and Madonna-like serenity. Yet as I stare, Mia somehow becomes Drew—not Drew as I know him now, but as the beautiful boy he was when he scorched across the firmament at St. Stephen's more than twenty years ago. I blink my eyes and Drew becomes Ellen, and then Ellen, Kate, until I lose my sense of balance though I'm sitting in my own car on **terra firma** ['dry land']. Throwing the Saab into gear, I spin onto Cemetery Road and race toward town. But one glance in the rearview mirror tells me what I already know: the Turning Angel is watching me go. [pp. 295-296]

Praised by his readers and peers alike, Greg Iles is unquestionably one of the most original, inventive and popular thriller writers of the younger generation. The Latin references encountered in his prose—primarily nouns or noun phrases of general or legal provenance, with or without a preceding preposition—offer a welcome contribution to the proposition that the ubiquity of the ancient language in modern European languages, English in particular, cannot be denied. The Latin motto of his alma mater, the University of Mississippi, is *Pro scientia et sapientia* ("For knowledge and wisdom").

19. Ian RANKIN (1960–)

Ian James Rankin was born on April 28, 1960, in Cardenden, Fife, Scotland, United Kingdom. After graduating from the University of Edinburg (1982), he taught there for a while before he moved to London and then spent some time in France. He wrote his first novel, *The Flood*, in 1986, and his first Inspector Rebus novel, *Knots and Crosses*, a year later. His other Rebus novels, which constitute the essence and majority of his writing credits, include *Hide and Seek* (1991), *Strip Jack* (1991), *The Black Book* (1993), *Mortal Causes* (1995), *Let It Bleed* (1995), *Black and Blue* (1997, Macallan Gold Dagger for Fiction), *The Hanging Garden* (1998), *Dead Souls* (1999), *Resurrection Men* (2002, Edgar Award), *Fleshmarket Close* (2004), *Exit Music* (2007, ITV3 Crime Thriller Award) and *A Song for the Dark Times* (2020, #23 and, so far, the last Rebus novel). Rankin's nonfiction book *Rebus's Scotland Yard: A Personal Journey* (2005) won the CWA Cartier Diamond Dagger. Among his other numerous awards and honors are honorary doctorates from the University of Abertay Dundee, the University of St. Andrews, the University of Edinburg and the Open University; Palle Rosencrantz Prize (2000, Denmark), Officer of the Order of the British Empire for services to literature (2002), Whodunnit Prize (2003, Finland), Grand Prix du Roman Noir (2003, France), CWA Lifetime Achievement Award (2005, Cartier Diamond Dagger), Grand Prix de Littérature Policière (2005, France) and Deutsche Krimi Prize (2005, Germany; for *Resurrection Men*); Hawthornden Fellow (1988) and Chandler-Fulbright Award (1991); and a couple of CWA Short Story Dagger awards.

The only (so far) screen adaptations based on Rankin's works are one television series, *Rebus* (2000-2007; with John Hannah and Ken Scott portraying the titular protagonist in different seasons), and two TV movies—John McKay's *Reichenbach Falls* (2007; featuring Alec Newman, Alastair Mackenzie, Nina Sosonya and Laura Fraser) and Marc Evans's *Doors Open* (2012; starring Douglas Henshall, Stephen Fry, Kenneth Collard and Lenora Crichlow).

Latin references have been discovered in two of Rankin's novels, *Mortal Causes* ([1995] 2005) and *Resurrection Men* ([2002] 2005). Since the latter book incorporates only one reference, and it happens to be one of its two mottos, it makes sense to present it first. It is a quotation from Vergil's *Aeneid* (see the entry on Wolfe), Book I, line 207 (the information provided by the author himself): **Durate et vosmet rebus servate secundis**, which means "Endure the hardships of your present state and reserve yourselves for better things." This line, used by Aeneas himself to address his despairing men after a lot of their ships are wrecked, may have, in addition to the obvious one, a personal meaning for Rankin as a possible inside joke, since the word *rebus*, being the dative/ablative plural form of the fifth-declension noun *res rei* ('a thing/object' or 'matter/affair/circumstance') is spelled exactly the same way as the protagonist's last name. To hypothesize that the Latin origin of his name can additionally be related or alluding to the inspector's ethnicity (Polish), as Poland is the country where Latin functioned as a spoken language (one of two, to be fair) for the longest time after it had developed into Italian in its original location, and where the word 'rebus' has been used for years to refer to a special type of a graphic puzzle, may probably be going too far.

In the other novel by Rankin, *Mortal Causes*, several Latin references have been found. Set, like most of the author's works, in Edinburg, the novel follows Inspector John Rebus as he investigates the activities of a dangerous terrorist group composed of a few cooperating gangs. A short Latin phrase comes up in a dialogue between Rebus and Mr. Peter Cave, a man offering his services to the church, both men taking a walk together across the playing fields (Father Conor Leary is the person mentioned by Cave):

'Your church doesn't seem so sure.'

Cave stopped in his tracks. 'Is that what this is about? You're in Conor's congregation, isn't it? He's sent you here to ... what's the phrase? Come down heavy on me?'

'Nothing like that.'

'He's paranoid. *He* was the one who wanted me here. Now suddenly he's decided I should leave, **ipso facto** ['by that very fact/act'] I must leave. [p. 59]

Rebus's interlocutor in the next excerpt is Inspector Ken Smylie (whose brother Calumn, working undercover, would get killed later in the novel). The conversation is about Inspector Abernathy from the Special Branch:

Smylie looked up. 'He went back yesterday, caught an evening plane. Did you want to see him?'

'Not really.'

'There was nothing here for him.'

'No?'

Smylie shook his head. 'We'd know about it if there was. We're the best, we'd've spotted it before him. **QED**.'

'***Quod erat demonstarndum*** ['What was to be shown/proven'].' [p.89]

One major Latin reference appears in three different places of the book (on pp. 2, 102, 261), and, since most of the information about it, suggesting an important clue, is provided in the second one, here is the pertinent excerpt, in which Rebus talks with Caroline Rattray, a woman working for the Prosecutor's Fiscal Office:

Caroline Rattray was dressed for work, from black shoes and stockings to powder-grey wig.

'I wouldn't have recognized you,' he said.

'Should I take that as a compliment?' She gave him a big smile, and held it as she held his gaze. Then she touched his arm. 'I see you've noticed.' She looked up at the stained glass. 'The royal arms of Scotland.' Rebus looked up too. Beneath the large picture there were five smaller square windows, each showing a coat of arms. Caroline Rattray's eyes were on the central panel. Two unicorns held the shield of the red Lion Rampant. Above on a scroll were the words IN DEFENCE, and at the bottom a **Latin** inscription. Rebus read it.

'***Nemo me impune lacessit*** ["No one provokes me with impunity"].' He turned to her. 'Never my best subject.'

'You might know it better as "Wha daur meddle wi' me?". It's the motto of Scotland or, rather, the motto of Scotland's kings.' [p. 102]

Except for *annus mirabilis* ('a remarkable/auspicious year'), a phrase found in two places, on pp. 151 and 153, these are all the Latin references encountered in *Mortal Causes*. Between these and the one found in *Resurrection Men*, they constitute an interesting diversity: a quotation from an ancient Roman epic, the motto of the Royal Stuart dynasty that can be found on the reverse side of Scottish merk coins minted in the sixteenth century, a popular clause and its abbreviation used, traditionally, in published documents at the end of a mathematical proof or a philosophical argument, and two simple phrases, one—*ipso facto*—a combination of an intensive pronoun and a noun, both in the ablative singular form, and one—*annus mirabilis*—a combination of a noun and an adjective, both in the nominative singular form. Out of the last two phrases, the first one is a widely used expression frequently encountered in art, philosophy, science and law, the second one, while originally used in reference to the year 1666 in which Isaac Newton (1643 – 1727), the most accomplished English mathematician, physicist, astronomer and theologian, twice visited his hometown Woolsthorpe in order to get away from the Great Plague affecting Cambridge, is nowadays quite a popular term applied to years of major significance.

Based on the number and variety of his international accolades, Ian Rankin does not seem to be in need of anyone else praising his writing achievements. The fact that his prose is occasionally embellished with some Latin phraseology is something to admire and be grateful for, even if his charismatic protagonist does not reveal a special knack for that particular subject.

20. Dennis LEHANE (1965–)

Dennis Lehane was born on August 4, 1965, in Boston, MA, and was educated at Eckerd College in St. Petersburg, FL, and Florida International University in Miami. His first novel, *A Drink Before the War* (1994), was at the same time the first item in his best-known series featuring the relentless Kenzie-Gennaro couple of private detectives and consisting of six books, the final one being *Moonlight Mile* (2010). His Coughlin series, which started with *The Given Day*, consists of three novels written between 2008 and 2015. Out of his other works, the most famous ones are probably *Mystic River* (2001), *Shutter Island* (2003) and *Since We Fell* (2017). He is a winner of many awards, including Shamus (the Private Eye Writers of America Award), Edgar (the Edgar Allan Poe Award), WGA (the Writers Guild of America Award) and OFTA (the Online Film & Television Association Award).

Many of Lehane's works have been turned into successful screen adaptations. The most prestigious ones include Clint Eastwood's Oscar-winning *Mystic River* (2003; featuring Sean Penn, Tim Robbins, Kevin Bacon, Laurence Fishburne, Marica Gay Harden and Laura Linney); Ben Affleck's *Gone Baby Gone* (2007; starring Casey Affleck, Michelle Monaghan, Morgan Freeman and Ed Harris)—from the Kenzie-Gennaro novel of the same name (1998); Martin Scorsese's *Shutter Island* (2010; featuring Leonardo DiCaprio, Mark Ruffalo, Ben Kinsley and Max von Sydow); Michaël R. Roskam's *The Drop* (2014; starring Tom Hardy, Noomi Rapace and James Gandolfini)—from Lehne's short story "Animal Rescue;" and Ben Affleck's *Live by Night* (2016; featuring Ben Affleck, Elle Fanning and Brendan Gleeson)—from the 2012 Coughlin novel of the same title.

While Lehane is not one of the authors whose works abound in Latin quotations or references, three have been discovered in his fifth novel featuring Patrick Kenzie and Angela Gennaro, *Prayers for Rain* ([1999] 2000), primarily set, like all of them, in Boston and its area. Split as both a romantic couple and business partners at the closing of the previous novel, *Gone, Baby, Gone*, the two protagonists have a chance to get together again due to a challenging case that Patrick (the narrator) has been voluntarily working on, an unusual suicide of a young woman named Karen Nichols he has helped to get rid of a dangerous stalker. The first Latin phrase appears in the context of Angie presenting her conditions/prerequisites of her consent to join efforts. (David Wetterau is Karen's boyfriend, who was killed by a car in circumstances that were concluded by the police as unsuspicious.)

She looked up at me and her face was tender and open. "Yeah. Yeah, it does, Patrick." She shook her hand free of water and stood up on the pavement beside me. "I'll make you a deal."

"Shoot."

"If you can prove that David Wetterau's accident deserves a second look, I'll come in on the case. **Pro bono**" ['out of good will/free of charge,' literally: 'for the good']. [pp. 116-117]

The second Latin expression is a part of a paragraph revealing the narrator's thoughts about a mysterious phone-call and the extent of the danger he is facing because of the case:

My car was parked four blocks down Commonwealth, and while the rain was light, it was steady, and the mist was threatening to turn into a fog. Whoever the guy was, I decided, he'd either chosen or been sent to rattle my cage, to let me know that he knew me, and I didn't know him, and that made me vulnerable and gave him a semblance of omnipotence.

I've had my cage rattled by pros, though—wiseguys, cops, gangbangers, and in one case a pair of **bona fide** ['genuine/real,' literally: 'in good faith'] serial killers—so the days when a disembodied voice on the other end of a phone line could give me the shakes and a dry mouth were gone. Still, it did have me guessing, which may have been the point. [p. 206]

The final Latin phrase is used by Dr. Christopher Dawe, Karen's stepfather, in his conversation with Patrick and Angie about his daughter Naomi:

He pulled his hands down from his head, covered his face with them, stared at me from between the fingers again.

"Naomi," Angie said. "Switched at birth."

A nod.

"Why?"

He dropped his hands. "She had a heart condition known as **Truncus Arteriosis**. Not something anyone picked up on in the delivery room, but she was my child, I did my own exams. I discovered a murmur and ran a few more tests. In those days, **Truncus Arteriosis** was thought to be inoperable. Even now, it's often fatal. [p. 260]

Except for the last one, which, by the way, may be misspelled here (other sources spell this congenital heart defect as *Truncus Arteriosus*, using the nominative, rather than genitive, form of the second word), the Latin expressions quoted above are phrases in the ablative case, with the preposition physically present in the first one and implied in the second. It is worth pointing out that they include two words derived from the same base but used as different parts of speech: 'bono' (in the first one) being the ablative singular form of the neuter noun 'bonum,' and 'bona' being the feminine/ablative singular form (thus, it should have a macron over the 'a' to distinguish it from the nominative case) of the adjective 'bonus/bona/bonum.'

All three examples of Latin in Lehane's work are expressions adapted without spelling alterations by the English language and thus not italicized. All three are used in a casual conversation (by, admittedly, educated people), which fact illustrates the intrinsic role that some Latin phrases play not only in English, but also in many other languages in Western culture. To conclude the entry on Lehane, it is appropriate to mention the motto of his second alma mater (Eckerd College does not seem to have one). The three magic words selected by the Florida International University in Miami are *Spes, Scientia, Facultas* ("Hope, Knowledge, Opportunity").

III.
Latin in Frontier and Western Fiction

1. Emerson HOUGH (1857–1923)

Emerson Hough was born on June 28, 1857, in Newton, Iowa, the son of Joseph Bond Hough (a schoolmaster) and Elizabeth Hough. A public school teacher after high school graduation, he studied law at the University of Iowa and started a law practice in Whiteoaks, New Mexico. However, fascinated with nature, outdoor living and the West, he soon gave up law in favor of traveling and journalism. He published his first book, *The Story of the Cowboy*, in 1897, and his first novel, *The Mississippi Bubble*, in 1902. His other major works include *The Magnificent Adventure* (1916), *The Man Next Door* (1917), *The Sagebrusher* (1919), *The Covered Wagon* (1922), *North of 36* (1923) and *The Ship of Souls* (1925). President of the Midland Society of Authors in the years 1917-1918, Hough died on April 30, 1923.

Hough's possibly greatest novel, *The Covered Wagon*, reached the screen only a year after its publication. Directed by James Cruze, the film (starring J. Warren Kerrigan, Lois Wilson, Ernest Torrence, Charles Ogle and Alan Hale) is regarded as a milestone of the genre. His other important western novel, *North of 36*, was filmed twice: the silent version (1925; featuring Jack Holt, Ernest Torrence, Lois Wilson and Noah Beery) was directed by Irvin Willat; the sound version, entitled *The Texans* (1938; featuring Randolph Scott, Joan Bennett, May Robson and Walter Brennan), was directed by James Hogan. Other notable screen adaptations of Hough's works include *The Sagebrusher* (1920; starring Roy Stewart, Marguerite de la Motte, Noah Beery and Betty Brice) and *The Conquering Horde* (1931; featuring Richard Arlen, Fay Wray and Claude Gillingwater), from a novel of the same name—both directed by Edward Sloman.

Several Latin references have been discovered in *The Covered Wagon* (1922), the story of two men, Will Banion and Sam Woodhull, vying for the heart and hand of Molly Wingate, told as a theme parallel to the adventures of a group of pioneers going west. Most of the references are rather self-explanatory and appear in descriptive and narrative passages. Here are two excerpts from the beginning of the novel:

> The west-bound paused at the Missouri, as once they had paused at the Don.
>
> A voice arose, of some young man back among the wagons busy at his work, paraphrasing an **ante-bellum** ['prewar'] air:

Oh, then, Susannah,
Don't you cry for me!
I'm goin' out to Oregon,
With my banjo on my knee! [p. 16]

They now were at the edge of the law. Organized society did not exist this side of the provisional government of Oregon, devised as a **modus vivendi** ['a way of living'] during the joint occupancy of that vast region with Great Britain—an arrangement terminated not longer than two years before. [p. 18]

While the first Latin phrase is a modifier related here to the time before the Civil War, the deeper, or more specific (in this context), meaning of the phrase *modus vivendi* is 'an arrangement or agreement allowing conflicting parties to coexist peacefully, either indefinitely or until a final settlement is reached.' The word *vivendi* is an example of the gerund in the genitive case.

The next Latin phrase, or two versions thereof, appears just several pages later:

Some of the bewhiskered men who sat about him stirred, but cast their eyes toward their own captain, young Banion, whose function as their spokesman had thus been usurped by his defeated rival, Woodhull. Perhaps few of them suspected the **argumentum ad hominem**—or rather **ad feminam**—in Woodhull's speech. [p. 25]

The bold-printed phrase, indirectly used in reference to the election of Molly's father as the trail boss, one more area where Woodhull, through flattery, hopes to win his rivalry with Banion, literally meaning 'against the man/woman', really refers to 'an argument that attacks a man's/woman's motives or character rather than his/her beliefs.'

The next excerpt is a part of Banion addressing the pioneers and talking about a number of issues related to the long journey and how the participants should have prepared for it:

"No man ought to be allowed to start this caravan with less supplies, for each mouth of his wagon, than one hundred pounds of flour. One hundred and fifty or even two hundred would be much better—there is loss and shrinkage. At least half as much of bacon, twenty pounds of coffee, fifty of sugar would not be too much in my belief. About double the **pro rata** ['proportionate allocation'] of the Santa Fé caravans is little enough, and those whose transport power will let them carry more supplies ought to start full loaded, for no man can tell the actual duration of this journey, or what food may be needed before we get across. One may have to help another. [p. 28]

Figure 3.1. The jacket of the first edition of *The Covered Wagon* (1922) by Emerson Hough (D. Appleton and Company, New York, MCMXXII).

In addition to mentioning the Latin language itself (p. 162), Hough's signature novel incorporates two more Latin references that are worth quoting outside of their contexts. Here they are:

> ***de gustibus*** (a shortened version of the popular proverb *De gustibus non est disputandum*, meaning literally: "There should be no discussion about tastes," or, better: "In matters of tastes, there can be no disputes." p. 161);

> ***spolia opima*** ('rich spoils' of war, this one referring to a beautiful woman, p. 212).

The last phrase, referring to the practice of Roman generals offering spoils after killing an enemy leader, according to Livy (1.10), was originally instituted by Romulus, the first of the Roman kings, who, after defeating King Acron of Caenina in a duel, stripped him of the armor and offered it to the temple of Jupiter Feretrius.

Hough's other epic western novel, *North of 36* (1923), a captivating story about the first cattle drive from Texas to Abilene, also brims with attributes of the genre, such as Indian attack, stampede and gunfights. Three Latin references have been found in it, two of which are parts of narrative paragraphs and are thus self-explanatory:

> North of the first unbridged river—the Colorado—the advance was over a country practically new, although now subdivided into organized counties. The main thrust of the early population was from the south and lower east, so that now the farther north they got the sparser grew the infrequent settlements. All North and Northwest Texas remained ***terra incognita*** '['unknown land'] even for Texans, and no map of it ever had been made, let alone of the wild Indian Territory that lay north of it. [p. 132]

> It was no great matter to rope the two broad-horn scows together side and side, and to lay a pole platform across to receive the carts, which were run by hand. Remained the question of propulsion, and none of these knew aught of sail or pole or oars. This meant falling back on the ***vade mecum***—the horse, without which in his day the railroads and bridges might as well never have been. [p. 136]

The Latin phrase in the last paragraph literally means 'go with me,' but it really stands (not only in Latin or English) for 'a handbook or guide that is kept at hand for consultation.' *Vade* (from the third-conjugation verb *vado vadĕre* – 'to hasten/rush/go/') is an example of the present imperative singular form; *mecum* is a sample of an unusual situation in Latin where a preposition, instead of preceding a pronoun, is attached to it.

The last Latin reference in the book appears in a conversation between two characters, Cal Dalhart, the cowboy riding on point (a minor character), and Anastasie (Taisie) Lockhart, the daughter of Colonel Burleson Lockhart and owner of the Laguna del Sol range (the female protagonist). The male protagonist is Jim Nabours, the foreman of del Sol for twenty-five years.

> "I'm top rod here just now, Miss Lockhart," said he, "and I want to talk with you a little while. This is my first chance."
>
> The girl looked at him. She had been in tears. Her nerves were going. She was no longer the daring Taisie Lockhart, "***dulce ridentem … dulce loquentem***" ['smiling/laughing sweetly … talking sweetly'], like the Lalage of Horace of old, always ready to chat and to laugh.
>
> "Drive them away!" Her glance was toward the distant row of solemn black birds, advancing, hopping staring. [p. 154]

The Latin quotation requires, once again, a further explanation. Hough puts it in quotation marks because it is a part of the famous excerpt "*Dulce ridentem Lalagen amabo, dulce loquentem*" from Horace's (see the entry on Wolfe) *Odes* 1.22, meaning "I will love [my] sweetly laughing, sweetly chatting Lalage." While *Lalagen*, the direct object of the sentence, is an example of the Greek accusative (in the Latin accusative singular, we would expect the ending '-m' rather than '-n'), the two samples of the present active participle, *ridentem* and *loquentem*, are also in the accusative case as they need to match (in number, gender and case) the noun that they modify. Consequently, in Hough's excerpt, the accusative case of the two forms is incorrect as those two words are supposed to modify Miss Lockhart, who is the subject of the sentence, and thus the present participles 'laughing and 'chatting' should be used in the nominative case, i.e., *ridens* and *loquens*. But, then, they would not match the famous reference.

An extremely interesting reference to the history of ancient Rome found in the book is definitely worth quoting here as well. Again, it is a part of a narrative/descriptive paragraph:

> Perhaps two hundred miles, as nearly as they could guess at an unmapped and unfamiliar portion of their own state—a land by no means yet redeemed from savagery—still lay between them and the Red River, **the Rubicon** of that day, the northern boundary of Texas. [p. 165]

The reason why the two rivers, one in North America and one in ancient Rome, are mentioned by the author side by side is their symbolic meaning as the crossing of both was a crucial milestone in the decision-making by the involved parties, Julius Caesar in 49 B.C. (precipitating the Roman Civil War) and the leaders of the cattle drive about nineteen centuries later (opening a new trail).

Despite his diminishing popularity among readers after his death, Emerson Hough's contribution to the development of Wild West literature and film is quite significant. While the numerous Latin and some Roman references encountered in his prose testify to his classical education, the diversity of those references offers an interesting and precious material to the students of the ancient language. Indirectly, they support the opinion that Latin and classical studies are far from being antiquated.

2. Paul HORGAN (1903–1995)

Born on August 1, 1903, in Buffalo, New York, Paul Horgan was educated at the Eastman School of Music (a part of the University of Rochester, New York) and the New Mexico Military Institute in Roswell. His principal fiction works include *The Fault of the Angels* (1933), *Main Line West* (1936), *A Lamp of the Plains* (1937), *The Habit of Empire* (1939), *Figures of the Landscape* (1940), *The Common Heart* (1942), *Devil in the Desert* (1950), *Give Me Possession* (1957), *A Distant Trumpet* (1960), *Memories of the Future* (1966), *Everything to Live For* (1968), *Whitewater* (1970), *The Thin Mountain Air* (1977) and *Mexico Bay* (1982). A two-time Pulitzer Prize winner for History: in 1955 with *Great River: The Rio Grande in North American History* (1954) and in 1976 with *Lamy of Santa Fe* (1975), Horgan died on March 8, 1995, in Middletown, Connecticut.

Even though Horgan himself wrote scripts for a few episodes of such TV series as *Fireside Theatre* (1954), *General Electric Theater* (1959) and *The United States Steel Hour* (1958-1959), the only movie based on his published work is Raoul Walsh's *A Distant Trumpet* (1964; featuring Troy Donahue, Suzanne Pleshette, Diane McBain, James Gregory and William Reynolds).

One of the author's prime fiction works, *A Distant Trumpet* ([1960] 1964), is a novel set in the Territory of Arizona (mostly in Fort Delivery) during the 1880s, and its main characters are Second Lt. Matthew Carlton Hazard (assigned to the Fort immediately after his commission from West Point), Laura Greenleaf (his fiancée, then, wife), Major General Alexander Upton Quait (Laura's uncle), First Lt. Theodore Mainwaring, Major Hiram Hyde Prescott, White Horn (a Chiricahua nicknamed "Joe Dummy") and two Chiricahua chiefs, Chief Rainbow Son and Chief Sebastian.

Even though the abundance of Latin references in the book is a direct result of Quait's tendency to quote original texts by Roman authors whenever he addresses his subordinates, the first Latin expression encountered in the book is uttered by Matt. It takes place in his conversation with Laura's parents regarding his plans to marry their daughter, an idea openly opposed by the mother, Drusilla Godwin Greenleaf (from a famous South Carolina family), and favored by the father, Colonel Huntleigh Greenleaf (from Philadelphia). However, the quoted excerpt is Matt's reaction to the opinion/advice offered by Laura's brother and Matt's college friend, Harvey:

"*Et tu, Brute* ['And you, Brutus'], said Matthew to his classmate, who laughed with delight at the classical learning of his friend. But he could see that there was something to recommend the proposal, for Laura's sake. He bowed to it. [p. 50]

After that, a long series of extensive and insightful Latin references starts to flow into the pages of the book as soon as Major General Qauit appears at the scene, that is, when he arrives at Fort Delivery with his adjutant, Captain Adrian Brinker. Here are his first words addressed to Matt and Major Prescott:

"***Anxius et intentus agere***," he declared, "as you will remember from Tacitus, which I translate to mean, '*Always active, never impulsive.*' How do you do, gentlemen." [p. 407]

The same two officers are addressed once again by Quait, with another quotation, before they are dismissed, rather impolitely, by his adjutant:

"***Omnia scire, non omnia exsequi***," he said. "Again Tacitus. I shall render it. '*He knew all, though he did not always act upon all he knew.*' I commend these words to you as a motto for the next several days, gentlemen." [p. 409]

The above two quotations are taken out of their contexts; consequently, Quait's (Horgan's) translations are not exactly literal, e.g., they turn the present active infinitive forms of the verbs (*agere, scire* – 'to do/act' and 'to know') into the third person singular forms of the Past Tense.

With a similar attitude and apparent arrogance, Quait, having dismounted from his horse, speaks to Major Prescott about the inspection of the troops:

"Though, like Agricola, **intravitque animum militaris gloriae cupido**, or, his heart was pierced by a craving for a soldier's glory, I shall nevertheless inspect your post on foot, major." [p. 441]

Later on, however, Quait recognizes the assets of both Prescott and Hazard, and he eagerly announces their promotion, admitting, at the same time, some obvious flaws in his adjutant who has been disagreeable to the other two officers:

"Ah, my good young man, Tacitus said it for us: **proprium humani ingenii est odiesse quem laeseries**, that is, it is a human trait to hate whom you harm. [sic, p. 460]

All the remaining Latin references found in the book, except for two lines from *Ars Amatoria*, Book II, by Ovid (see the entry on Adams), quoted along with the translation by Dr. Jonson (on p. 557), are listed below. The translation of the last three is done by the author himself, i.e., by Quait, who continues quoting his favorite author Tacitus (the first of the three), then Vergil's *Aeneid* (*Aeneis*, with Dryden's translation) and, finally, *The Gallic Wars* (*Commentarii de bello Gallico*) by Julius Caesar (see the entries on Lewis and Hilton for more information on Vergil and Caesar, respectively).

vade mecum (literally: 'go with me,' better: 'a handbook or guide that is kept at hand for consultation,' p. 444);

totus porcus ('the whole hog,' p. 450);

verbena bipinatifida (name of a flower, p. 450);

senecio canescens (name of a flower, p. 450);

cassia bauhinoides (name of a flower, p. 450);

edere ('to eat,' p. 450);

id est ('that is,' p. 451);

Veritas, veritas ('Truth, truth,' p. 459);

inter somnum ac trepidationem vigilibus irrupere ('overwhelming the sentries, they struck terror into the sleeping camp,' 464);

Possunt quia posse videntur. ("They can conquer who believe they can." *The Aeneid*, Book V, line 231; p. 501);

Diligebat idoneos homines huic rei. ("He selected suitable men for this affair!" *The Gallic Wars*, Book VII, Chapter 31; pp. 536-537).

The second item on the list, *totus porcus*, is an example of 'fake Latin,' also known as 'Dog Latin' (*Canis Latinicus*), 'Cod Latin,' 'macaronic Latin' or 'mock Latin.' It usually refers to a phrase or another expression composed of Latin words, made up as a literal translation of an expression in another language, thus, not originating from ancient Roman culture. Occasionally, those expressions also follow the rules of Latin syntax, with verbs being conjugated and nouns and adjectives declined, but the purpose of such an effort is only to imitate the original Latin language. The motivation behind this phenomenon is to create a proverb or metaphorical expression, not infrequently humorous, and evoke, at the same time, scholarly seriousness or parody thereof. This kind of Latin, however, should not be confused with 'Pig Latin,' which is a form of playful code and in fact has no relation to the ancient language.

Since Publius Cornelius Tacitus is quoted by Quait a few times, each time testifying as much to the general's educational background as to his pomposity (also accentuated by James Gregory's performance in the screen adaptation), it is appropriate to finish the discussion of the references in Horgan's remarkable novel with a few words about the famous Roman historian and politician. Born in 56 A.D. in Gallia Narbonensis, he died in 120 A.D. in the territory of the Roman Empire. Praised for his wisdom and superior prose style, he wrote several important historical and oratory works, such as *Annals* and *Histories*. Gnaeus Julius Agricola (40 A.D.–93 A.D.), also quoted by Quait, was Tacitus's father-in-law and a Roman Italo-Gallic general significantly contributing to the conquest of Britain.

One of the most distinguished Western writers, focused more on historical details than fictitious adventures, Paul Horgan deserves, additionally, to be recognized for his classical background, as well as his readiness to share his fascination and wisdom with the reader. While writers like Hough and Henry/Fisher incorporate Latin expressions into their narrative prose without giving their characters a chance to brag about their erudition, Horgan, just like McMurtry (a writer three decades younger), skillfully utilizes Latin references as one extra means/opportunity to portray a character of fiction in a more original way. Consequently, Horgan's example can serve as a strong argument in the thesis that Latin does not deserve to be included among dead languages.

While the motto of the Eastman School of Music is simply "Eat, Sleep, Music," the Latin motto of the University of Rochester (which the school is a part of) is *Meliora* ("Ever better"). Since the motto of the New Mexico Military Institute (the author's other alma mater) is "Duty, Honor, Achievement" – no Latin equivalent used, Horgan's competence in the Latin language and his impressive knowledge of Roman history are to be appreciated and admired even more.

3. Will HENRY/Clay FISHER (1912–1991)

Will Henry and Clay Fisher are the pen names of Henry Wilson "Heck" Allen, who was born in Kansas City, Missouri, on September 29, 1912. Having attended Kansas City Junior College (1929-1930), the young Allen went west and—after a number of odd jobs there—became a columnist for the Santa Monica *Sunset Reporter*, a story man for an animation film company and a junior writer for MGM, where he worked for nine years. He turned to writing western fiction in the late 1940s, and his first novel, *No Survivors*, was published in 1950 under the name Will Henry. The major novels he wrote under the same name include *To Follow a Flag* (1952; condensed in *Zane Grey's Western Magazine* under the title *Frontier Fury*, subsequently assumed the title of its film version), *Who Rides with Wyatt* (1954), *From Where the Sun Now Stands* (Spur Award for best historical novel, 1960), *Journey to Shiloh* (1960), *Gates of the Mountains* (Spur Award for best historical novel, 1963), *Mackenna's Gold* (1963), *Chiricahua* (Spur Award for best historical novel, 1972), *The Bear Paw Horses* (1973) and *Summer of the Gun* (1978). His principal works published under the name Clay Fisher include novels *Santa Fe Passage* (1952), *The Tall Men* (1954), *Yellowstone Kelly* (1957), *The Crossing* (1960), *Apache Ransom* (1974), *Black Apache* (1976) and a short story collection *Seven Legends West* (1983). In addition to the Spur Awards received (from the Western Writers of America) for his novels and short stories ("Isley's Stranger," 1962, and "The Tallest Indian in Tolepec," 1965), he won the Wrangler Trophy of the National Cowboy Hall of Fame and the first (lifetime achievement) Levi Strauss Golden Saddleman Award. He died on October 26, 1991, in Van Nuys, Los Angeles, California.

An impressive number of films have been made from Allen's works. The most successful screen adaptations include William Witney's *Santa Fe Passage* (1955; featuring John Payne, Faith Domergue and Rod Cameron)—from an Esquire Magazine story, Raoul Walsh's *The Tall Men* (1955; starring Clark Gable, Robert Ryan, Jane Russell and Cameron Mitchell), George Marshall's *Pillars of the Sky* (1956; featuring Jeff Chandler, Dorothy Malone, Ward Bond and Lee Marvin)—from the novel *To Follow the Flag*, Gordon Douglas's *Yellowstone Kelly* (1959; starring Clint Walker, Edd Byrnes, John Russell and Ray Danton), William Hale's *Journey to Shiloh* (1969; featuring James Caan, Michael Sarrazin, Brenda Scott, Don Stroud and Harrison Ford), Burt Kennedy's *Young Billy Young* (1969; starring Robert Mitchum, Angie Dickinson and Robert Walker, Jr.)—from the novel *Who Rides with Wyatt*, and Nils Gaup's

North Star (1996; featuring James Caan, Christopher Lambert and Catherine McCormack)—from the novel *The North Star* (1956).

Figure 3.2. Polish poster for Raoul Walsh's *The Tall Men* (1955), designed by Wiktor Górka (1965). Courtesy of the "Ikonosfera" Gallery and Transart Collection.

3. Will HENRY/Clay FISHER (1912–1991)

One of the author's best-known books, *The Tall Men* ([1954] 1970), is an epic novel depicting a cattle drive through the Seven Sioux Nations, from Texas all the way to Montana. The titular protagonists are two Southern brothers, Ben and Clint Allison, and a Yankee named Nathan Stark, who, despite being robbed by the other two, persuades them to join forces with him on the big undertaking, hoping to double-cross them once it is accomplished. An additional catalyst of the conflict between Ben and Nathan is the female protagonist, Nella Torneau, an unusual, tough but loving woman from Texas, who seems to be unable to choose between the two men until the very end. The book incorporates two minor Latin references.

Both Latin phrases appear in descriptive/narrative paragraphs of the novel, the first one, quite well-known in English and other languages, in the opening of Chapter Thirteen, the second one in the middle of Chapter Fourteen:

> Not counting Stark, there were twenty-odd men in his drive crew; eighteen fulltime cowboys, two horse wranglers, a cook and two halfbreed assistants, a jack-of-all-trades farrier and graduate of doubtful ***cum laude*** ['with praise'] "cow doctor," and Ben and Clint Allison. Not barring Nella and excepting only Stark himself, every member of the Montanan's trail outfit was as deep-Texas as range beef and refried red beans. [p. 75]

> For Stark's part of the report, they had the unofficial good wishes of the U.S. Army, as indeed he had guaranteed the Texas brothers the night above Alder Gulch. But beyond the ***sub rosa*** [happening or done 'in secret'] extension of the wish, he got only a field-grade frown of the professional opinion that his chances of getting through were highly questionable. [p. 87]

The last phrase, denoting secrecy or confidentiality, comes from ancient mythology, where it is stated that Cupid gave a rose to Harpocrates, the god of silence, to keep him from revealing goddess Venus's indiscretions.

Another book by the author, *Yellowstone Kelly* ([1957] 1988), also published under the pseudonym Clay Fisher, is set mostly in Montana, and the protagonist, Luther Sage Kelly, better known as "Yellowstone" Kelly, repeatedly faces death and earns respect from both the Cavalry and the Sioux while searching for his Crow Girl, "H'tayetu Hopa" ("Beautiful Evening"), his Absaroka mate.

The first Latin phrase appears in a descriptive paragraph regarding geography, the Cavalry and their relationship with the protagonist:

Thus it was that the most the Irish scout received for his perilous sixty days in the Sioux wilderness was a detailed edition to his former knowledge of the unexplored lands north of the Yellowstone. These were the same lands which history even at that moment was leading George Crook's erudite adjutant, John Bourke, to label **terra incognita** ['unknown land']. And they were the same whose blankness on the existing military maps was at that identical August hour causing Colonel Nelson A. Miles to dispatch up and down the river his historic summons for Luther Kelly to join him in his camp on the banks of the Yellowstone at the mouth of Tongue River. [pp. 158-159]

The second phrase, quite well-known and even popular in English and several other languages, is used by the narrator in another narrative passage, in a scene that is a continuation of the previous excerpt, referring to Kelly and, first of all, Colonel Miles:

Miles was an enigma to many men. But Kelly had to assay him and assay him fast, or miss his chance to make his difficult point, perhaps for good.

First off, a man could see that the famed Comanche fighter actually did not like to talk. Accordingly, when he had to, as with Kelly now, he lied to get it done in uninterrupted bursts. This suggested that his ordinary **modus operandi** ['a particular way/method of doing something'] was action. Quite clearly he suffered neither from Crook's fussy infatuation with delaying logistics, nor Custer's fatal mania for blowing Garry Owens before his support came up. His military philosophy was apparently quite simple; seek, find, destroy. But before putting this philosophy into active effect, to judge from Kelly's short contact with him, he was a man who would want to make sure his men understood the dangers ahead. [p. 170]

Will Henry/Clay Fisher was one of the most celebrated writers of western fiction. His perhaps most acclaimed work, *From Where the Sun Now Stands*, was selected as the #23 western novel by the Western Writers of America in their 1997 poll, and as one of the best twelve western novels in their 1995 survey, in which Allen himself was voted #2 (a tie with Louis L'Amour) western author. While the Latin references found in his prose are neither overly numerous nor insightful, and they come out from the narrator's (meaning the author's) mouth rather than any of the characters', they are still significant as they show that popular expressions adopted from the ancient language were a natural part of the writer's vocabulary and style.

4. Larry McMURTRY (1936–)

Born in Wichita Fall, Texas, on June 3, 1936, Larry Jeff McMurtry is a son and grandson of cattlemen. Educated at North Texas State College, Denton (B.A. 1958), Rice University, Houston (M.A. 1960) and Stanford University, California (Wallace Stegner Fellowship), he published his first novel, *Horseman, Pass By*, in 1961, winning the Jesse H. Jones Award of the Texas Institute of Letters for Best Work of Fiction. He became internationally famous for his modern "Thalia/Duane" saga consisting of five parts—*The Last Picture Show* (1966), *Texasville* (1987), *Duane's Depressed* (1999), *When the Light Goes* (2007) and *Rhino Ranch* (2009)—and even more for his "Texas Rangers" tetralogy composed of *Lonesome Dove* (1986, Pulitzer Prize, Spur Award from the Western Writers of America), *Streets of Laredo* (1993), *Dead Man's Walk* (1995) and *Comanche Moon* (1997)—written in this order but telling the story in the 3-4-1-2 chronological sequence. His other notable works include *Leaving Cheyenne* (1963), *All My Friends Are Going to Be Strangers* (1972), *Terms of Endearment* (1975) and *The Evening Star* (1992), the last two linked by the character Aurora Greenway.

McMurtry's movie credits are equally impressive. In addition to three remarkable theatrical pictures based on his novels—Martin Ritt's *Hud* (1963; starring Paul Newman, Patricia Neal, Melvyn Douglas and Brandon de Wilde) from *Horseman, Pass By*, Peter Bogdanovich's *The Last Picture Show* (1970; featuring Timothy Bottoms, Jeff Bridges, Cybill Shepherd and Ben Johnson) and James L. Brooks's *Terms of Endearment* (1983; with Shirley MacLaine, Debra Winger, John Lithgow and Jack Nicholson), winning ten Academy Awards altogether, there are a number of major television adaptations of his works. While all four of the TV versions of the "Texas Rangers" tetralogy have been great hits, Simon Wincer's miniseries *Lonesome Dove* (1989; featuring Robert Duvall, Tommy Lee Jones, Danny Glover, Diane Lane and Anjelica Huston), winning two Golden Globes and seven Emmy Awards, is widely regarded as a TV sensation and has successfully competed for praise with theatrical productions.

The novel *Lonesome Dove* (1986) emerged as a gem of western fiction in the mid-1980s and was immediately recognized as one of the masterpieces of the genre. It reveals the author's unlimited imagination manifested in the richness of characters and the complexity of the plot. An absolutely original work, it can be treated as a creative summary of the genre's best elements. Its most fascinating characters are unquestionably Augustus McCrae and Woodrow F. Call, but charismatic are also some female characters, particularly Clara Forsythe and Lorena Wood.

The whole story about Latin, or rather Augustus's fascination with it, begins early in the book, in a scene where Call and Augustus are considering "crossing some stock" at night and Lewt, Call's illegitimate and never acknowledged son, is trying to get included in this relatively dangerous mission:

> "You should have let him sit," Augustus said, a little later. "After all, the boy's only chance for an education is listening to me talk."
>
> Call let that float off. Augustus has spent a year in a college, back in Virginia somewhere, and claimed to have learned his Greek letters, plus a certain amount of **Latin**. He never let anyone forget it. [p. 28]

The idea is resumed and expanded later in the book, in a part related to the famous sign designed by Augustus:

> However, it was his view that **Latin** was mostly for looks anyway, and he devoted himself to the mottoes in order to find one with the best look. The one he settled on was ***Uva uvam vivendo varia fit***, which seemed to him a beautiful motto, whatever it meant. One day when nobody was around he went out and lettered it onto the bottom of the sign, just below "We Don't Rent Pigs." Then he felt that his handiwork was complete. The whole sign read:
>
> HAT CREEK CATTLE COMPANY
AND LIVERY EMPORIUM
>
> CAPT. AUGUSTUS MC CRAE and CAPT. W. F. CALL   PROPS.
>
> P. E. PARKER
> WRANGLER
> DEETS, JOSHUA
> FOR RENT: HORSES AND RIGS
> FOR SALE: CATTLE AND HORSES
> GOATS AND DONKEYS NEITHER BOUGHT NOR SOLD
> WE DON'T RENT PIGS.
> **UVA UVAM VIVENDO VARIA FIT.**
>
> ...
>
> "So what's it say, that **Latin**?" Call asked.
>
> "It's a motto," Augustus said. "It just says itself." [pp. 90-92]

4. Larry McMURTRY (1936–)

The Latin sign Augustus so proudly displays, *Uva uvam vivendo varia fit*, is a somewhat incorrect or revised version of a well-known Latin quotation *Uva uvam videndo varia fit*, which means "A grape changes by seeing another grape." The discrepancy between this and Augustus's version, where the gerund *videndo* (from the second-conjugation verb *video vidēre* – 'to see') has been replaced by the gerund *vivendo* (from the third-conjugation verb *vivo vivĕre* – 'to live'), almost maintaining the grammaticality of the whole clause (preposition *ad* in front of *uvam* would make it perfect), thus suggesting that "A grape changes by living next to another grape," can be explained in three different ways. It can be attributed to McMurtry's mistake or typo, which was not caught by the editor or proofreader. It can suggest the writer's purposeful mistake in order to imply Augustus's more than "rusty" Latin. Or, which seems to be most likely, it was meant exactly the way it was spelled so that the revised meaning of the sentence, obviously understood metaphorically (the grapes standing for human beings), could serve as the book's hidden motto or intentionally misplaced message. For, after all, *Lonesome Dove*, more than any of the other three parts of the tetralogy, uses the motif of the journey (in fact, several journeys, parallel and consecutive, overlapping and crossing each other) as much to draw exciting adventures as to carry out the study of characters and the complex relationships between them. Tragedies pile up, people die under a variety of circumstances, but living life to the fullest seems to be the idea behind the rich episodes of the epic novel, Augustus being its perfect example. He dies at the end of the road, but, before he goes, he makes a wish of being buried back in Texas—a wish that compels his best friend, Call, to experience a new series of challenging adventures that would gradually lead to reviving his temporary dead soul or numb spirit.

A different Latin reference appears later in the book (p. 105), this time an outsider, Wilbarger (educated at Yale), is the person that introduces it, and the word, used for a horse brand, is **HIC** (the masculine nominative singular form of the personal pronoun 'he' or the demonstrative 'this'). The word 'Latin' itself is used twice in that particular excerpt and twice more later in the book, on pp. 522 and 620. The last excerpt, being a part of a moving scene where the dying Wilbarger unexpectedly readdresses the infamous sign one more time, is definitely worth quoting:

> "McCrae, I'll give you credit for having written a damn amusing sign," he said. "I've laughed about that sign many a time, and laughing's a pleasure. I've got two good books in my saddlebags. One's Mister Milton and the other's a Virgil. I want you to have them. The Virgil might improve your **Latin**."
>
> "I admit it's rusty," Augustus said. "I'll apply myself, and many thanks."

> "To tell the truth, I can't read it either." Wilbarger said. "I could once, but I lost it." [p. 620]

No Latin words have been found in the pages of *Streets of Laredo* ([1993] 1994), the sequel to *Lonesome Dove*, but the word "Latin" does appear there. It is used by McMurtry, the narrator at the very beginning of Part II of the book, entitled "The Manburner." Lorena, who was Gus's sweetheart in the prequel, is now, after Gus's death, married to Pea Eye Parker, who at some point joins Captain Woodrow Call to help him track down a Mexican bandit. That is when Lorena receives a letter from Clara with an unusual suggestion:

> Lorena was reading a letter from Clara when Clarie came in to tell her that Mr. Goodnight was at the door.
>
> In the letter, Clara was urging her to make a beginning in **Latin**, advice that caused Lorena to feel doubtful. She thought she could do quite well with English grammar now, but she didn't know if she was up to **Latin**, or if she ever would be. The baby had been sick most of the time since Pea Eye left, and she had been sleeping tired and waking tired, worrying about the baby and worrying about Pea. [p. 209]

In *Comanche Moon* ([1997] 1998), the second (and last) prequel to *Lonesome Dove*, McMurtry incorporates only one, but quite meaningful, Latin quotation. The two men that watch the Indians hunt buffalo in the quoted episode are Captain Inish Scull, a very-well educated, tough and eccentric Texas Ranger, and Augustus, here still young relative to the other rangers:

> Looking down on the scene from high above, Augustus, though he couldn't say why, felt a mood of sadness take him. He knew he ought to be going, but he could not stop looking at the scene far below. A line of Indian women were moving out from the camp, ready to help cut up the meat.
>
> Inish Scull paused a moment. He saw that his young ranger had been affected by the chase they had just observed, and its inevitable ending.
>
> "***Post coitum omne animal triste***," he said, leaning over to put a hand, for a moment, on the young man's shoulder. "That's Aristotle."
>
> "What, sir?" Augustus asked. "I expect that's **Latin**, but what does it mean?"

4. Larry McMURTRY (1936–)

> "'After copulation every animal is sad,'" the Captain said. It's true, too—though who can say why? The seed flies, and the seeder feels blue."
>
> "Why is it?" Augustus asked. He knew, from his own memories, that the Captain had stated a truth. Much as he like poking, there was that moment, afterward, when something made his spirits dip, for a time. [p. 80]

Another, perhaps more correct, version of the above reference is *Post coitum omne animalium triste*, which means "After sexual union, each of the animals is sad," the difference being significant as it addresses the concept of 'genitive partitive,' which is illustrated by the genitive plural form of the noun *animalium*. The maxim is attributed to Galen (full name: Aelius Galenus or Claudius Galenus; born in 129 A.D.), a Greek-Roman doctor, philosopher and writer.

The word 'Latin' itself appears in the book once again fifty pages later, when the author/narrator reveals Captain Scull's thoughts regarding the education level of the two protagonists, Gus (Augustus) McCrae and Woodrow F. Call:

> At moments he missed the learned talk of Cambridge; at times he grew depressed when he considered the gap in knowledge between himself and the poor dull fellows he commanded—they were brave beyond reason, but, alas, untutored. Young Call, it was true, was eager to learn, and Augustus McCrae sometimes mimicked a few lines of **Latin** picked up in some Tennessee school. But the truth was, the men were ignorant, which is why, from time to time, with no immediate enemy to confront, he had started giving little impromptu lectures on the great battles of history. [p. 130]

In addition to the ones found in his western novels, McMurtry makes use of Latin quotations in a couple of his main-stream works, *Some Can Whistle* (1989) and *The Evening Star*. The former, a sequel to *All My Friends Are Going to Be Strangers* (1972), is a moving story, somewhat uplifting but tragic toward the end, of a belated relationship between a father, successful Texas writer Danny Deck (the narrator), and his long-lost daughter, life-loving and unpredictable T.R. The passage quoted below is a part of a conversation between Danny and his English friend, Godwin, shortly before Dee shoots Godwin, T.R. and security guard Buddy at a filling station. Eventually, Dee gets caught, sentenced and, a few years later, killed by an inmate. Ironically, the topic of the conversation is Earl Dee, the cause of the upcoming tragedy:

> Several times I'd been on the point of asking T.R. what attracted her to a man who would threaten her life, but at the last second I had always pulled back and left the question unasked. Attraction didn't have to mean, it only had to be. Why was I attracted to women so high-strung and brilliant that if you looked at them twice it would usually prompt a fit? Was it the brilliance that attracted me, or was it the fits, or was it the combination? Who knew? And if I could not answer such a question for myself, there was no point in asking T.R. to try to explain what she had seen in Earl Dee.
>
> "***De gustibus***," I said to Godwin as we raced toward Wichita Falls. [p. 300]

McMurtry, in his own conclusion, offers here just the beginning of a very well-known Latin quotation *De gustibus non est disputandum* ("About tastes there is no disputing."), sometimes somewhat expanded into *De gustibus et coloribus non est disputandum*. The singular forms of both the verb *est* ('is') and the gerundive *disputandum* ('about to be disputed'), meaning, together with the negative *non*, 'one must not dispute,' do not need to be put in the plural form regardless of how many nouns (in the ablative form) precede, due to the impersonal form of the whole expression. In terms of the context of the quotation, no comments seem necessary.

In his sequel to *Terms of Endearment* (1975), *The Evening Star* ([1992] 1993), McMurtry follows the life of Aurora Greenway, now, after her daughter Emma's death of cancer, taking care of her grandchildren, Tommy (who ends up in prison doing fifteen years to life), Teddy and Melanie. The quoted passage regards Patsy Carpenter, a long-time friend of Aurora's family:

> Patsy, at fifty, was still a beautiful woman, or would have been if she could have managed not to look disappointed, Aurora thought. Disappointment, particularly self-disappointment—the variety Patsy suffered from—did not do good things for the female face. Tragedy might have added a kind of ***gravitas*** ['dignity/authority/seriousness'] that would have made Patsy commandingly beautiful, but self-disappointment was merely making her look irrelevantly sad. [pp. 99-100]

Despite the fact that the motto of Rice University, from which McMurtry graduated— *Letters, Science, Art*—is not in Latin, and that the eventually accepted Latin motto of Stanford University, where he studied on Wallace Stegner Fellowship—*Semper virens* ("Ever flourishing")—had been preceded by a German version (*Die Luft der Freiheit weht*, meaning "The winds of freedom blow"), the distinguished writer must have been effectively exposed to Vergil's language given the relative abundance of Latin references found in his writing.

While all those quotations intellectually enrich his remarkable novels, the ones that appear in his westerns, especially in *Lonesome Dove*, play multiple roles. In addition to providing humor and insightful information regarding some characters, they, or at least one of them, constitute a philosophical commentary on the complex story.

Appendix

Lists of Fiction Books by Other Authors with Minor/Few Latin Reference

A. Mainstream Literature

Albee, Edward. *Who's Afraid of Virginia Woolf?* ([1962] 1966): **Dies Irae** ('Day of the Wrath,' p. 117), **Et lucis aeternae beautitudine perfrui.** ('And to enjoy the blessedness of everlasting light.' p. 221), **Libera me, Domine, de morte aeterna, in die illa tremenda: Quando caeli movendi sunt et terra: Dum veneris judicare saeculum per ignem. Tremens factus sum ego, et timeo, dum discussio venerit, atque ventura ira. Quando caeli movendi sunt et terra. Dies illa, dies irae, calamitatis et miseriae; dies magna et amara valde. Dum veneris judicare saeculum per ignem. Requiem aeternam dona eis, Domine: et lux perpetua luceat eis.** ("Deliver me, O Lord, from eternal death, on that fearful day: When the heavens and the earth shall be moved: When thou shalt come to judge the world by fire: I am made to tremble, and I fear, till the judgment be upon us, and the coming wrath. When the heavens and the earth shall be moved. That day, day of wrath, calamity and misery, day of great and exceeding bitterness. When thou shalt come to judge the world by fire. Rest eternal grant unto them, O Lord, and let perpetual light shine upon them." p. 227—from "Libera Me.").

Algren, Nelson. *The Man with the Golden Arm* ([1949] 1956): **Ad Electrica Necessitas Vitae** (meaning unclear; quotation probably incorrect, p. 101).

Allen, Woody. *Without Feathers* (1983): **Deus ex machina** ('A god from a machine,' i.e., 'a plot device able to solve a seemingly unsolvable problem,' p. 148).

Barth, John. *Lost in the Funhouse* ([1963] 1969): **ergo me** ('therefore, I,' p. 35); **deus ex machina** ('a god from a machine,' p. 35).

Bromfield, Louis. *The Rains Came* ([1937] 1955): **virgo intacta** ('intact virgin,' p. 163).

Busch, Niven. *California Street* (1959): **Tempus fugit.** ("Time flies." p. 68), **"Coelum, non animum mutant, qui trans mare currunt.** ("Those who run across the sea, change the sky, not their soul." p. 207—Horace).

Busch, Niven. *Continent's Edge* (1980): **pro tempore** ('for the time being,' pp. 21, 342), **requiescat in pace** ('rest in peace,' p. 76).

Cheever, John. "The Sorrows of Gin" (1978): **non compos mentis** ('insane/out of one's mind,' p. 199).

Conroy, Pat. *Beach Music* (1995): **"Pax huic domui."** ("Peace be to this house!" p. 142), **"Et omnibus habitantibus in ea."** ("And to all its inhabitants." P. 143), **"Semper Fidelis"** ('Always faithful,' pp. 279, twice, and 280), **'O Solutaris Hostia'** ('O Saving Sacrifice,' p. 431—Hymn).

DeLillo, Don. *Underworld* (1997): **Dominus vobiscum** ("The Lord be with you." p. 107).

Doctorow, E. L. *Ragtime* ([1974] 1976): **prisca theologia** ('ancient theology,' pp. 170, 171), **"Gaudeamus Igitur"** ("So Let Us Rejoice." p. 228).

Flagg, Fannie. *Coming Attractions* ([1981] 1992): **bona fide** ('genuine/real,' p. 65), **"Semper Fidelis"** ('Always faithful,' p. 195).

Ford, Richard. *Independence Day* (1995): **status quo** ('the existing state of affairs,' p. 129).

Greene, Graham. *The Human Factor* (1978): **aspergillus flavus** (name of a saprotrophic and pathogenic fungus, p. 70); **prima facie** ('on the first impression,' p. 195).

Guterson, David. *Our Lady of the Forest* (2003): **Ecce ancilla Domini. Fiat mihi secundum verbum tuum.** ("Behold the handmaid of the Lord. Be it done unto me according to Thy word." p. 235).

Haddon, Mark. *The Curious Incident of the Dog in the Night-Time* (2003): **Entia non sunt multiplicanda praeter necessitatem** (literally: "Entities should not be multiplied without necessity." or, according to Haddon: "No more things should be presumed to exist than are absolutely necessary." p. 90).

Hartley, L. P. *The Go-Between* ([1953] 1984): **delenda est** ('must be destroyed,' an allusion to *Carthago delenda est*, p. 267).

Heggen, Thomas. *Mister Roberts* ([1946] 1966): **in absentia** ('while not present,' p. 12).

Heller. Joseph. *God Knows* (1984): **Vita brevis, ars longa** ("Life is short, and art is long." p. 26), **mirabile dictu** ('wonderful to relate,' p. 278).

Innes, Michael. *Candleshoe* ([1953] 1978): **de mortuis nil nisi bonum** ('about the dead nothing but good,' p. 73).

Kaufman, Bel. *Up the Down Staircase* ([1964] 1965): **in toto** ('as a whole/in all/overall,' p. 164).

Kazan, Elia. *The Arrangement* ([1967] 1968): **in flagrante delicto** ('in the act of wrongdoing,' p. 463).

Kazan, Elia. *The Assassins* ([1972] 1973): **pro forma** ('as a matter of form or politeness,' p. 310).

Keillor, Garrison. *Lake Wobegon* ([1985] 1986): **Sumus quod sumus.** ("We are what we are." p. 6, 8, 90).

Kennedy, Adam. *Just Like Humphrey Bogart* ([1978] 1979): **Mea culpa** ('my fault,' p. 3).

Kennedy, William. *Billy Phelan's Greatest Game* ([1978] 1983): **Mea maxima culpa** ('throughmy most grievous fault,' p. 171).

Kerouac, Jack. *Designation Angels* ([1960] 1980): **lacrimae rerum** ('tears of things,' p. 318—from Vergil's *Aeneid*, Book I, line 462).

Latham, Aaron. *Riding with John Wayne* (2006): **semper** ('always,' p. 187).

Maclean, Norman. "Logging and Pimping and 'Your Pal, Jim'" ([1976] 2001): **Nemo me impune lacessit** ("No-one provokes me with impunity." p. 119).

Mailer, Norman. *Tough Guys Don't Dance* ([1984] 1985): **Inter faeces et urinam nascimur** ("Between shit and piss are we born."—Mailer's own translation—pp. 77, 190), **Quid pro quo** ('one thing for another,' p. 351).

Marquand, John P. *Point of No Return* (1949): **status quo** ('the existing state of affairs,' p. 439).

Maugham, W. Somerset. *The Razor's Edge* ([1943] 1946): **Si monumentum quoeris, circumspice.** ("If you seek his monument, look around." Sir Christopher Wren's epitaph, p. 199).

Michener, James R. *The Fires of Spring* ([1949] 1984): **Gaudeamus Igitur** ("So Let Us Rejoice" p. 193).

O'Connor, Edwin. *The Last Hurrah* ([1956] 1957): **memento mori** ("Remember that you will die." p. 24), **Quid pro quo** ('one thing for another,' p. 175), **"Accipe Viaticum corporis Domini ..."** ("Accept the Eucharist of the Lord's body." p. 352), **Miserere** ("Be Merciful," p. 356—Psalm 51), **De Profundis** ("Out of the Depth," p. 356—Psalm 130), **Dies Irae** ("Day for The Wrath," p. 357—Hymn).

Odets, Clifford. *The Country Girl* (1951): **non compos mentis** ('out of one's mind,' 43).

O'Hara, John. *From the Terrace* ([1958] 1984): **in absentia** ('while not present,' p. 215).

O'Hara, John. "Our Friend the Sea" ([1963] 1984): **Cogito, ergo sum.** ("I think; therefore, I am." p. 280, twice).

O'Kane, Leslie. *Finding Gregory Peck* (2015): **Carpe diem** ("Seize the day." p. 97).

O'Neill, Eugene. *The Great God Brown* ([1926] 1954): **in flagrante delicto** ('in the act of wrongdoing,' p. 332).

Rand, Ayn. *The Fountainhead* ([1943] 1993): **Mea culpa—mea culpa—mea maxima culpa** ('through my most grievous fault,' p. 663).

Ritchie, Ron M. *The Day Burt Lancaster Died* (2008): **sanctum sanctorum** ('the holy of holies' or 'holy place/shrine,' p. 212)

Rosten, Leo. *Captain Newman, M.D.* ([1954] 1964): **Cogito ergo sum** ("I think; therefore, I am." p.193), **Semper fidelis!** ('Always faithful!' p. 223), **mirabile dictu** ('wonderful to relate,' p. 225).

Schulberg, Budd. *The Disenchanted* (1950): **homo somnus ambulatus** ('sleepwalker,' p. 101), **qui vive** ('on the alert/lookout,' p. 101).

Segal, Erich. *Man, Woman and Child* ([1980] 1981): **in loco parentis** ('in place of a parent,' pp. 170, 171).

Sheldon, Sidney. *Nothing Lasts Forever* ([1994] 1995): **Quid pro quo** ('one thing for another,' p. 143), **Pro bono** ('out of good will/free of charge,' p. 179), **Virgo** (literally: 'virgin," here: 'a person born when the sun is in the sign of Virgo,' p. 241).

Shulman, Max. *Rally Round the Flag, Boys!* (1954): **status quo** ('the existing state of affairs,' pp. 48, 49, 175).

Singer, Isaac Bashevis. *Shadows on the Hudson* (1998): **Homo sapiens** ('sensible human being,' p. 141), **'Qui Pro Quo'** ('one person for/instead of another,' the name of a small theater/cabaret in pre-WW II Warsaw, p. 434).

Styron, William. *Sophie's Choice* (1979): **mea culpa** ('my fault,' p. 5), **mirabile dictu** ('wonderful to relate,' p. 248).

Vonnegut, Jr. Kurt. *Breakfast of Champions* ([1973] 1975): **locomotor ataxia** ('last stages of syphilis,' p. 3), **"E pluribus unum"** ('One out of many,' p. 9).

Wallace, Irving. *The Word* ([1972] 1973): **tablinum** ('main room/study/library,' pp. 78, 585), **caudex** ('trunk of a tree,' p. 132), **dominus** ('Lord/master,' p.

345), ***Quid est veritas?*** ("What is truth?" p. 362), ***Historia Augusta*** ('Augustan History," p. 401).

Weidman, Jerome. *Other People's Money* (1967): ***Festina Lente*** ("Rush slowly." p. 139), ***Ceterum censeo Carthaginem esse delendam*** ("For the rest I vote that Carthage should be destroyed." p. 426—Cato the Censor).

Wellman, Paul I. *Magnificent Destiny* (1962): ***Georgius III, Dei Gratia Britanniarum Rex, Fidei Defensor*** ('George III, by the grace of God, king of the Britons, Defender of the Faith,' p. 29).

Wolff, Tobias. *This Boy's Life: A Memoir* (1989): ***pro forma*** ('as a matter of form or politeness,' p. 141).

Wouk, Herman. *The Winds of War* ([1971] 1973): ***persona non grata*** ("unwelcome person,' p. 46), ***Pax Romana*** ('Roman Peace,' p. 303).

B. Crime & Detective Fiction

Baldacci, David. *The Simple Truth* ([1998] 1999): ***in forma pauperis*** ('in the form of a pauper, pp. 70, 234), ***quid pro quo*** ('one thing for another,' p. 120), ***sui generis*** ('one of a kind' or 'unique,' p. 375), ***stare decisis*** ('to stand by decided matters,' i.e., 'to determine points according to precedent,' p. 376).

Baxt, George. *The Clark Gable & Carole Lombard Murder Case* (1995): **non sequitur** ('does not logically follow,' pp. 65, 81), ***in flagrante delicto*** ('in the act of wrongdoing,' p. 166).

Blatty, William Peter. *Dimiter* (2010): ***Mea culpa, mea culpa!*** ('through my most grievous fault,' p. 54), **non sequitur** ('does not logically follow,' p. 92), **"Gloria in Excelsis Deo"** ('Glory to God in the Highest,' p. 101), **"Noli me tangere"** ("Do not touch me." p. 137).

Bloch, Robert. *Psycho* ([1959] 1960): ***corpus delicti*** ('the dead body of the victim,' 48).

Brown, Sandra. *Smash Cut* (2009): **"In vino veritas."** ("In wine lies the truth." p. 164).

Caspary, Vera. *Laura* ([1942] 1961): ***Lacrymae Christi*** ('Tears of Christ,' type of wine, p. 67), ***corpus delicti*** ('the dead body of the victim,' pp. 89, 99).

Cornwell, Patricia. *From Potter's Field* ([1995] 1996): ***Tacent Colloquia Effugiat Risus Hic Locus Est Ubi Mors Gaudet Succurrere Vitae*** ("Let conversation cease; let the laughter flee; this is the place where death delights to help the living." p. 47).

Cornwell, Patricia. *Isle of Dogs* ([2001] 2002): ***sapidus*** ('tasty/savory,' p. 277).

Cornwell, Patricia. *The Scarpetta Factor* (2009): ***In vina veritas*** ("In wine lies the truth." p. 243).

Crider, Bill. *We'll Always Have Murder: A Humphrey Bogart Mystery* (2001): ***vice versa*** ('the other way around,' p. 135).

Deaver, Jeffery. *The Twelfth Card* ([2005] 2006): ***inter alia*** ('among others,' p. 219).

Dickey, Eric Jerome. *Resurrecting Midnight* (2009): ***Faber est suae quisque fortunae.*** ("Every man is the artisan of his own fortune." p. 394), ***Audaces fortuna iuvat.*** ("Fortune favors the bold." p. 395).

Diehl, William. *Primal Fear* ([1993] 1994): **malum in se** ('wrong/evil in itself,' pp. 117, twice, 210, 313), **malum prohibitum** ("crime prohibited by statute,' pp. 117, twice, 210, four times, 211), **rigor mortis** ('stiffness after death,' pp. 161, 336), **mens rea** ('intention/awareness of wrongdoing,' pp. 313, twice, 314, twice).

Grisham, John. *Time to Kill* ([1989] 1992): **in limine** ('on the threshold' or, when used for motions, 'as the preliminary matter,' p. 240), **summa cum laude** ('with the highest distinction,' p. 367).

Hall, James W. *Body Language* ([1998] 1999): **Carpe diem.** ("Seize the day." p. 94), **antecubital fossa** ('elbow pit,' p. 127), **Periplaneta americana** (a type of cockroach, p. 247).

Hammett, Dashiell. *The Continental Op* ([1923] 1974): **cacoethes carpendi** ('uncontrollable urge,' p. 246).

Harr, Jonathan. *A Civil Action* (1996): **res ipsa loquitur.** ("The thing speaks for itself." p. 46).

Harris, Thomas. *Hannibal* (1999): **Semper fi** (a short for 'Semper fidelis,' meaning 'Always faithful,' p. 332).

Healy, Jeremiah. *The Stalking of Sheilah Quinn* (1998): **genus Felis** ('a genus of small and middle-sized cats,' p. 125).

Hughes, Dorothy B. *Ride the Pink Horse* ([1946] 1988): **O Salutaris Hostia** ("O Saving Sacrifice," p. 117), **Laudate** ("Praise," Psalm 117, p. 118), **habeas corpus** ('in the act of wrongdoing,' p. 183).

Isaacs, Susan. *Red, White and Blue* (1998): **E pluribus unum** ('Out of many, one,' p. 14), **Semper Fi** ('Always Faithful,' p. 163).

James, P. D. *A Certain Justice* ([1977] 1998): **memento mori** ("Remember that you will die." p. 296), **Vigiles non timendi sunt nisi complures adveniunt.** ("Police are not to be feared unless many arrive." p. 426).

James, P. D. *Death of an Expert Witness* (1977): **Ex umbris et imaginibus in veritatem** ('From shadows and images to the reality,' p. 207), **Contra mundum** ('against the world,' p. 241, twice, and 244).

Kellerman, Faye. *Grievous Sin* ([1993] 1994): **Pseudocyesis** ('false pregnancy,' p. 310).

Kellerman, Jonathan. *When the Bough Breaks* ([1985] 1986): **In Memoriam** ('in memory' of a dead person, p. 229).

Lanier, Virginia. *Blind Bloodhound Justice* ([1998] 1999): **Et tu, Brute** ('And you, Brutus,' p. 219).

Leonard, Elmore. *The Big Bounce* ([1969] 1986): **Sursum corda** ("Lift up your hearts." p. 16), **Habemus ad Dominum** ("We are lifting them up to the Lord." p. 16), **Gratias agamus Domino, deo nostro** ("Let us give thanks to the Lord, our God." p. 16), **Dignum et justum est** ("It is right and fitting." p. 16).

Maron, Margaret. *Long Upon the Land* (2015): **Carpe diem** ("Seize the day." p. 173).

Maron, Margaret. *Sand Sharks* (2009): **ex post facto** ('backdated/retroactive,' p. 101), **ca. AD** ('around the year of the Lord,' pp. 45, 55, 73, 147, 153, 225, 231, 259), **se defendendo** ('in self-defense,' p. 287).

Maron, Margaret. *Take Out* (2017): **quid pro quo** ('one thing for another,' 295).

McBain, Ed. *Rumpelstiltskin* ([1981] 1989): **in flagrante delicto** ('in the act of wrongdoing,' p. 2).

McGivern, William P. *Caprifoil* ([1972] 1973): **Ego te absolvo** ("I absolve you." p. 134).

Palmer, Michael. *A Heartbeat Away* (2011): **Res ipsa loquitur.** ("The thing speaks for itself." pp. 130, 131).

Parker, Robert B. *Chance* ([1996] 1997): **pro bono** ('for the public good,' or 'free of charge,' p. 89).

Parker, Robert B. *Potshot* ([2001] 2002): **In memoriam** ('In memory of ...,' p. 241).

Patterson, James. *Black Friday* ([1986] 2000): **prima facie** ('based on the first impression,' p. 266).

Patterson, James. *Kiss the Girls* (1995): **quid pro quo** ('one thing for another,' p. 235).

Patterson, James. *Violets Are Blue* ([2001] 2002): **Tempus fugit** ("Time flies." p. 40).

Puzo, Mario. *The Fourth* (1990): **Mens sana in corpore sano.** ('A sound mind in a healthy body,' p. 199).

Roosevelt, Elliott. *Murder in the Red Room* ([1992] 1994): **malum in se** ('wrong/evil in itself,' p. 233), **malum prohibitum** ('unlawful act only by virtue of statute,' p. 233).

Sanders, Lawrence. *McNally's Trial* ([1995] 1996): **cum grano salis** ('with a grain of salt,' p. 188).

Sanders, Lawrence. *Timothy's Game* (1988): **Sic transit ...** ('Thus passes ...,' p. 497).

Sayers, Dorothy. *Murder Must Advertise* ([1933] 1993): **de mortuis ...** ('about the dead [nothing but good],' p. 36).

Scottoline, Lisa. *Moment of Truth* ([2000] 2001): **Mea culpa** ('my fault,' p. 19), **Et cum spiritu tuo** ('and with your spirit,' p. 95), **Sui generis** ('one of a kind' or 'unique,' p. 197).

Thompson, Jim. *After Dark, My Sweet* ([1955] 1990): **Quod erat demonstrandum** ("What was to be shown." p. 34).

Thorp, Roderick. *Rainbow Drive* (1986): **Semper fi** (a short for 'Semper fidelis,' meaning 'Always faithful,' p. 35).

Truman, Margaret. *Murder at the National Cathedral* ([1990] 1992): **primus inter pares** ('first among equals,' p. 9).

Truman, Margaret. *Murder in the Supreme Court* ([1982] 1992): **Fide, sed cui vide.** ("Trust, but watch whom you trust." p. 194).

Westlake, Donald E. *Don't Ask* ([1993] 1994): **Quid lucrum istic mihi est?** ("What's in it for me?" pp. 16, 177, 331), **sic transit gloria ...** ('thus passes the glory of ...,' p. 122).

C. Frontier & Western Fiction

Abbey, Edward. *The Brave Cowboy* ([1956] 1982): **nolo contendere** ("I do not wish to contest." p. 89).

Beach, Rex. *The Silver Horde* (1909): **persona non grata** ('an unwelcome person,' p. 192, twice).

Busch, Niven. *Duel in the Sun* ([1944] 1963): **Semper fidelis** ('Always faithful,' 29).

Curwood, James Oliver. *God's Country and the Woman* ([1914] 1925): **terra incognita** ('unknown land,' p. 23).

Grey, Zane. *Wild Horse Mesa* ([1924] 1956): **terra firma** ('firm/dry land,' p. 302).

Kiefer, Warren. *Outlaw* (1991): **versus** ('against,' p. 491).

Raine, William MacLeod. *Ridgeway of Montana* ([1909] 1913): ***fidus Achates*** ('faithful/devoted Achates,' a metaphor for a 'faithful/devoted friend,'—from *The Aeneid*, p. 102, ***apologia*** ('apology,' p. 130).

Rhodes, Eugene Manlove. *Good Men and True* ([1910] 1920): ***modus vivendi*** ('a way of life,' p. 88).

Figure 4.1. Polish poster for King Vidor's *Duel in the Sun* (1946), designed by Jakub Erol (1970). Courtesy of the "Ikonosfera" Gallery and Transart Collection.

D. Other Genres

Brown, Dan. *Angels & Demons* ([2000] 2003): **Quid pro quo** ('one thing for another,' p. 156).

Clancy, Tom. *Patriot Games* ([1987] 1988): **Arma virumque cano, Trojae qui primus ab oris ...** ("I sing of the wars and the man who first came from the shores of Troy ..." p. 90); **Conticuere omnes, intentique ora tenebant.** ("All became silent and were listening attentively." p. 91)—both quotations from Vergil's *Aeneid*, Book One, line 1, and Book Two, line 1, respectively.

Crichton, Michael. *Congo* ([1980] 1993): **persona non grata** ('an unwelcome person,' p. 87), **bona fortuna** ('good luck,' p. 106), **terra incognita** ('unknown land,' 159).

Grady, James. *Six Days of the Condor* ([1974] 1975): **post facto** ('after the fact,' p. 104).

Hamilton, Donald. *The Terminators* (1975): **modus operandi** ('a way of doing something,' pp. 144, 146), **Quid pro quo** ('one thing for another,' p. 198).

Wilson, F. Paul. *The Select* ([1994] 1995): **ipso facto** ('by the very fact,' p. 180), **Cogito, ergo sum** ("I think; therefore, I am." p. 304).

Conclusions

The goal of this publication was to prove the prevalence of the Latin language in modern fiction by presenting pertinent references encountered in fiction books written in the twentieth and twenty-first centuries and set in the nineteenth, twentieth and twenty-first centuries. The quotations have been extracted from novels, short stories and plays that I have read, or reread (in some cases), in the period of about twenty-five years, starting in the mid-1990s (when I began teaching Latin) and selected either randomly or according to criteria unrelated to the thesis of this publication, a fact important in the process of establishing the statistical basis applied in further conclusions. Because in the same period I have been working on a variety of film and literature-related projects, the genre of the books on my reading lists covered, in addition to significant mainstream titles, many items of the frontier and western fiction (included in the scopes of my first two books) and plenty of mysteries, the genre that I have been fond of for a long time and am still hoping to write about in the near future.

Assuming that during that twenty-five-year period I have read about 1200 books (approximately fifty books a year), the number of works that have been quoted in this project, over 220, constitutes about 20%, which would suggest that every fifth book I have read (without applying any Latin-related favoring criteria in the choice) contained one or more Latin references. Compared to that, the number of references to any other languages, e.g., French, German, Spanish, Italian, Russian, Polish or Sanskrit (and I have paid attention to those as well and made a note of most of the cases), is by far less impressive. There are quite a lot of instances of single expressions or brief dialogue in those languages, but, if, for instance, a line (or several lines) is quoted from a French, German or Italian book (fiction or nonfiction), it is usually automatically translated into English. Thus, it is probably quite safe to conclude that Latin has a special place among languages, that the writers quoting it in their works, more or less extensively, make a certain assumption as to how many people may recognize those words or lines without being helped.

The main body of the book consists of forty-five entries, divided into three genre-dependent parts, each entry corresponding to one writer (in one case, Ellery Queen, it is a team of two authors hiding under one pen name). Those are the writers whose contribution to the main thesis of the book is most impressive; they either incorporated samples of Latin in more than one book or, if it happens to be only one work, it is certainly filled with an overwhelming number of references. One way or another, these writers—whom I would like to grant the honorable epithet of the major advocates of the ancient language—are the ones that deserve more attention than the authors (about a hundred of them) quoted in the Appendix, where the number/quality of references per name would not justify creating a separate entry or the presented data do not require extra explanation or commentary. While books brimming with Latin references are certainly the welcome core of the publication, in one way, they are a mixed blessing. Because of the 300-word restriction related to the copyright law (seeking publisher's permissions for quoting excerpts exceeding that limit has turned out to be rather discouraging), I was compelled to present only some of the references in their contexts and put the rest of them (from the same source) on a comprehensive list—along with their translations but outside of the contexts, which, as a result, deprived some of those samples of their profundity.

What needs to be clarified here is that the size of an entry does not correspond to the rank/prestige of a given author; rather, it illustrates the number of Latin references found in his/her work(s) that I happen to have read. Thus, the writers featured in the main body are not necessarily in any way superior to those quoted in the Appendix. Furthermore, it would be false to conclude that writers completely excluded in the book are unlikely to show any Latin references in their works. On the other hand, if someone is determined to find out the names of authors/titles of books "unfriendly" or indifferent to the ancient language, I would advise that person to compare the writers/works listed in the bibliographies of my previous books against the Bibliography of this publication.

While most of the writers quoted here are American, there are a few among them that, even though they write/wrote in English, are/were foreigners, e.g., Scotsman Ian Rankin and Australasians Morris L. West and C. K. Stead. Some of the writers, such as James Hilton and Aldous Huxley, were born in England but concluded their careers and lives in the USA. Jerzy Kosinski was born in Poland but died in America after an impressive career on this side of the Atlantic. Dermot McEvoy was born in Dublin, Ireland, but immigrated to America as a child and became writing in the USA. The list of English-language writers of dual nationality is closed with Ross Macdonald, a Canadian-American. The unambiguously international flavor among the writers is provided by Argentinian Julio Cortázar, writing in Spanish, and Italian Umberto Eco, whose books have been translated all over the world from Italian, of course.

The prestige of the authors that have provided the data can be illustrated, among other things, by some of their accolades. The list includes three Nobel Prize winners (Sinclair Lewis, John Steinbeck and Saul Bellow) and several Pulitzer Prize winners (Herman Wouk, Edwin O'Connor, William Styron, Saul

Bellow, Norman Mailer, William Kennedy, Larry McMurtry and John Updike). Among the crime and detective fiction writers, there are many with multiple awards, such as Edgar or Master's, and many of those authors have held the position of the President of the Mystery Writers of America—six out of those that are featured in the main body (Raymond Chandler, Ellery Queen, John Dickson Carr, Ross Macdonald, Joe Gores, Sara Paretsky) and eight out of those quoted in the Appendix (Robert Bloch, William P. McGivern, Elmore Leonard, Elizabeth Maron, Lisa Scottoline, Sandra Brown, Donald E. Westlake and Jeffery Deaver).

Many of the writers graduated from, or at least attended for some time, prestigious universities, and because of that, you can find quoted in the book Latin mottos of four Ivy League schools—Harvard (the alma mater of Wolfe, Updike, Van Dine, Turow and Finder), Yale (Lewis and Finder), Princeton (Fitzgerald and Dunne) and Columbia (Kosinski). While other prestigious U.S. school mentioned in the book for the same reasons include, first of all, Stanford (Steinbeck, Gores, Turow, McMurtry) and New York University (Raucher, Queen), some famous foreign schools are also represented here—University of Oxford (Huxley, Updike), University of Buenos Aires (Cortázar), University of Melbourne (West), University of Bristol (Stead), University of Turin (Eco) and University of Łódź (Kosinski).

The Latin references presented in the book, all listed in the Index (the size of which itself is a strong argument for the thesis), can be classified according to their theme or provenance into the following categories: literature, philosophy, history, mythology, culture (including the film industry), education, religion, medicine, law, sciences (including biology, zoology, botany and psychology/psychiatry), politics, military and others. The last category covers general, everyday expressions, and among those, I would include most of the proverbs. The category that has collected the largest number of examples is religion, and the authors that provided extensive or numerous citations of that kind include Fitzgerald, Hilton, Steinbeck, Shaw, West, O'Connor, Raucher, Updike, Dunne, Irving, McEvoy, Queen, Kienzle, Gores and Finder. While the legal phraseology is rather obvious—such references dominate primarily but not exclusively the entries on the crime and detective fiction writers—the category most interesting to Latin students is probably literature. In addition to some citations from Ovid and Lucretius, the reader can enjoy numerous quotations from Vergil (to be found mostly in the entries on Hilton, Wolfe, Cortázar, Levine, Rankin, McMurtry), Horace (Wolfe, Steinbeck, Hough) and Catullus (Huxley, Wolfe). Of interest should also be the references to other famous names related to ancient Rome, such as Marcus Tullius Cicero, a statesman, lawyer and scholar who has been quoted by Paul Levine, and

Publius Cornelius Tacitus, a historian and politician admired, ad nauseam, by a character in Paul Horgan's novel *A Distant Trumpet*.

Another area worth analyzing is the variety of roles that the Latin references play in the works of fiction. Two of them are quite obvious: whether representing a general expression or a legal term, a lot of Latin phrases and, occasionally clauses, are used in literature to imitate the everyday language, and certain lexical items adopted from Latin without any spelling changes (the meaning may occasionally be somewhat different) are a natural part of it simply because they better or more easily address the ideas/notions that a speaker wants to refer to. It is especially true in the case of the legal terms, where one, two or three Latin words (e.g., 'alibi,' *habeas corpus* or *in flagrante delicto*, or, even more so, 'subpoena' *duces tecum*) would have to be replaced by a sentence or a paragraph if the idea were to be explained without the help of the Latin phrase or clause.

The role of religious references is almost diametrically different. Here the Latin quotations serve at least a couple of purposes: they are either absolutely necessary in order to address certain issues related to the Church or its philosophy (like in West's *The Shoes of the Fisherman* or Updike's *Roger's Version*), or they illustrate religious routines and/or the language of the believers, Catholics first of, either in their communication with other representatives of the same belief or in the documentation of their everyday life. Sometimes, religious references lead to intentional humorous effects, e.g., in Steinbeck's *Tortilla Flat*. A discipline closely related to religion is philosophy, and the role of such references in fiction (as illustrated, again, in *Roger's Version*) is simply to quote published philosophers in support of one's argument in a discourse.

A literary work unique in many respects, escaping all classification criteria, is Umberto Eco's speculative and occult novel *Foucault's Pendulum*. The author tells a fascinating and haunting story, covering a vast territory and an extensive period of time, and, while unveiling its enormously complex mystery, rather than creating it (as it appears to have been perpetually hanging there, somewhere in the clouds, dormant and unlikely to be discovered because of its absolute secrecy), he consciously uses Latin references to provide the irresistible impression of authenticity. Who needs evidence stronger than that to demonstrate the special role that Latin has been incessantly playing in many areas of Western culture? To illustrate its own expression, Latin is definitely *sui generis* among the languages of the PIE group. Such a conclusion is also made clear, or at least insinuated, by Aldous Huxley in his novel *Island*, where one's competence in Latin appears to be treated as an exception among the Western culture values inflicted by stereotypical thinking and thus rejected by the progressive faction of the characters.

Conclusions

In many books, the purpose of a Latin reference, or references, is to testify to a character's background, i.e., to his/her thorough and/or classical education, the best or most apparent example of which is probably Wolfe's *Look Homeward, Angel*. The overuse of Latin by one character can, however, imply arrogance and/or pomposity, as in the books by Van Dine and Horgan, and a caricature in depicting one's enthusiasm towards the language, inevitably evoking humor, is also possible, as illustrated by McMurtry's *Lonesome Dove*. Thus, we could go further in our reasoning and say that Latin is frequently used to limn a literary character in more than one way. In the case of ranger McCrae, his pretentious Latin sign testifies to his vanity rather than his erudition. But, it needs to be admitted that Latin itself, or its mere notion, is frequently associated with a good education. And, it is probably why no one seems to be surprised that it takes Latin expressions, such as *cum laude*, *magna cum laude* and *maxima cum laude*, to express one's distinction in academic performance, or a phrase adopted from Latin, *alma mater*, to refer to one's educational institution. An excellent example of the best use of the ancient language (in the area of education), both to refer to the material covered and to entertain the audience, is the speech given by Chips in James Hilton's *Goodbye, Mr. Chips*, which, additionally, testifies to the teacher's unique relationships with his former and present students.

Last but not least, another role of Latin references, rather obvious when one gets to think of it, is quoting a certain line from a literary work or an aphorism as an analogy to what goes on at a given moment or in a given scene of a book. It takes both creativity and good knowledge of both literature in Latin and the Latin language itself on the writer's part in order to apply this device properly, but the effects are usually quite rewarding. A good example is a scene in Elizabeth George's mystery *Well-Schooled in Murder* where senior prefect Chas Quilter, facing serious consequences because of his tragic negligence (and some serious sins to be revealed later in the book), all of a sudden remembers the line *Nam tua res agitur, paries cum proximus ardet* ("For it is your business, when the wall door catches fire."). Furthermore, several instances of such a role of references can be found in *Goodbye Mr. Chips*. One of the authors quoted by Chips is Vergil, the great poet whose numerous lines—e.g., *Durate et vosmet rebus servate secundis* ("Save yourselves for better times.")—embellish a host of literary works, usually in a context fitting the situation, such as a period of hardships in the case of the line quoted here.

One thing in the book that should appeal to Latin students is the diversity of grammatical forms offered by the references. The quotations contain many examples of verbs (regular, irregular, deponent and semi-deponent) in a variety of forms, covering almost all six tenses in the indicative mood, both active and passive voice, and some instances of the subjunctive mood, mostly in the Present Active Tense. There is also an abundance of examples of nouns and adjectives in practically all cases, singular and plural, quite a lot of pronouns in different cases and numbers, and several instances of such verbal forms as gerund, gerundive and all three participles. There may be one or two examples of the Accusative and Infinitive Construction, several instances of Indirect Commands/Requests and some examples of Ablative Absolute.

Something that has come up between the time I started working on this project and now, when I am about to conclude it, is the appearance of the pandemic, a worldwide disaster originally attributed to a contagion labeled 'coronavirus.' Ironically, but not predictably (considering that epidemiology is one of the sciences), the neologism is composed (in the German manner of creating compound nouns) of two Latin words, *virus viri* (a second-declension neuter noun meaning 'slime/slimy liquid/poison'), a word adopted by medicine and widely used in many modern languages in its self-explanatory sense, and *corona coronae* (a first-declension feminine noun meaning 'crown'), which became a part of the compound in order to describe the shape of the virus. Thus, 'coronavirus,' which soon received a more specific code, 'COVID-19,' has become one more unwelcome—in this case, vivid—example of the popularity or ubiquity of the Latin language in modern life all over the world, just like the linguistic phenomenon of 'computer,' which has already been discussed in the Preface.

While the Preface is full of examples of the use of Latin in many different areas of modern life, one area, very important to me, is not addressed there as, truly, it is not directly included in the scope of this book. However, since the arguments have already been exhausted and the job (I hope to believe) done, I feel it is appropriate to get less strict now and talk a little bit about some other matters. Also in the Preface, I do mention two films—*Balls of Fire* and *People Will Talk*—to illustrate the familiarity of "Gaudeamus Igitur" among the American academia. Well, I wrote the Preface several months ago, and, in the meantime, I have seen another movie where that famous song is sung by a group of students. It takes place in Richard Thorpe's *The Student Prince* (1954; starring Edmund Purdom, Ann Blyth, Louis Calhern and Edmund Gwenn), a musical film set in the nineteenth century and the pertinent scene taking place in Heidelberg. The movie is a remake of a silent film, which was based on an operetta with book and lyrics by Dorothy Donnelly and music by Sigmund Romberg, itself based on a stage play and novel by Wilhelm Meyer-Förster. Thus, now, I can use the movie as an example of the popularity of the song in Europe, which was mentioned in the Preface but not documented.

Conclusions 261

But *The Student Prince* is not the only film that I would like to mention here. Since, after all, this is a book about Latin, I would like to give some instances of movie titles that use Latin words or phrases, rather than English or any other language, regardless of which part of the world they were made and/or distributed. Here they are: two versions of *Solaris*—Andrei Tarkovsky's (1972; featuring Natalya Bondarchuk and Donatas Banionis) and Steven Soderbergh's (2002; starring George Clooney and Natascha McElhone)—both based on the novel by Stanisław Lem, a Polish science fiction master; Volker Schlöndorff's *Homo Faber* (a.k.a. *Voyager*, 1991; starring Sam Shepard and Julie Delpy; based on the novel by Max Frisch, a Swiss writer); and James Gray's *Ad Astra* (2019; featuring Brad Pitt, Tommy Lee Jones, Ruth Negga and Donald Sutherland). The form *solaris* is a third-declension, two-termination adjective, masculine or feminine, derived from the noun *sol solis* (thus, meaning 'sunny' or 'related to the sun'); *Homo Faber*, meaning 'Man the Maker,' consists of the third-declension masculine noun *homo hominis* ('man/human being') in the nominative singular case and the second-declension masculine substantive *faber* (genitive *fabri* – 'worker'), also in the nominative case; and *ad astra* ('to the stars') is a phrase composed of the preposition *ad* ('to/toward') and the second-declension neuter noun (*astrum*, *astri* – 'star/constellation') in the accusative plural form (for destination/place to which). Two of the titles are most likely shortened versions of famous lines: *Homo Faber* of *Homo faber suae quisque fortunae* ("Every man is the artifex of his destiny"), a line originally used by Appius Claudius Caecus (340 B.C. – 273 B.C., a distinguished statesman of the Roman Republic) in his *Sententiae*; and *Ad Astra* of *Ad astra per aspera* ("Through thorns/hardships to the stars"), which happens to be the motto of Kansas (a fact attributed to John James Ingalls, 1861).

There are two more films that are worth mentioning here for different reasons—*Dead Poets Society* (1989) and *Tombstone* (1993). The former, directed by Peter Weir, is of interest because of the way the English teacher (played by Robin Williams, who, ironically, appears also in the movie version of Saul Bellow's novel *Carpe Diem*) uses the Latin quotation *Carpe diem* ("Seize the day") as one of the ways to inspire his students to live their lives to the fullest, as well as because of the scene where the Latin instructor is trying to teach his students the forms of the first-declension, masculine noun *agricola agricolae* and thoughtlessly recites with them all the cases. George P. Cosmatos's *Tombstone* (starring Kurt Russell, Val Kilmer, Sam Elliott, Bill Paxton and Michael Biehn), on the other hand, has (unexpectedly in a western movie) a relatively brief exchange in Latin between Doc Holliday (Kilmer) and Johnny Ringo (Biehn). The reason why I am able to include the whole excerpt here verbatim is its existing novelization by Giles Tippette (from the screenplay by Kevin Jarre). Thus, here is the famous scene that takes place in a

Tombstone saloon (Kate is Holliday's girlfriend, in the movie portrayed by Polish actress Joanna Pacula; Wyatt Earp is played by Kurt Russell):

> Ringo stepped up to the table. He had been hanging back. He said softly, "Then you must be Doc Holliday."
>
> Doc smiled that mysterious smile of his and said, "That's the rumor."
>
> "You retired too?"
>
> Doc said, "Not me. I'm in my prime."
>
> Ringo looked at him with his dead eyes. He said, "Yeah, you look it."
>
> Kate made her way through the crown and up to Doc's chair. She put her hand on his shoulder,
>
> Doc said, "And you must be Ringo. Look, darling, Johnny Ringo. The deadliest pistoleer since Wild Bill, they say. What do you think, darling? Should I hate him?"
>
> Kate said, "You don't even know him."
>
> He said, "Yes, but there's just something about him. Something about the eyes, I don't know, reminds me of ... me. No, I'm sure of it, I hate him."
>
> Wyatt spoke up to Ringo, "Don't mind what he said, he's drunk."
>
> Doc looked into Ringo's eyes and said, "***In vino veritas***" ["In wine lies the truth."].
>
> Ringo answered him back in **Latin**, "***Age quod agis***" ["Do what you're doing."].
>
> Doc said, "***Credat Judaeus Apella***" ["Let the Jew Apella believe it," meaning: "Tell it to someone else, not me."].
>
> With his dead eyes, Ringo patted his gun. He said, still speaking **Latin**, "***Eventus stultorum magister***" ["Events are the teacher of fools," meaning "Fools have to learn through experience."]

> The Cheshire-cat smile was back on Doc's face. He said meaningfully, "*In pace requiescat*" ["Let him rest in peace," meaning "It's your funeral."]
>
> Fred White had come up and said appeasingly, "Come on now, we don't want any trouble, not in any language."
>
> Doc laughed. "Evidently, Mr. Ringo is an educated man. Now I really hate him." [pp. 56-57]

The above excerpt from *Tombstone* is just one example of how Latin has also penetrated the performing arts. References found in films, though undoubtedly numerous, are not, however, the topic of this book, and neither are those encountered in other media, including magazines, newspapers, broadcasting, the internet and nonfiction books. But they all exist and all can be studied as part of separate projects that would provide further evidence of the ubiquity of the ancient language in modern times. Since I have just finished reading Lee Server's biographical book *Robert Mitchum: "Baby, I Don't Care"* (for my next project), I can share several examples of Latin references that I was only moderately surprised to have found in its pages, either used by the author/narrator (e.g., **habeas corpus** – pp, 169 and 221; **ad hoc** – p. 174; **ad hominem** – p. 177; **pro bono** – p. 189; **per diem** – pp. 301 and 451), Mitchum himself in one of his quoted comments (**homo sapiens** – p. 352) or other people quoted, e.g., film critic Pauline Kael (using the epithet **sui generis**, p. 448, when praising the actor in *The New Yorker*)—not required to be translated as all have been presented on many occasions in the main body. The idea behind this paragraph is to show that *Latin in Modern Fiction* is just one of many options available to illustrate/prove the unique nature of Latin, just a threshold of the doorway leading to a big chamber of endless possibilities.

Now that I am in the course of quoting Latin references from sources outside of the project's scope, I would like to finish the Conclusions, and the whole book, with an insightful quotation from *Quo Vadis* (1896), a great novel by highly-acclaimed Polish writer Henryk Sienkiewicz (1846 – 1916), one more Nobel Prize-winner. Set in the turbulent times of the reign of Nero, the novel is a love story on the surface but, truly, it depicts the persecutions of Christians in a manner that none other fiction book has ever done. The two excerpts quoted below come from the end of the book, after its denouement, and refer to Apostle Peter who, accompanied by a boy named Nazarius, is about to leave Rome as well as his martyred co-religionists:

It was perfectly still all around. Nazarius saw only that the trees were quivering in the distance, as if someone were shaking them, and the light was spreading more broadly over the plain. He looked with wonder at the Apostle.

"Rabbi! what ails thee?" cried he, with alarm.

The pilgrim's staff fell from Peter's hands to the earth; his eyes were looking forward, motionless; his mouth was open; on his face were depicted astonishment, delight, rapture.

Then he threw himself on his knees, his arms stretched forward; and this cry left his lips,—

"O Christ! O Christ!"

He fell with his face to the earth, as if kissing someone's feet.

The silence continued long; then were heard the words of the aged man, broken by sobs,—

"**Quo vadis, Domine?**" ["Where are you going, Lord?"]

Nazarius did not hear the answer; but to Peter's ears came a sad and sweet voice, which said,—

"If thou desert my people, I am going to Rome to be crucified a second time."

The Apostle lay on the ground, his face in the dust, without motion or speech. It seemed to Nazarius that he had fainted or was dead; but he rose at last, seized the staff with trembling hands, and turned without a word toward the seven hills of the city.

The boy, seeing this, repeated as an echo,—

"**Quo vadis, Domine?**"

"To Rome," said the Apostle, in a low voice.

And he returned. [p. 537]

Conclusions

Figure 5.1. The author standing in front of a store named "Quo Vadis" in Potsdam, Germany (March 2020). Photo by Betsy Hoffmann.

And so Nero passed, as a whirlwind, as a storm, as a fire, as war or death passes; but the basilica of Peter rules now, from the Vatican heights, the city, and the world.

Near the ancient Porta Capena stands to this day a little chapel with the inscription, somewhat worn: ***Quo vadis, Domine?*** [p. 654]

Acknowledgments

In addition to being genuinely indebted to two popular websites, Wikipedia and IMDb, which I have been referring to on a regular basis to find and/or verify information regarding the authors of the books quoted in this publication, I would like to express my gratitude to:

- Brash Books, the publisher of Tom Kakonis's *Flawless* (2014), for allowing me to quote extensive excerpts from the book;

- Daniel Kakonis for providing detailed biographical information about his father, Tom Kakonis; and

- Jacek Jaroszyk, the Director of the "Ikonosfera" Gallery, Transart Collection and Transart Production, for his enormously kind and comprehensive response to my inquiry as to the law regulating the issues of reproducing Polish film posters, which allowed me to include in this publication copies of four: the poster for Michelangelo Antonioni's *Blow-Up* (1966, based on the short story by Julio Cortázar), designed by Waldemar Świerzy (1968); the poster for King Vidor's *Duel in the Sun* (1946), designed by Jakub Erol (1970); the poster for Raoul Walsh's *The Tall Men* (1955), designed by Wiktor Górka (1965); and the poster "The Cinema According to Chandler," designed by Waldemar Świerzy (1988) for the retrospective organized by the Film Society "Kinematograf 75."

Bibliography

Abbey, Edward. *The Brave Cowboy*. New York: Avon, (1956) 1982.

Adams, Samuel Hopkins. *Tenderloin*. New York: Signet/New American Library, 1960.

Albee, Edward. *Who's Afraid of Virginia Woolf?* New York: Pocket Cardinal, (1962) 1966.

Algren, Nelson. *The Man with the Golden Arm*. New York: Pocket Cardinal, (1949) 1956.

Allen, Woody. *Without Feathers*. New York: Ballantine Books, 1983.

Baldacci, David. *The Simple Truth*. New York: Grand Central Publishing, (1998) 1999.

Barth, John. *Lost in the Funhouse*. New York: Bantam Books, (1963) 1969.

Baxt, George. *The Clark Gable & Carole Lombard Murder Case*. New York: St. Martin's Press, 1995.

Beach, Rex. *The Silver Horde*. New York: A. L. Burt Company, 1909.

Bellow, Saul. *More Die of Heartbreak*. New York: William Morrow and Company, 1987.

Bellow, Saul. *Mr. Sammler's Planet*. New York: The Viking Press, 1970.

Blatty, William Peter. *Dimiter*. New York: Tom Doherty Associates, 2010.

Bloch, Robert. *Psycho*. Greenwich, CT: Fawcett Publications, (1959) 1960.

Bromfield, Louis. *The Rains Came*. New York: Signet/New American Library, (1937) 1955.

Brown, Dan. *Angels & Demons*. New York: Atria Books, (2000) 2003.

Brown, Sandra. *Smash Cut*. New York: Simon & Schuster, 2009.

Busch, Niven. *California Street*. New York: Simon and Schuster, 1959.

Busch, Niven. *Continent's Edge*. New York: Simon and Schuster, 1980.

Busch, Niven. *Duel in the Sun*. New York: Popular Library, (1944) 1963.

Carr, John Dickson. *The Blind Barber* (1934). In *John Dickson Carr: Four Complete Dr. Fell Mysteries*. New York: Avenel Books, 1988.

Carr, John Dickson. *The Case of the Constant Suicides* (1941). In *John Dickson Carr: Four Complete Dr. Fell Mysteries*. New York: Avenel Books, 1988.

Carr, John Dickson. *The Crooked Hinge* (1938). In *John Dickson Carr: Four Complete Dr. Fell Mysteries*. New York: Avenel Books, 1988.

Carr, John Dickson. *To Wake the Dead*. (1938). In *John Dickson Carr: Four Complete Dr. Fell Mysteries*. New York: Avenel Books, 1988.

Caspary, Vera. *Laura*. New York: Dell Books, (1942) 1961.

Chandler, Raymond. *The Long Goodbye*. New York: Vintage Crime/Black Lizard, (1953) 1981.

Chandler, Raymond. "Mandarin's Jade" (1937). In *Killer in the Rain*. New York: Ballantine Books, 1977.

Chandler, Raymond. "The Man Who Liked Dogs" (1934). In *Killer in the Rain*. New York: Ballantine Books, 1977.

Cheever, John. "The Sorrows of Gin." In *The Stories of John Cheever*. New York: Borzoi/Alfred A. Knopf, 1978.

Clancy, Tom. *Patriot Games*. New York: Berkley Books, (1987) 1988.

Conroy, Pat. *Beach Music*. New York: Nan A. Talese/Doubleday, 1995.

Cornwell, Patricia. *From Potter's Field*. New York: Berkley Books, (1995) 1996.

Cornwell, Patricia. *Isle of Dogs*. New York: Berkley Books, (2001) 2002.

Cornwell, Patricia. *The Scarpetta Factor*. New York: G. P. Putnam's Sons, 2009.

Cortázar, Julio. *The Winners*. Translated from the Spanish by Elaine Kerrigan. New York: Pantheon Books, (1960) 1965.

Crichton, Michael. *Congo*. New York: Ballantine Books, (1980) 1993.

Crider, Bill. *We'll Always Have Murder: A Humphrey Bogart Mystery*. New York: ibooks/Simon & Schuster, 2001.

Curwood, James Oliver. *God's Country and the Woman*. New York: Doubleday, Page & Company for P. F. Collier & Son Company, (1914) 1925.

Deaver, Jeffery. *The Twelfth Card*. New York: Pocket Books, (2005) 2006.

DeLillo, Don. *Underworld*. New York: Scribner, 1997.

Dickey, Eric Jerome. *Resurrecting Midnight*. New York: Dutton, 2009.

Diehl, William. *Primal Fear*. New York: Gunn Productions, (1993) 1994.

Doctorow, E. L. *Ragtime*. New York: Bantam Books, (1974) 1976.

Dunne, John Gregory. *True Confessions*. New York: Pocket Books, (1977) 1978.

Eco, Umberto. *Foucault's Pendulum*. Translated from the Italian by William Weaver. New York: Helen and Kurt Wolff/Harcourt Brace Jovanovich, (1988) 1989.

Finder, Joseph. *Buried Secrets*. New York: St. Martin's Press, 2011.

Finder, Joseph. *Guilty Minds*. New York: Dutton/Penguin Random House, 2016.

Finder, Joseph. *Vanished*. New York: St. Martin's Press, 2009.

Finder, Joseph. *Z premedytacją* (a translation of *Guilty Minds* by Przemysław Hejmej). Katowice, Poland: Wydawnictwo Sonia Draga, 2019.

Fitzgerald, F. Scott. "Absolution." In *The Stories of F. Scott Fitzgerald*." New York: Charles Scribner's Sons, (1924) 1969.

Fitzgerald, F. Scott. *The Beautiful and the Damned*. New York: A Signet Classic/Collier Books, (1922) 1986.

Fitzgerald, F. Scott. "Financing Finnegan." In *The Stories of F. Scott Fitzgerald*." New York: Charles Scribner's Sons, (1938) 1969.

Fitzgerald, F. Scott. *Tender Is the Night*. New York: Charles Scribner's Sons, (1934) 1962.

Flagg, Fannie. *Coming Attractions* (as *Daisy Fay and the Miracle Man*). New York: Warner Books, (1981) 1992.

Ford, Richard. *Independence Day*. Toronto: Little Brown and Company, 1995.

Gardner, Erle Stanley. *The Case of the Daring Decoy* (1957). In *A Perry Mason Casebook*. New York: William Morrow and Company, 1993.

Gardner, Erle Stanley. *The Case of the Golddigger's Purse*. New York: Pocket Books, (1945) 1962.

Gardner, Erle Stanley. "The Case of the Irate Witness" (1953). In *Sleuths of the Century*. New York: Carroll & Graf Publishers, 2000.

Gardner, Erle Stanley. *The Case of the Stuttering Bishop*. New York: Ballantine Books, (1936) 1988.

George, Elizabeth. *A Traitor to Memory*. New York: Bantam Books, (2001) 2009.

George, Elizabeth. *Well-Schooled in Murder*. New York: Bantam Books, (1990) 1991.

Gores, Joe. *Hammett*. New York: Ballantine Books, (1975) 1976.

Gores, Joe. *Spade & Archer: The Sequel to Dashiell Hammett's The Maltese Falcon*. New York: Alfred A. Knopf, 2009.

Grady, James. *Six Days of the Condor*. New York: Dell Publishing, (1974) 1975.

Greene, Graham. *The Human Factor*. New York: Simon and Schuster, 1978.

Grey, Zane. *Wild Horse Mesa*. Roslyn, NY: Walter J. Black, (1924) 1956.

Grisham, John. *Time to Kill*. New York: Island Books/Dell, (1989) 1992.

Guterson, David. *Our Lady of the Forest*. New York: Alfred A. Knopf, 2003.

Haddon, Mark. *The Curious Incident of the Dog in the Night-Time*. New York: Vintage Contemporaries/Random House, 2003.

Hall, James W. *Body Language*. New York: St. Martin's Paperbacks, (1998) 1999.

Halliday, Brett. *Murder Takes No Holiday*. New York: Dell, 1960.

Halliday, Brett. *This Is It, Michael Shayne*. New York: Dell, (1950) 1968.

Hamilton, Donald. *The Terminators*. Greenwich, CT: Fawcett Publications, 1975.

Hammett, Dashiell. *The Continental Op*. New York: Vintage Books/Random House, (1923) 1974.

Harr, Jonathan. *A Civil Action*. New York: Vintage/Random House, 1996.

Harris, Thomas. *Hannibal*. New York: Delacorte Press, 1999.

Hartley, L. P. *The Go-Between*. New York: Stein and Day *Publishers*, (1953) 1984.

Healy, Jeremiah. *The Stalking of Sheilah Quinn*. New York: St. Martin's Press, 1998.

Heggen, Thomas. *Mister Roberts*. New York: Bantam Books, (1946) 1966.

Heller. Joseph. *God Knows*. New York: Alfred A. Knopf, 1984.

Henry, Will (writing as Clay Fisher). *The Tall Men*. New York: Bantam Books, (1954) 1970.

Henry, Will (writing as Clay Fisher). *Yellowstone Kelly*. New York: Bantam Books, (1957) 1988.

Hilton, James. *Goodbye, Mr. Chips*. New York: Bantam Books, (1934) 1986.

Hilton, James. *Random Harvest*. Boston: Little, Brown and Company, 1941.

Horgan, Paul. *A Distant Trumpet*. Greenwich, CT: Third Crest/Fawcett, (1960) 1964.

Hough, Emerson. *The Covered Wagon*. New York: D. Appleton and Company, 1922.

Hough, Emerson. *North of 36*. New York: McKinlay, Stone & Mackenzie, 1923.

Hughes, Dorothy B. *Ride the Pink Horse*. New York: Carroll & Graf Publishers, (1946) 1988.
Huxley, Aldous. *Island*. New York: Perennial Library, (1962) 1989.
Iles, Greg. *Black Cross*. New York: Signet/New American Library, 1995.
Iles, Greg. *The Quiet Game*. New York: Signet/New American Library, (1999) 2005.
Iles, Greg. *Sleep No More*. New York: Signet/New American Library, 2002.
Iles, Greg. *Turning Angel*. New York: Scribner, 2005.
Innes, Michael. *Candleshoe* (originally: *Christmas at Candleshoe*). New York: Penguin Books, (1953) 1978.
Irving, John. *A Prayer for Owen Meany*. New York: Ballantine Books, (1989) 1990.
Irving, John. *A Son of the Circus*. New York: Ballantine Books, 1995.
Irving, John. *Until I Find You*. New York: Random House, 2005.
Irving, John. *A Widow for One Year*. New York: Ballantine Books, (1998) 2001.
Isaacs, Susan. *Red, White and Blue*. New York: HarperCollins*Publishers*, 1998.
James, P. D. *A Certain Justice*. New York: Ballantine Books, (1977) 1998.
James, P. D. *Death of an Expert Witness*. Boston: G.K. Hall & Co., 1977 (Large Print).
Kakonis, Tom. *Flawless*. Leawood, KS: Brash Books, 2014.
Kakonis, Tom. *Michigan Roll*. New York: St. Martin's Press, 1988.
Kaufman, Bel. *Up the Down Staircase*. Englewood Cliff, NJ: Prentice-Hall, (1964) 1965.
Kazan, Elia. *The Arrangement*. New York: Avon, (1967) 1968.
Kazan, Elia. *The Assassins*. Greenwich, CT: Fawcett Crest, (1972) 1973.
Keillor, Garrison. *Lake Wobegon*. New York: Viking, (1985) 1986.
Kellerman, Faye. *Grievous Sin*. New York: Ballantine Books, (1993) 1994.
Kellerman, Jonathan. *When the Bough Breaks*. New York: Signet/New American Library, (1985) 1986.
Kennedy, Adam. *Just Like Humphrey Bogart*. New York: Signet/New American Library, (1978) 1979.
Kennedy, William. *Billy Phelan's Greatest Game*. New York: Penguin, (1978) 1983.
Kerouac, Jack. *Designation Angels*. New York: Wideview/Perigee, (1960) 1980.
Kiefer, Warren. *Outlaw*. New York: Signet/Penguin Group, 1991.
Kienzle, William X. *No Greater Love*. New York: Fawcett Books, (1999) 2000.
Kienzle, William X. *The Rosary Murders*. New York: Ballantine Books, (1978) 1989.
Kosinski, Jerzy. *The Hermit of 69th Street*. New York: Zebra Books, (1988) 1991.
Lanier, Virginia. *Blind Bloodhound Justice*. New York: Harper, (1998) 1999.
Latham, Aaron. *Riding with John Wayne*. New York: Simon & Schuster, 2006.
Lehane, Dennis. *Prayers for Rain*. New York: HarperTorch/HarperCollins Publishers, (1999) 2000.

Leonard, Elmore. *The Big Bounce.* New York: Mysterious Press/Warner Books, (1969) 1986.
Levine, Paul. *Bum Deal.* Seattle: Thomas & Mercer, 2018.
Levine, Paul. *Fool Me Twice.* New York: William Morrow, 1996.
Levine, Paul. *Mortal Sin.* New York: William Morrow and Company, 1994.
Lewis, Sinclair. *Babbitt.* New York: P. F. Collier & Son Corporation, 1922.
Lewis, Sinclair. *Dodsworth.* New York: Pocket Books, (1929) 1941.
Lewis, Sinclair. *Elmer Gantry.* New York: Dell Publishing, (1927) 1960.
Lewis, Sinclair. *Kingsblood Royal.* New York: Random House 1947.
Macdonald, Ross. *Black Money* (1966). In *Archer at Large: Three Great Lew Archer Novels of Suspense by Ross Macdonald.* New York: Alfred A. Knopf, 1970 (Bok Club edition).
Macdonald, Ross. *The Galton Case* (1959). In *Archer at Large: Three Great Lew Archer Novels of Suspense by Ross Macdonald.* New York: Alfred A. Knopf, 1970 (Book Club edition).
Macdonald, Ross. *The Three Roads.* New York: Warner Books, (1948) 1991.
Macdonald, Ross. *The Zebra-Striped Hearse.* New York: Warner Books, (1962) 1993.
Maclean, Norman. "Logging and Pimping and 'Your Pal, Jim'". In *A River Runs Through It and Other Stories.* Chicago: The University of Chicago Press, (1976) 2001.
Mailer, Norman. *Tough Guys Don't Dance.* New York: Ballantine Books, (1984) 1985.
Maron, Margaret. *Long Upon the Land.* New York: Grand Central Publishing, 2015.
Maron, Margaret. *Sand Sharks.* New York: Grand Central Publishing, 2009.
Maron, Margaret. *Take Out.* New York: Grand Central Publishing, 2017.
Marquand, John P. *Point of No Return.* Boston: Little, Brown and Company, 1949.
Maugham, W. Somerset. *The Razor's Edge.* Philadelphia: Triangle Books/The Blakiston Company, (1943) 1946.
McBain, Ed. *Rumpelstiltskin.* New York: Ballantine Books, (1981) 1989.
McEvoy, Dermot. *Our Lady of Greenwich Village.* New York: Skyhorse Publishing, 2008.
McGivern, William P. *Caprifoil.* New York: Pyramid Books, (1972) 1973.
McMurtry, Larry. *Comanche Moon.* New York: Pocket Books, (1997) 1998.
McMurtry, Larry. *The Evening Star.* New York: Pocket Books/Simon and Schuster, (1992) 1993.
McMurtry, Larry. *Lonesome Dove.* New York: Pocket Books, 1986.
McMurtry, Larry. *Some Can Whistle.* New York: Simon and Schuster, 1989
McMurtry, Larry. *Streets of Laredo.* New York: Pocket Books, (1993) 1994.
Michener, James R. *The Fires of Spring.* New York: Fawcett Crest/Ballantine, (1949) 1984.
O'Connor, Edwin. *The Last Hurrah.* New York: Bantam Books, (1956) 1957.

O'Connor, Flannery. "A Temple of the Holy Ghost." In *A Good Man Is Hard to Find and Other Stories*. Garden City, NY: Image Books/Doubleday & Company, (c. 1954) 1970.

Odets, Clifford. *The Country Girl*. New York: The Viking Press, 1951.

O'Hara, John. *From the Terrace*. New York: Carrol & Graf Publishers, (1958) 1984.

O'Hara, John. "Our Friend the Sea" (1963). In *Collected Stories of John O'Hara*. New York: Random House, 1984.

O'Kane, Leslie. *Finding Gregory Peck: Life's Second Chances*. Scotts Valley, CA: CreateSpace Independent Publishing Platform, 2015.

O'Neill, Eugene. *The Great God Brown*. In *Nine Plays by Eugene O'Neill*. New York: The Modern Library/Random House, (1926) 1954.

Palmer, Michael. *A Heartbeat Away*. New York: St. Martin's Press. 2011.

Paretsky, Sara. *Bitter Medicine*. New York: Ballantine Books, (1987) 1988.

Paretsky, Sara. *Blood Shot*. New York: Dell/Bantam, (1988) 1989.

Paretsky, Sara. *Fire Sale*. New York: Signet/New American Library, (2005) 2006.

Paretsky, Sara. "Grace Notes" (1995). In *Sleuths of the Century*. New York: Carroll & Graf Publishers, 2000.

Paretsky, Sara. *Tunnel Vision*. New York: Delacorte Press, 1994.

Parker, Robert B. *Chance*. New York: Berkley Books, (1996) 1997.

Parker, Robert B. *Potshot*. New York: Berkley Books, (2001) 2002.

Patterson, James. *Black Friday*. New York: Warner Books, (1986) 2000.

Patterson, James. *Kiss the Girls*. Boston: Little, Brown and Company, 1995.

Patterson, James. *Violets Are Blue*. New York: Warner Vision Books, (2001) 2002.

Pharr, Clyde. *Vergil's Aeneid: Books I-VI*. Wauconda, ILL: Bolchazy-Carducci Publishers, 1964.

Puzo, Mario. *The Fourth*. New York: Random House, 1990.

Queen, Ellery. *Calamity Town*. New York: ImPress, (1942) 2003.

Queen, Ellery. *The Dutch Shoe Mystery*. Signet Books/The New American Library, (1931) 1968.

Queen, Ellery. *The Fourth Side of the Triangle*. New York: Random House, 1965.

Queen, Ellery. *The Origin of Evil*. New York: Signet Books/New American Library, (1951) 1972.

Raine, William MacLeod. *Ridgeway of Montana* (1909). In *The Big Book of the Ranges*. New York: Grosset & Dunlap Publishers, 1913.

Rand, Ayn. *The Fountainhead*. New York: Signet/Penguin, (1943) 1993.

Rankin, Ian. *Mortal Causes*. London: Orion, (1995) 2005.

Rankin, Ian. *Resurrection Men*. London: Orion, (2002) 2005.

Raucher, Herman. *A Glimpse of Tiger*. Greenwich, CT: Fawcett Crest, (1971) 1975.

Raucher, Herman. *Summer of '42*. New York: Dell, 1971.

Rhodes, Eugene Manlove. *Good Men and True*. New York: Grosset & Dunlap Publishers, (1910) 1920.

Ritchie, Ron M. *The Day Burt Lancaster Died*. Renfrew, Ontario, Canada: General Store Publishing House, 2008.

Roosevelt, Elliott. *Murder in the Red Room.* New York: Avon Books, (1992) 1994.

Rosten, Leo. *Captain Newman, M.D.* Greenwich, CT: Crest/Fawcett Publications, (1954) 1964.

Sanders, Lawrence. *McNally's Trial.* New York: Berkley Books, (1995) 1996.

Sanders, Lawrence. *Timothy's Game* (1988). In *Lawrence Sanders: Three Complete Novels.* New York: G. P. Putnam's Sons, 1999.

Sayers, Dorothy. *Murder Must Advertise.* New York: HarperPerennial/Harper Collins*Publishers,* (1933) 1993.

Schulberg, Budd. *The Disenchanted.* New York: Random House, 1950.

Scottoline, Lisa. *Moment of Truth.* New York: HarperTorch/HarperCollins Publishers, (2000) 2001.

Segal, Erich. *Man, Woman and Child.* New York: Ballantine Books, (1980) 1981.

Server, Lee. *Robert Mitchum: "Baby, I Don't Care."* New York: St. Martin's Press, 2001.

Shaw, Irwin. *Acceptable Losses.* New York: Avon Books, (1982) 1983.

Shaw, Irwin. *Beggarman, Thief.* New York: Delacorte Press, 1977. (Book Club Edition)

Sheldon, Sidney. *Nothing Lasts Forever.* New York: Warner Books, (1994) 1995.

Shulman, Max. *Rally Round the Flag, Boys!* Garden City, NY: Doubleday & Company, 1954.

Sienkiewicz, Henryk. *Quo Vadis: A Narrative of the Time of Nero.* Translated from the Polish by Jeremiah Curtin. Garden City, New York: International Collectors Library, 1925.

Simpson, D. P. *Cassell's Latin Dictionary.* New York: Macmillan Publishing Company, 1968.

Singer, Isaac Bashevis. *Shadows on the Hudson.* New York: Farrar, Straus, Giroux, 1998.

Sondel, Janusz. *Słownik łacińsko-polski dla prawników i historyków.* Kraków, Poland: Universitas, 2001.

Stead, C. K. *Sister Hollywood.* New York: St. Martin's Press, (1989) 1990.

Steinbeck, John. *Tortilla Flat.* In The Short Novels of Steinbeck, John. New York: The Viking Press, (1935) 1953.

Steinbeck, John. *Travels with Charley.* New York: Bantam Books, (1962) 1963.

Steinbeck, John. *The Winter of Our Discontent.* New York: The Viking Press, 1961.

Styron, William. *Sophie's Choice.* New York: Random House, 1979.

Tanenbaum, Robert. K. *Corruption of Blood.* New York: Signet Books/Penguin, (1995) 1996.

Tanenbaum, Robert. K. *Escape.* New York: Vanguard Press/Perseus Books Group, 2008.

Thompson, Jim. *After Dark, My Sweet.* New York: Vintage/Black Lizard, (1955) 1990.

Thorp, Roderick. *Rainbow Drive.* New York: Summit Books, 1986.

Tippette, Giles. *Tombstone* (Based on the screenplay by Kevin Jarre). New York: Berkley Books, 1994.

Truman, Margaret. *Murder at the National Cathedral*. New York: Fawcett Books, (1990) 1992.

Truman, Margaret. *Murder in the Supreme Court*. New York: Fawcett Crest, (1982) 1992.

Turow, Scott. *The Burden of Proof*. New York: Farrar, Straus, Giroux, 1990.

Turow, Scott. *The Laws of Our Fathers*. New York: Farrar, Straus, Giroux, 1996.

Turow, Scott. *Personal Injuries*. New York: Farrar, Straus, Giroux, 1999.

Updike, John. *Bech Is Back*. New York: Alfred A. Knopf, 1982.

Updike, John. *The Centaur*. Greenwich, CT: Crest/Fawcett Publications, (1963) 1964.

Updike, John. *Couples*. Greenwich, CT: Crest/Fawcett Publications, 1968.

Updike, John. *Rabbit Is Rich*. New York: Fawcett Crest/Ballantine, (1981) 1982.

Updike, John. *Roger's Version*. New York: Alfred A. Knopf, 1986.

Updike, John. *S*. New York: Fawcett Crest/Ballantine, (1988) 1989.

Updike, John. *The Witches of Eastwick*. New York: Fawcett Crest/Ballantine, (1984) 1985.

Van Dine, S. S. *The Canary Murder Case*. New York: Pocket Books, (1927) 1945.

Van Dine, S. S. *The Kennel Murder Case*. Boston: Gregg Press, (1933) 1980.

Van Dine, S. S. *Piosenka śmierci* (a translation of *The Bishop Murder Case* by Janina Sujkowska). Warszawa, Poland: Czytelnik, (1929) 1991.

Vidal, Gore. *The Best Man*. New York: Dramatists Play Service, (1960) 2001.

Vidal, Gore. *Myra Breckenridge*. New York: Bantam Books, 1968.

Vonnegut, Jr. Kurt. *Breakfast of Champions*. New York: Dell Publishing, (1973) 1975.

Wallace, Irving. *The Word*. New York: Pocket Books, (1972) 1973.

Wambaugh, Joseph. *Hollywood Station*. New York: Little, Brown and Company, 2006.

Wambaugh, Joseph. *The Secrets of Harry Bright*. New York: Perigord Press/Bantam Books, (1985) 1986.

Weidman, Jerome. *Other People's Money*. New York: Random House, 1967.

Wellman, Paul I. *Magnificent Destiny*. Garden City, NY: Doubleday & Company, 1962.

West, Morris L. *The Shoes of the Fisherman*. New York: Dell, (1963) 1968.

Westlake, Donald E. *Don't Ask*. New York: The Mysterious Press/Warner Books, (1993) 1994.

Wilson, F. Paul. *The Select*. New York: Dell, (1994) 1995.

Wolfe, Thomas. *Look Homeward, Angel*. New York: Charles Scribner's Sons, (1929) 1957.

Wolfe, Thomas. *You Can't Go Home Again*. New York: Perennial Classics/HarperPerennial, (1940) 1998.

Wolff, Tobias. *This Boy's Life: A Memoir*. New York: Grove Press, 1989.

Wouk, Herman. *The Winds of War*. New York: Pocket Books, (1971) 1973.

Index

A

Abhorrendum, 25
ab initio, 52
Ab ovo usque ad mala, XV
Acceptasne electionem?, 56
Accepto ... Miserere mei Deus, 56
Accipe Viaticum corporis Domini ... 249
A.D., XIV, 108
Ad Astra, 261
Ad astra per aspera, XV, 92, 261
Ad Electrica Necessitas Vitae, 247
ad hominem, 166, 263
ad hoc, XIV, 157, 209, 263
ad infinitum, XIV, 32, 48, 200
a divinis, 107
ad libitum, 48
ad nauseam, XIV
advocatus diabolis, 4
a fortiori, 159
Age quod agis, 262
Agnus Dei, 89, 104
Alea iacta est, XV
alibi, XIV, 190, 258
Aliquod crastinus dies ad cogitandum dabit, 119
alma mater, XIV, 15, 190, 259
alter ego, 134
a.m., XIV
Amantes sunt amentes, 189
amicus curiae, 117
Amo, amas, amat, 32
Amores, 30
amor fati, 72
Amor vincit omnia, XV

Amphitheatrum sapientiae aeternae, 73
amplexus reservatus, 156
anima naturaliter christiana, 83
Anno Domini, XIV
Annuntio vobis gaudiam magnum. Habemus Papam!, 158
annus mirabilis, 217
ante-bellum, 32, 225
antecubital fossa, 251
ante meridiem, XIV
ante mortem, 112
Anxius et intentus agree, 232
Apello ad Petrum, 57
apologia, 253
Apologia compendiaria Fraternitatem de Rosea Cruce suspicionis et infamiis maculis aspersam, veritatem quasi Fluctibus abluens et abstergens, 73
arbiter elegantarum, 118
Arcana arcanissima, 73
Argentum virtus robur et stadium, 49
argumentum ad feminam, 226
argumentum ad hominem, 6, 226
Arma virumque cano, Trojae qui primus ab oris ... 254
Ars est celare Artem, 37
Ars Gratia Artis, 91
Artes, Scientia, Veritas, 153
aspergillus flavus, 248
Audaces fortuna iuvat, 250
Ave, Caesar!, 138
avertens, 79
axis mundi, 166

B

Bona, 157
bona fide, XIV, 17, 99, 130, 146, 172, 175, 180, 183, 190, 220
bona fortuna, 254

C

ca. AD, 251
cacoethes carpendi, 251
Caelum non animam mutant qui trans mare currunt, 6
Cannabis indica, 116
Cardinalem, 159
Carpe diem, XV, 54, 249, 251
cassia bauhinoides, 233
cassus belli, 10
caudex, 249
causa finite, 159
caveat, 178, 194
Certum est quia impossibile est, 84, 116
Ceterum censeo Carthaginem esse delendam, 26, 250
Christo et Ecclesiae, 85
Civis Romanus sum, 6
Civitas Dei, 153
Claudicat ingenium, delirat lingua, labat mens, 75
Claudite jam rivos, pueri, sat prata biberunt, 145
Coelum, non animum mutant, qui trans mare currunt, 247
Cogitata, 30
Cogito ergo sum, XV, 249, 254
coitus interruptus, 162
coitus reservatus, 11
Commune vinculum omnibus artibus, 167
compos mentis, 150

CONDOLEO ET CONGRATULATOR, 74
Confessio fraternitatis Roseae Crucis, ad aruditos Europae, 73
Confiteor, 89
congressus subtilis, 97
consensus, 157
Contincuere omnes, intenque ora tenebant, 254
Contra mundum, 251
Cor ad cor loquitur, 57
corona, 260
corpus delicti, XV, 118, 123, 190, 192, 250
Corpus Domini nostri Jesu Christi custodiat animam tuam in vitam aeternam, 20
Corpus Hermeticus, 73
Corpus Juris Secundum, 194
Credat Judaeus Apella, 262
Crede firmiter et pecca fortiter, 73
Credo, 33, 89
Credo in unum Deum, Patrem omnipotentem … 87-88
Crescat scientia; vita excolatur, 54, 186
cui bono, 188, 194, 208
Cui placet obliviscitur, cui olet meminit, 188
Culpa, 103
Cum, 140, 184
cum grano salis, 212, 252
cum laude, 100, 237, 259
Cur, quomodo, quando, 73
curriculum vitae, 48

D

Datum, 11
De Amicitia, 30
"De Brevitate Vitae", XIX
de facto, XIV, 85, 171, 209

Index 279

De gustibus, 228, 244
Dei gratia, 192
Deinde ego te absolvo a peccatis tuis, 57
De insolentia Templariorum, 73
Dei Sub Numine Viget, 22, 90
delenda est, 248
delenda est Carthago, 26
Delirium Tremens, 33
de minimis, 191
De mortuis, 11, 119, 252
De mortuis hihil nisi bonum, 150, 188
de mortuis nil nisi bonum, 248
De Naturae Secretis, 74
de obligatione sigilli, 156
Deo volente, 190
De poenitentia, 156
De Profundis, 249
De Rerum Natura, 82
De resurrectione carnis, 85
De revolutionibus orbium coelestium, XII
De Senectute, 30
Detur gloria soli Deo, 114
Deus absconditus, 84
deus ex machina, XV, 157, 247
Deus misereatur!, 192
dictum, 93, 163
Diem, 80
Dies illa, dies irae, calamitatis et miseriae; dies magna et amara valde. Dum veneris judicare saeculum per ignem, 247
Dies Irae, 53, 247, 249
Dies Irae. Lacrimosa, 43
Dignum et justum est, 251
Diligebat idoneos homines huic rei, 233
Disputatur apud peritus, 155
Dixit, et avertens rosea cervice refulsit ... 78

Doctrina sed vim promovet insitam, 93
doctus cum libro, 191
Domine, non sum dignus; ut inters sub tectum meum; sed tantum dic verbo, et sanabitur anima mea, 20
dominus, 249
Dominus illuminatio mea, 85
Dominus vobiscum, XV, 247
Donum, 11
Doryphora decemlineata, 138
dramatis personae, 120, 190
duces tecum, 124, 177, 195, 203, 204, 258
Dulce et decorum est pro patria mori, 31
dulce ridentem ... dulce loquentem, 229
duplex status, 83
Durate et vosmet rebus servate secundis, 259

E

Ecce ancilla Domini. Fiat mihi secundum verbum tuum, 248
Ecce Homo, 81, 97, 120
Ecclesiasticus, 33
edere, 233
e.g., XIV
Ego sum qui sum, 72
Ego te absolvo, 89, 252
Eheu, 118, 120
Entia non sunt multiplicanda praeter necessitate, 248
Episcopum, 159
E pluribus unum, XVI, 249, 251
Ergo, 190
ergo me, 247
Errare humanum est, XVI, 102
Esse, 84

Esse est percipi, 84
Esse quam videri, XIX
et cetera, XIV
Et cum spiritu tuo, 252
Et ego in Arcadia, 32
Et incarnatus est, 53
Et lucis aeternae beautitudine perfrui, 247
Et omnibus habitantibus in ea, 247
Et tu, Brute?, 196, 232, 251
Et tu Brute contra me, XVI
Et verbum caro factum est, 89
Eventus stultorum magister, 262
exempli gratia, XIV
Ex oriente lux, 57
ex post facto, 119, 251
Ex umbris et imaginibus in veritatem, 251

F

Faber est suae quisque fortunae, 250
facies hermetica, 72
Fama, 73
fama, malum qua non aliud velocius ullum, 208
fecundi calices quem non fecere disertum?, 207
Felici brevis!, 137
Festina lente, XVI, 116, 182, 250
Festinatio tarda est, 116
Fiat Lux, 180, 201
Fide, sed cui vide, 252
filioque, 15
finis, 69
flexor digitorum longus, 196
fidus Achates, 253
Floreat Domus de Balliolo, 12
Floreat scienia!, 146
Fuimus fumus, 32

G

"Gaudeamus Igitur", XIX, 248, 249, 260
Genus hoc erat pugnae quo se Germani exercuerant, 25
Georgius III, Dei Gratia Britanniarum Rex, Fidei Defensor, 250
Gladiator in arena consilium capit, XVI
Gloria in excelsis Deo, XII, 250
Gratias agamus Domino, deo nostro, 251
gratis, 193
gravitas, 244

H

habeas corpus, XV, 21, 123, 124, 130, 144, 152, 251, 258, 263
Habemus ad Dominum, 251
Habemus papam, 209
Haec olim meminisse juvabit, 24
Hic, 241
Hic erat demonstrandum, 37
Hic est enim calix sanguinis mei, 82
Hic jacet, 120
hinc illae lacrimae, 14
Historia Augusta, 250
Hoc est enim corpus meum, 82
Homo, 138
Homo Faber, 261
Homo faber suae quisque fortunae, XVI, 261
homo sapiens, 11, 54, 85, 174, 249, 263
homo somnus ambulatus, 249
Honor sit et baculum et ferula, 198
Horresco referens, 47

Index 281

Huc venite pueri ut viri sitis, 101, 102
Humanum Genus, 74
Hyla regilla, 139

I

Id, Ego, Superego, 85
Id est, XIV, 135, 233
i.e., XIV
Ille ubi matrem agnovit, 79
illo tempore, 49
impotentia coeundi, 72
imprimis, 144
in absentia, 85, 171, 248, 249
inane profundum, 82
in carnem, 84
ineptum, 84
in extremis, 15, 208
in flagrante, 204
in flagrante delicto, XV, 3, 42, 64, 104, 151, 190, 213, 248, 249, 250, 252, 258
in forma pauperis, 250
Ingenio et labore, 93
In hanc utilitatem angeli saepe figuras, characteres, formas et voces invenerunt ... 72
in humane dignitatis opprobrium, 72
in limine, 196, 251
in loco parentis, XV, 249
In luce tua videmus lucem, 127
In lumine Tuo videbimus lumen, 97
In manus tuas, Domine, 57
in medias res, XV
in memoriam, XIV, 251, 252
innascibilitas, 14
In Nomine Patris et Filii et Spiritus Sancti, 39
In pace requiescat, 262
in posteriori parte spine dorsi, 72
In principio erat verbum, 89
in re, 136
in situ, XIV, 170
in statu quo, 117
inter alia, 250
Inter faeces et urinam nascimur, 248
inter somnum ac trepidationem vigilibus irrupere, 233
in terrorem, 206
in toto, XIV, 248
intravitque animum militaris gloriae cupido, 232
In vino veritas, XVI, 250, 262
in vitro, XV
in vivo, XV
Ipsa scientia potestas est, XVI
ipso facto, 49, 118, 216, 254
Ira furor brevis est, 192

J

Janua, 52
Juris Doctor, 196

L

lacrimae rerum, 16, 248
Lacrymae Christi, 250
Lapis, 52
lapis exillis, 72
lapsus linguae, 5, 140, 159
(Latino) sine flexion, 74
Laudate, 251
Lavabo inter innocentes ... 88
Liber AL vel legis, 74
Libera me, Domine, de morte aeterna, in die illa tremenda: Quando caeli movendi sunt et terra: Dum veneris judicare saeculum per ignem. Tremens

factus sumego, et timeo, dum discussio venerit, atque ventura ira, 247
liquor vitae, 96
locomotor ataxia, 249
locus delicti, 190
locus standi, 118
Lux et Veritas, 18, 209
Lux Libertas, 33

M

Magisterium, 80, 159
magna cum laude, 259
magna cum sane, 163
Magna est veritas, 196
Magna est ... vis humanitatis, XI
magnum opus, XV
magnus Apollo!, 118
malum in se, 251, 252
malum prohibitum, 251, 252
Manus manum lavat, XVI
Mater Dolorosa, 108
maxima cum laude, 259
mea culpa, XV, 79, 170, 248, 249, 250, 252
Mea culpa. Mea maxima culpa, 89, 249
Mea maxima culpa, 248
Meliora, 234
Melior video proboque; deteriora sequor, 4
memento mori, 11, 161, 249, 251
mens rea, 208, 209, 251
mens sana, 156
Mens sana in corpore sano, XVI, 10, 156, 165, 209, 252
Mihi cura futuri, 108
mirabile dictu, 248, 249
miranda sextae aetatis, 72
Miserere, 249
M.O., 157

Modus, 140
modus operandi, XIV, 118, 119, 139, 174, 238, 254
modus vivendi, 226, 253
mons veneris, 89
Morituri te salutamus, XVI
Morte, morte, morte, 82

N

Nam tua res agitur, paries cum proximus ardet, 198
Natura veneranda est, non erubescenda, 84
Nemo malus felix, XVI
Nemo me impune lacessit, 217, 248
Nequaquam vacui/vacuum, 74
Nihil sub sole novum, XVI
Nil igitur mors est ad nos neque pertinent hilium, quandoquidem natura animi mortalis habetur, 81
Nil nisi bonum, 150
Nil quam difficile est, quin quaerendo investigari possit, 120
Nil sine magno labore, 44
Noli me tangere, 11, 250
Nolo, 159
non compos mentis, 247, 249
non confusus sed conjunctus in una persona—deus et homo, 83
nolo contendere, 193, 195, 252
Non doctior, sed meliore doctrina imbutus, 147
Non fumum ex fulgore, sed ex fumo dare lucem cogitat, et speciosa dehinc miracula promat, 39
Non semper ea sunt quae videntur, 190, 191, 194

non sequitur, 120, 164, 169, 190, 194, 250
Non Timebis a Sagitta Volante in Die, 21
Novus ordo seclorum, XVI
Nox est perpetua. Una dormienda. Luna dies et nox, 30
Nulla potest mulier tantum se dicere amatam vere, quantum a me Lesbia amata mea est, 31

O

Odi et amo: quare id faciam fortasse requires. Nescio, sed fieri sentio et excrucior, 30-31
O mihi praeteritos referat si Jupiter annos, 24
Omnia Movens, 74
Omnia post obitum fingit majora vetustas, 117
Omnia scire, non omnia excequi, 232
Omnia vincit amor, 138
Opus Dei, 57, 108
Orate fratres, 88
Ordo Templi Orientis, 74
Oremus, 88
'O Salutaris Hostia', 247, 251
Otium sine litteris mors est et hominis vivi sepultura, XVI
O vita, misero longa! Felici brevis!, 137

P

pars pro toto, XV
particeps criminis, 6
pater, 197
Patriciam, 158
Paulus PP VI, 108
Pax huic domui, 247
Pax Romana, 250
Pax vobiscum, 70
Pecca fortiter, 11
Per Angusta, Ad Augusta, 92
per annum, 11
per capita, XV
per diem, 79, 114, 263
Periplaneta Americana, 251
Per mortes eorum vivimus, 199
per omnia saecula saeculorum, 17
personae, 32
personae gratae, 118
persona grata, 21
persona gratis, 21
persona non grata, XV, 6, 85, 180, 250, 252, 254
Perstare et Praestare, 70, 140
pervigilium veneris, 49
Placetne, fratres?, 57
p.m., XIV
Possunt quia posse videntur, 233
post CXX annos patebo, 73
Post coitum omne animal triste, 242
post hoc ergo ante hoc, 72
Postera Crescam Laude, 58
post facto, XV, 190, 254
post meridiem, XIV
post mortem, XV, 31, 119, 120, 123, 134, 135, 197
postpartum, 179, 180
prima facie, 118, 120, 180, 184, 196, 248, 252
Primum non nocere, 103
primus inter pares, 252
prisca theologia, 248
pro bono, XV, 180, 183, 220, 249, 252, 263
Pro bono publico, 53, 64, 96
pro forma, XV, 157, 248, 250
Pro Patria Omnia, 212

proprium humani ingenii est odiesse quem laeseries, 232
pro rata, 226
Pro scientia et sapientia, 214
prospectus, 197, 198
pro tem, 157
pro tempore, 120, 247
Pseudocyesis, 251
pudibundus, 84

Q

Quadrupedante putrem sonitu quatit ungula campum, 31
Quaecumque sunt vera, 54
Quaere verum, 189
Qualis Artifex Pereo, 74
quam primum famam audieram, 185
Quantum mortalia pectora ceacae noctis habent, 74
Quem enim naturae usum, quem mundi fructum ... 84
Quercus agrifolia, 139
Quid est veritas?, 74, 250
Quid lucrum istic mihi est, 252
quid pro quo, XV, 66, 152, 184, 191, 199, 201, 248, 249, 250, 251, 252, 254
Quid sum miser tunc dicturus, 53
Quid vobis videtur?, 57
Qui Pro Quo, 249
Quis fallere possit amantem?, 189
qui vive, 249
Quo, 30
Quocunque jeceris stabit, 179
Quod avertat Deus!, 191
Quod erat demonstrandum, 11, 38, 47, 53, 119, 136, 217, 252
Quod potui perfeci, 32
Quorum, XIV
quota, XIV, 131, 164

Quo Vadis, 263, 265
Quo vadis, Domine?, 264, 266

R

reductio ad absurdum, 21, 119
Religio Medici, 163
Requiem aeternam dona eis, Domine, et lux perpetua luceat eis, 44
Requiescat in pace, 135, 247
Res Gestae, 122, 125
Res ipsa loquitur, 205, 251, 252
Respice finem, 188
res sacramenti, 14
rete mirabile, 83
Rident stolidi lingua Latina, XI
rigor mortis, XV, 119, 125, 126, 136, 196, 251
Risus Sardonicus, 162

S

Sacerdos, 159
Sagitta Volante in Dei, 20
Sagitta Volante in Die, 21
Sanctae Romanae Ecclesiae, 159
sanctum sanctorum, 48, 213, 249
Sanctus, 89, 104
Sanguis eius super nos et super filios nostros, 146
Sapidus, 250
Sapiens nihil affirmat quod non probat, 191
se defendendo, 251
Sedes Sapientiae, 158
sede vacante, 55
Semper, 175, 248
Semper fi, 108, 180, 251, 252
Semper Fidelis, 108, 247, 248, 249, 253
Semper Paratus, 68, 69

Semper virens, 40, 172, 206, 244
senecio canescens, 233
sensus fidelium, 80
Sero sapiunt Phryges, 5
sexta hora, 96
Sic transit, 120, 252
Sic transit Gloria, 137, 252
Sic transit gloria mundi, 74, 96
Sic volvere parcae!, 144
Sigillum confessionis, 207
Sigillum Universitatis Dominae Nostrae a Lacu, 172
Silentium post clamores, 74
Si monumentum quoeris, circumspice, 249
sine flexione, 74
sine qua non, 8, 66, 157
Solaris, 261
Soles occidere et redire possunt nobis cum semel occidit brevis lux, nox est perpetua una dormienda. Da mi basia mille, 9
Solvitur vivendo, XIX
Spes, Scientia, Facultas, 221
spolia opima, 228
stare decisis, 250
status quo, XIV, 130, 159, 172, 248, 248, 249
Steganographia, hoc est ars per occultam scripturam animi sui voluntatem absentibus Certa, 72
Stultum est timere quod vitare non potes, XVI
sua sponte, 179
subpoena duces tecum, 124, 177, 195, 203, 204, 258
sub rosa, 237
Sub umbra alarum tuarum, Jehova, 72
sui generis, XV, 85, 195, 250, 252, 263

Summa cum laude, 138, 150, 251
Summa Theologiae Moralis, 156
Sumus quod sumus, 248
Sunt superis sua iura, 190
Sursum corda, XVI, 120, 251

T

tablinum, 249
Tacent Colloquia Effugiat Risus Hic Locus Est Ubi Mors Gaudet Succurrere Vitae, 250
Tantum ergo Sacramentum ... 59, 61, 88-89
Tegenaria domestica, 114
Telluris Theoria Sacra, 73
Templi Resurgentes Equites Synarchici, 74
Tempus fugit, XVI, 247, 252
terra cognita, 52
terra firma, 100, 214, 253
terra foetida, 72
terra incognita, 52, 228, 238, 253, 254
terrarius, 119
Terras Irradient, 206
Theatrum Chemicum, 74
the Rubicon, 229
timor mortis, 53, 151
Timor mortis conturbat me, 53
totaliter aliter, 83
totus porcus, 233
Tractatus apologeticus integritatem societatis de Rosea Cruce defendens, 73
Trinitas, 83
Truncus Arteriosis, 220, 221
Truncus Arteriosus, 221
Turris Babel, 74
tutior pars, 157

U

Ubi argumentum?, 181
Ubi concordia, ibi victoria, XVI
Ubi opes, ibi amici, XVI
Ubi Petrus, ibi Ecclesia, 158
Ulmis hollandicis, 79
Ultima, 16
Umbilicus Telluris, 74
una substantia, tres personae, 83
Usus Antiquior, XII
Utriusque cosmi historia, 73
Uva uvam videndo varia fit, 241
Uva uvam vivendo varia fit, 240

V

vade mecum, 73, 228, 233
Vae misero mihi, 118
Vanitas Vanitatum!, 103
Veni, Sancte Spiritus, 56
Veni, vidi, vici, XVI, 67
Venite exultemus domino, 104
vera doctrina, 159
verbatim, 65
verbena bipinatifida, 233
Veri iustique scientia vindex, 120
Veritas, 33, 85, 120, 167, 206, 209
Veritas et Libertas, 97
Veritas et Utilitas, 153
Veritas, veritas, 233
Veritas Vincat, 153
versus, 178, 214, 253
Vias, 83
vice versa, 250
Videbo visionem hanc manam quare non comburatur rubus, 186
Vigiles non timendi sunt nisi complures adveniunt, 251
Vim promovet insitam, 93
vincit omnia veritas, 136

Vincit qui patitur, 193
Vincit veritas, 190
Virgo, 249
virgo intacta, 139, 247
Virtus mille scuta, XVI
virus, 260
vis medicatrix naturae, 11
vis movendi, 74
Vita brevis, ars longa, 248
Vita, Dulcedo, Spes, 172
Vitae excelsioris limen, XIX
Volo, 159
Vox populi, vox Dei, 48
Vox, Veritas, Vita, 176, 201
vultus est index animi, 116

www.ingramcontent.com/pod-product-compliance
Lightning Source LLC
Chambersburg PA
CBHW072124290426
44111CB00012B/1767